Philosophy, Rhetoric, Literary Criticism: (Inter)views

Edited by
Gary A. Olson

Foreword by
Clifford Geertz

Introduction by
Patricia Bizzell

Commentary by
David Bleich

SOUTHERN ILLINOIS UNIVERSITY PRESS
Carbondale and Edwardsville

For Marlyne S. Olson and Joseph David Olson

4 3 2 1   97 96 95 94

Library of Congress Cataloging-in-Publication Data

Philosophy, rhetoric, literary criticism: (inter)views /
        edited by Gary A. Olson; foreword by Clifford Geertz,
        introduction by Patricia Bizzell, commentary by David Bleich.
                p.   cm.
        Includes bibliographical references.

        1. Literature—Philosophy.   2. Rhetoric.   3. Criticism
        4. Intellectuals—United States—Interviews.
        I. Olson, Gary A., date.

        PN45.P516   1994
        801—dc20
        ISBN 0-8093-1908-X

                                        93-38349
                                        CIP

The paper used in this publication meets the minimum requirements of the
American National Standard for Information Sciences—Permanence of Paper
for Printed Library Materials. ANSI Z39.48-1984. ∞

Contents

Acknowledgments ix

Foreword
    Clifford Geertz xi

Introduction
    Patricia Bizzell 1

Donald Davidson

Language Philosophy, Writing, and Reading:
A Conversation with Donald Davidson
    Thomas Kent 9

The Malaprop in Spite of Herself:
A Desperate Reading of Donald Davidson
    Susan Wells 29

A Response to "Language Philosophy, Writing,
and Reading: A Conversation with Donald Davidson"
    Reed Way Dasenbrock 35

Stanley Fish

Fish Tales: A Conversation with "The Contemporary Sophist"
    Gary A. Olson 43

A Response to "Fish Tales: A Conversation
with 'The Contemporary Sophist'"
    Patricia Bizzell 68

"Fish Tales" and the Politics of Anti-Professionalism
    John Trimbur 72

bell hooks

bell hooks and the Politics of Literacy: A Conversation
  Gary A. Olson 81

bell hooks on Literacy and Teaching: A Response
  Joyce Irene Middleton 100

Literacy and Activism: A Response to bell hooks
  Tom Fox 105

J. Hillis Miller

Rhetoric, Cultural Studies, and the Future of Critical Theory:
A Conversation with J. Hillis Miller
  Gary A. Olson 115

On Transforming the English Department:
A Response to J. Hillis Miller
  Patricia Harkin 144

Learning About Learning About Deconstruction:
An Epi(tryingtobe)gone
  Jasper Neel 152

Jane Tompkins

Jane Tompkins and the Politics
of Writing, Scholarship, and Pedagogy
  Gary A. Olson 161

Encounters with Jane Tompkins
  Susan C. Jarratt 178

Lit/Comp: A Response to Jane Tompkins
  Elizabeth A. Flynn 184

Stephen Toulmin

Literary Theory, Philosophy of Science, and Persuasive Discourse:
Thoughts from a Neo-premodernist
  Gary A. Olson 193

"The Good Man Speaking Well," or Business as Usual
Arabella Lyon 220

Novissimum Organum: Phronesis on the Rebound
C. Jan Swearingen 227

Commentary: The Performance Model of Teaching and Scholarship
David Bleich 235

Acknowledgments

I'd like to thank Kenney Withers for his support both of the two interviews projects and of rhetoric and composition in general, Curtis Clark for editorial advice, Tom Ross and Rollin Richmond for substantial encouragement and financial support, Marilyn Minor for expert editorial assistance, and Sid Dobrin and Todd Taylor for what must have seemed interminable research. This project was supported in part by research leave generously granted by the University of South Florida.

Foreword

CLIFFORD GEERTZ

The vexed relationship between speech and writing has come sharply into focus in recent years. The linguist's or the anthropologist's tendency to see spoken language as primary and written language as derivative, a pale and parasitic reflection of "direct" communication going on in "actual" conversations carried on between "real" people, has come up against the literary critic's or the philosopher's tendency to see "inscribed discourse" of one sort or another as the heart of the matter and the flow of utterance as but the noisy background from which such discourse separates into its own sort of autonomy. Instead of words and things, talk and text.

Attempts to negotiate this uncertain boundary between language as a vocal performance and as an inscriptional object are nowadays quite common—discussions of code and design in conversation, of voice and dialogue in literature; and genres which seem to hover somehow between the two—letters, diaries, fieldnotes, and, the case at hand, interviews—are getting looked at with renewed interest. Printed interviews, especially, recounting as they do verbal exchanges in literary form, questions and answers arranged into essays, seem both to bring the speech and writing relationship plainly into view and to tackle its perplexities in a frontal way.

There are, of course, interviews, oral and printed, all around us these days: talk shows on television, call-in programs on radio, press briefings in newspapers, celebrity chats in magazines. But the sort of interviews reprinted from the *Journal of Advanced Composition* in the pages of this collection and of its predecessor, *(Inter)views*—extended, detailed, and systematic efforts to expose at once a line of argument and the speech ways of the person advancing it—are still not all that common. European intellectuals are somewhat more given to publishing such interviews, often at book length and with a fair amount of second-thought revision which rather spoils the effect. But the form, with its capacity to connect the words of the scholar with the words of the work, is only beginning to flourish here.

This curious, in-between quality of the essay-interview as a form, at once free flowing on the respondent's side, where most of the talking occurs, and carefully constructed on the questioner's, where most of the text building does, encourages the appearance of subjects and concerns not normally prominent in scholarly work: the development of a particular individual's thought against the pressure of that of other individuals, aligned or competing; the way in which ideas and standpoints react to changing circumstances, narrowly professional and broadly general; the play of the social, ropes-and-pulleys dimensions of academic life on its substance; and the construction of a scholarly persona to fit a desired audience. When all this is supplemented, as it is here, with response essays, also personal and also free-ranging, by other players in the game (*chers collègues, mais néanmoins amis*), the result is a vivid, *n*-dimensional view of contemporary intellectual life elsewhere presented in a warier, dressed-for-the-occasion form.

That so much of the impetus for this sort of talking-writing should come from composition studies is hardly surprising. The intense concern in such studies with how texts come into being, with how to build them, what they are built out of, and how, once built, they have their effects, naturally conduces to a realistic view of a process—"composition"—generally ignored, mystified or reduced to an ancillary matter. The cross-disciplinary character of such studies, trained as they are on how the thing is done or botched, wherever it is done or botched, makes of them a general inquiry into the practical task of, in the plain-man words of Paul Ricoeur, "saying something about something." In pursuing that inquiry wherever it leads, and to whomever, they are making of the interview a powerful tool.

Institute for Advanced Studies
Princeton, New Jersey

Introduction

PATRICIA BIZZELL

It would be risky to claim to identify any common theme in the six interviews in *Philosophy, Rhetoric, Literary Criticism: (Inter)views*, other than that all six are indeed interesting to scholars in composition and rhetoric. But I will offer a few remarks here about a common theme, drawn from my own preoccupations, that I read into the interviews as I paged through them. I would call this the theme of democratization of literacy and interpretation. I see recurring issues here related to who gets access to literacy education, what "taxes" are levied against entrants, what this education is used for, and more. I see recurring issues of who gets to determine what important cultural texts mean—or what cultural texts are important, what conventions need to be followed for communication to take place across cultural groups, if any, and more. Bound up in these issues is another concern, too, that of the social mission or purpose, if any, of professional educators, particularly in English studies.

Donald Davidson's strictures against the concept of discourse community, for example, can be seen as a move against the supposedly closed and elitist world of discourse communities such as the academic community. He offers ways for people to communicate effectively even if they don't share the conventions of a discourse community. Such sharing is not necessary, he suggests. Instead, all we need is for his "principle of charity" to operate, such that we simply acknowledge that our interlocutors are indeed "sharing a world with" us and are "logical in the way that [we] are." With these assumptions in place, we can form "passing theories" about what other people mean, enlightening enough to allow communication and not so rigid as to bar new interlocutors with new perspectives. Whereas looking at human communication in terms of discourse communities can tend to emphasize the barriers between groups, Davidson's approach can be seen as minimizing the barriers, especially barriers that are group-related or culturally constructed, and as suggesting that it really isn't that difficult for any two mentally normal humans to communicate. This would appear to make the democratization of interpretation easier.

Stanley Fish is often cast as the opponent of democratizing interpretation, due to his praise for professionalism in English studies and his apparent comfort at operating within its interpretive discourse communities without concern for who might be left outside. But both John Trimbur and I offer somewhat revisionist views of Fish in this regard, and Trimbur's observations on Fish and professionalism are particularly instructive. Trimbur rejects the idea that Fish's views on professionalism can be attacked from the position that we can "dismantle the boundaries between the popular and the academic." This alternative is simply not possible, Trimbur says. Rather, says Trimbur, what we have to look at, if we are concerned about democratizing literacy and interpretation, is "the ongoing interplay of the academic and the popular, the high and the low, the expert and the public." Trimbur points out that Fish would say there is no reason to assume that professionalism is necessarily elitist. And he suspects, due to Fish's cogent critique of liberalism, that Fish would not be averse to seeing professionalism rearticulated in engagement with the current "culture wars": "It all depends on what you want and how persuasive you are. It's a matter of rhetoric."

The theme of democratization is perhaps stated most persuasively in the interview with bell hooks. She speaks eloquently about how hard it was for her to find a written voice in which to do her intellectual work because the styles of the traditional academy seemed so closed to her. I would contend that by the very style of writing and "being" as a professional academic that she has evolved, she has democratized the academy, enlarged its possibilities for inclusion. Moreover, she speaks explicitly about the need for academics to work toward more democratization, more inclusion—for example, by allowing Spanish as well as English in their classrooms or by engaging in basic literacy education as part of their feminist agenda:

> If we truly want to empower women and men to engage in feminist thinking, we must empower them to read and write, but I really don't see any large group of committed feminists making that a central agenda. . . . Who decides that sexual harassment is more central than the question of literacy? A lot of privileged women who already read and write, who don't encounter anybody in their life who doesn't read or write, and who therefore don't even think about literacy.

This is a dramatic engagement with the issue of democratizing literacy—a populist agenda in hooks, as Tom Fox points out in his response—linking the democratizing of literacy directly to the social usefulness, and indeed self-respect, of academic feminists and other academics.

This address to the social responsibility of the academic is logically linked in hooks' thought with the issue of the teacher's appropriate authority. Hooks argues that academics will not be able to accomplish the democratizing agenda she sets if they mistakenly think it requires their abdicating all control over the direction of their classes. Thus, hooks establishes a distinction between "authority" and "power," with authority being legitimate in that it "does not necessarily imply a positionality that leads to dominance" because both her authority as a teacher and the limitations of her authority are openly acknowledged and negotiated. This sort of authority-open-to-question might be seen as a kind of democratic authority. Indeed, this is exactly how Joyce Middleton sees it in her response. It is reminiscent of Trimbur's interpretation of the possibilities for professionalism in Fish's view—an authority that allows, even centers on, interplay across boundaries.

Hooks describes one basis of her authority as the projection of care for her students, even as she acknowledges that this sometimes sets up emotionally charged situations of rivalry in her classroom. Both Middleton and Fox comment on this "erotic" element, Fox especially with some discomfort. Fox sees hooks as able to generate "passion" between herself and her students as a function of her institutional position as the teacher, thus creating a situation in which she remains in a power hierarchy over students. While I see what he means, I also wonder if hooks is not drawing here on extra-academic models of how authority gets established, models that precisely because they offer non-academic grounds for the relationship between student and teacher act to democratize the academy, to make it more welcoming to students more familiar with the sources of authority models on which hooks draws.

J. Hillis Miller could hardly seem farther from bell hooks in style and interest, and yet they are perhaps very similar in their willingness to talk about structural change in English studies. Whereas the changes hooks recommends could be seen as centering on democratizing literacy, Miller advocates a number of changes that could be seen as democratizing interpretation. For example, he hails cultural studies as the hopeful future of English studies and he traces its rise to this concern: "The young people teaching literature now are anxious to make what they do have some importance in our society." This is like the anxiety hooks addresses directly in her literacy agenda (and, again, Trimbur's discussion of professionalism in Fish comes to mind). Evidently as part of this making of literary studies into something with social significance, Miller praises the diversification of the canon in American literature to include a number of ethnic literatures, including literatures not written in English. His only caution about this trend is that he hopes scholars will indeed learn the diverse languages needed to study these literatures and otherwise prepare themselves rigorously for the new approach—a caveat reminiscent of bell hooks's discussion of the need to accept a variety of languages, such as Spanish, in the English classroom. Also, Miller speaks several times of the "excitement about the methodological and theoretical aspects of the discipline" of composition, and he urges that composition remain an important part of English departments. He sees composition as fitting quite compatibly in his predicted English departments devoted to cultural studies. From his point of view, this inclusion of composition probably also represents a gracious democratizing of interpretation.

Jane Tompkins has gotten a lot of attention in literary studies recently for calling attention to issues of pedagogy, a kind of populist or democratizing gesture in itself, and other moves she makes in the interview here can be seen as relating to the theme I am tracing. For example, like hooks she calls for activism on behalf of basic literacy. To illustrate her notion of a specifically feminist pedagogy, she cites a North Carolina literacy program for pregnant high school students. Evidently, this program illustrates feminist pedagogy in that it goes beyond the traditional academy to engage in a sort of direct social intervention, just as hooks recommends. Also, Tompkins advances a metaphor of the safe, comforting home as a good model for what a school should be. Although this metaphor has limitations, which she notes, it can be seen as democratizing in that it reduces the distance between home and school. Insofar as it could be made to work as a model, it would perhaps facilitate school access for more people and thus aid the democratizing of literacy. Again, I am reminded of hooks' willingness to project care and emotional connection between teacher and students as perhaps a more non-academic, more home- or community-like model of authority.

There is a certain coziness about this image that looks forward to an image in the interview with Stephen Toulmin in which he imagines a return to the (presumed) epistemological simplicities of village life after the demise of rationalism: "I think the thing to do after rejecting Cartesianism is not to go on through the wreckage of the temple but to go back into the town where this heretical temple was built and rediscover the life that was lived by people for many centuries before the rationalist dream seized hold of people's minds." It seems from this image that Toulmin sees his own contribution to philosophy as a kind of populist endeavor, freeing "the people" from rationalist mandarins and enabling them to live a more collective, more democratic life. He evokes this image while acknowledging the justice of labeling him a "neo-premodern." His vision is perhaps distinctive among the contributors to this volume in that he finds his utopia by looking backward.

There is, of course, one major area in which democratization really does not seem to be operating in this volume, and that is in the understanding and acknowledging of scholarship in composition and rhetoric shown by those interviewed. One might particularly expect more citations of composition scholarship from Fish, hooks, Miller, and Tompkins, since they are all in American universities with composition colleagues and so have no excuse for their ignorance. Patricia Harkin and Jasper Neel take Miller to task—correctly, in my view—for essentially treating composition as a "service" field that helps students find the right words for ideas generated elsewhere (for example, by contact with literature scholars). But I would add that we should not be surprised at his misconception given his lack of citation of composition scholarship. The lack is more striking in view of his advocacy of learning more languages: this is possible, but reading composition scholarship is not? Literature scholars would justifiably react with outrage if, for example, someone were to refer to "all those feminist critics who are doing great work!" without naming any of them. Such a form of reference is patronizing, not to mention lacking in scholarly rigor. But this is how composition scholarship is routinely treated in the works of literature scholars *who consider themselves friends to composition studies.*

Perhaps literature scholars need to know this in order to understand the anger expressed in the responses to Jane Tompkins by both Susan Jarratt and Elizabeth Flynn. I confess that I had exactly the same reaction as Jarratt to "Pedagogy of the Distressed." It is infuriating to see literature scholars garner éclat for producing as great "discoveries" theoretical and pedagogical insights that have been discussed among composition scholars for years—especially infuriating as meanwhile literature scholars have been disrespectful, and in many cases downright damaging, to composition scholars' professional careers. References by literature scholars to the work of Paulo Freire have become a kind of locus classicus for me of these infuriating moments. Freire has been discussed among composition scholars for at least twenty years. But now Tompkins, hooks, and, in his Presidential address at the 1992 national Modern Language Association convention, Houston Baker, among others, announce with great fanfare their "discovery" of Freire's application to the problems we composition scholars have so long been discussing. And it's not as if we were in a distant discipline, with no contact. Witness the anecdotes shared by Flynn and Neel, for example, to show how literature people *ought* to know who we are.

I don't mean to say that literature scholars should not be allowed to discuss Freire, that he is somehow our property. On the contrary, I believe that the issues raised by discussion of Freire—many of the issues of democratization that I have been tracing here—are so crucial to the future of English studies that the more people discussing and working on them, the better. But literature people need the benefit of the work that has already been done by composition scholars. Too often, *their* "great discoveries" sound to *us* like reinventing the wheel. This is why your graduate professor sends you to the library to do a review of the scholarship before approving your brilliant thesis idea on *Moby-Dick*. You should avail yourself of the work done by other scholars.

I choose to end with this complaint because it speaks in a small, local way to the pain of being excluded. I'm willing to project a theme of democratization as running through the interviews in this collection—thus blurring many significant distinctions between them and leaving out a great deal of substance both in the interviews and in the responses—because I just want to take the little space of the Introduction to focus attention on the need for more discussion on these issues. And we definitely need more action on them.

College of the Holy Cross
Worcester, Massachusetts

Donald

Davidson

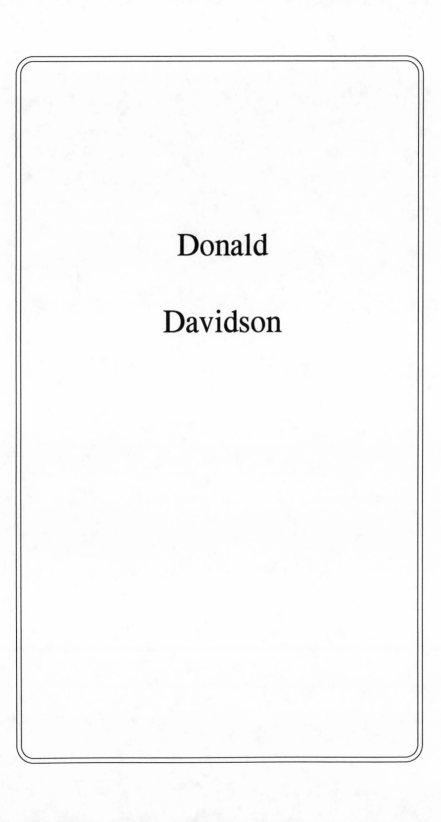

Language Philosophy, Writing, and Reading: A Conversation with Donald Davidson

Thomas Kent

Donald Davidson is an analytic philosopher in the tradition of Wittgenstein and Quine, and his formulations of action, truth, and communicative interaction have generated considerable debate in philosophical circles. In the areas of composition studies and rhetoric, however, Davidson is relatively unknown; he possesses neither the name recognition nor the influence of other contemporary philosophers of language to whom we regularly look for support and guidance, philosophers like Noam Chomsky, John Searle, Stephen Toulmin, Jacques Derrida, or Jürgen Habermas. Although Davidson does not occupy a conspicuous place in composition and rhetoric's pantheon of heroes, his ideas have nonetheless influenced—albeit indirectly—the study of writing. Davidson has entered our lives primarily through his influence on Richard Rorty, who, in turn, stands along with Thomas Kuhn as one of the two most prominent progenitors of social constructionist theory.

Davidson's important and largely unheralded contribution to rhetorical theory and, consequently, to composition studies resides in his elaboration of a vigorously anti-foundationalist conception of language and communicative interaction. In this interview, Davidson maintains that he has "departed from foundationalism completely," and in his version of anti-foundationalism, Davidson breaks with the Cartesian philosophical tradition that understands language to be a medium of either representation or expression. According to Rorty, Davidson's philosophy of language constitutes "the first systematic treatment of language which breaks *completely* with the notion of language as something which can be adequate or inadequate to the world or to the self. For Davidson breaks with the notion that language is a *medium*—a medium either of representation or of expression." If language does not mediate between us and the world, as Davidson claims, and if we cease to imagine that a split exists between an inner world of thought and feeling and an outer world of objects and events, as Davidson advocates, then nothing exists "out there" or "in here" that will serve as an epistemological foundation for either a theory of meaning or a theory of truth; all we have to authorize our utterances are other utterances. As Rorty puts it, "only sentences can be true

...and...human beings make truths by making languages in which to phrase sentences."

Of course, the claim that "human beings make truths" could serve as a motto for social constructionist writing theory, and by endorsing an assiduously anti-foundationalist conception of meaning and truth, Davidson clearly concurs with social constructionists when he tells us that "there is an irreducibly social element in determining what it is that we mean." However, what Davidson gives with one hand, he takes back with the other. Breaking with many philosophers, rhetoricians, and composition theorists who argue that utterances are social constructs that are convention bound, Davidson maintains that we are mistaken to think of language as a "single repertoire of expressions—with their meanings and their semantic interpretation—which everybody shares. . . . There is no such thing that's shared." Through his attack on what he calls conceptual schemes—the idea of a shared language governed by social conventions—Davidson rejects a central tenet of social constructionist thought: the possibility that discourse communities shape and control communication and, consequently, our knowledge of the world. He tells us, for example, that "there is no master key or framework theory that you can have prior to a communicative interaction or situation. You've got to work your way into the whole system at the same time."

In place of a shared language, Davidson posits a thoroughly hermeneutical and intersubjective account of communicative interaction. He emphasizes repeatedly that "communication is always incomplete. It's not as though anybody ever gets everything right. It's a matter of degree." Sharing much in common with Derrida's formulations of deferral and the supplement, Davidson's account of the indeterminate and always incomplete nature of communicative interaction requires us to think of utterances—both written and spoken—as thoroughly intersubjective and interpersonal relations through which we acquire access to unmediated contact with other minds and objects in the world. According to Davidson, even "our concept of objectivity ... is an idea that we would not have if it weren't for interpersonal relations. In other words, the source of objectivity is intersubjectivity." Intersubjectivity, in turn, is a property of individuals and not discourse communities, so, for Davidson, "understanding other cultures is no different from understanding our next door neighbor, except in degree."

With his insistence that "communication is always incomplete," Davidson challenges us to reexamine some of our most fundamental assumptions about the nature of writing. For example, when we accept Davidson's conception of communicative interaction as an uncodifiable and intersubjective activity, we are compelled to modify radically or to drop completely the central claims made both by adherents to cognitivist theory—who claim that mental processes largely define the writing act—and by adherents to social constructionist theory—who claim that writing primarily constitutes a conventional act. Moving beyond the inherent Cartesianism present in cognitivist and social constructionist theory, Davidson invites us to imagine writing as a hermeneutical interaction among language users, a conception of writing that does not require us to posit a split between a knowing subject and an imperturbable world of objects and events.

In addition to his important discussion of the nature of communicative interaction, Davidson addresses in this interview a wide range of topics, including his conception of externalism, radical interpretation, the principle of charity, triangulation, and the passing theory. Through his lucid explanations of these key concepts integral to his philosophy of language, Davidson also creates in this interview a portrait of a philosopher dedicated to the clarity of thought as he strives to make his ideas accessible to rhetoricians and composition specialists who may not possess a technical background in analytic philosophy. In other words, Davidson practices what he preaches. In this interview, he exemplifies the attempt, as he says, "to discover the common ground on which we can make whatever sense we can make of one another."

Q. In your essays, you seem intentionally to cultivate a kind of conversational and even colloquial tone. How would you describe your writing style?

A. A friend of mine, Arnold Isenberg, once told me—I think before I had written anything—that the way to write a paper in philosophy was to begin by asking a question that anybody could understand or by posing a problem in such a way that anyone would see that it was a problem. I followed that advice for a long time and began most of my papers with either a problem or a question, so I have attempted always to write my essays in such a way that the reader does not require any special background in philosophy in order to understand my meaning. I'm often told that my papers are difficult, but that was certainly never my aim. My aim was quite in the other direction. I'm gratified by the fact that people who don't have any technical background in philosophy do seem to make something of my ideas. I think the only other thing I can say about my style is that I sometimes find it incredibly hard to start writing. I often imagine the first sentence and then ask myself, "Wait! What comes next?" Pretty soon, I'm writing the whole paper in my head, and any problem in the composition or organization of the text stops me from even writing the first sentence for fear I would be somehow trapped. When I do finally write something, I often find that the first couple of pages, which usually sort of ease me into the subject, are better left out. So, I'll throw away these painfully constructed early pages completely.

Q. You've already anticipated my second question. How would you describe your writing process? Do your essays undergo several revisions?

A. I hope you won't hold this against me, but I don't do a great deal of revising. I always believe that I have a pretty clear idea about how a paper is going to go together before I start writing. However, in the throes of composing a paper, I find that I regularly think about the paper. When I'm trying to go to sleep or when I'm half asleep, ways of putting things often occur to me, or when I'm not in the midst of writing, a new idea or a solution for some problem of organization sometimes will come to me. I find that these relaxed moments—when I am not actually writing—are absolutely essential in my composing process.

Q. Do editors help you very much when you write an essay?

A. I don't think I've ever had any substantial help from an editor. I've often wished I had. The kind of thing I usually get from editors is advice on how to punctuate. For example, I've had several battles with the *Journal of Philosophy*. Concerning the first piece of mine that they published, the editors insisted that periods and commas go inside quotation marks and semi-colons and colons go outside. They said that this method of punctuation is absolutely standard practice in the United States. I wrote back and said, "Not so: the *New Yorker* does it the way I do it." Whereupon, they backed down. Aside from the fixation that the editor of the *Journal of Philosophy* had about punctuation and "whiches" and "thats," I can't remember much guidance from an editor. I should point out, however, that I often circulate a paper to colleagues and friends and ask them to make suggestions or comments, but they never do. The suggestions usually come years later after the paper has been published. Where I do receive a lot of help is from reading my papers aloud to audiences. In these presentations, I almost always get good ideas about what is difficult, what could be phrased in a better way, and so forth. Such feedback is extremely valuable because I see what it is that troubles people, and I realize there are difficulties I hadn't noticed.

Q. How would you describe your philosophical genealogy? That is, who are the thinkers who loom large in your own history?

A. As an undergraduate, I was first an English major and then went into comparative literature. I was interested in the history of ideas, and I did a lot of philosophy. By the time I finished my undergraduate work, I was in a combined field of classics and philosophy. So, I covered a great many different topics in those four years. For example, in my second year, Whitehead was teaching for the last time at Harvard, so I took both his undergraduate course and his graduate seminar, thinking I mustn't miss the great man. I was inspired both by his personality and by his writing, but he also encouraged me personally. He encouraged me in a way of thinking which was very congenial to me. Putting it very roughly, he taught me that I could learn from great figures of all sorts—both literary and philosophical. I learned, too, that the question of agreeing or disagreeing is subordinate to the question of getting an insight into various ways of looking at things; so, early on, I didn't think of philosophy as a subject where you tried to get it right; rather, I thought of it as a lot of interesting ideas, all of which you should take in as far as you could. So I'd say, Whitehead had quite an influence on me, not one that I now think of as altogether good.

The person who aroused me from my undogmatic slumbers was Quine. He was just starting his teaching career, and I felt as if I had discovered a new subject when I came under his influence. I was fascinated by mathematical logic and logical positivism which he was discussing and criticizing. Then I went into the Navy and there was a big hiatus. When I came back, I did my dissertation on something I had already started, namely Plato's *Philebus*, because I felt that I didn't know enough of the sort of thing that Quine was doing to write on his work. In 1951, I was hired by Stanford, and during the time I was there, I taught almost every course that appears in the catalog of a large philosophy department. So, I worked up one subject after another—philosophy of language, ancient philosophy, medieval philosophy, modern philosophy, epistemology, ethics—and I started formulating ideas in all these areas. In the philosophy of language, however, I found myself going back and reading Quine with a new eye, and as I started teaching, he slowly became more and more a guiding figure in my thinking. So, he entered my life twice over, so to speak, and has never departed; we've always been friends. My intellectual debt to him is greater than to anybody else.

Q. One of the intellectual developments that has directly influenced the study of writing is what has come to be called anti-foundationalism. In your survey of the passing philosophical scene, how would you assess the importance and the impact of anti-foundationalism? Has anti-foundationalism won the field in the philosophy of language?

A. The answer to the last question is no. It hasn't won the field. Foundationalism is alive. I'd like to think it isn't well, but it is certainly alive. There is a question as to exactly what one means by foundationalism. The British empiricists were foundationalists of one kind; according to them, everything comes from the senses in one way or another and this provides a foundation for epistemology. Another version is the Cartesian idea that what we know for certain is what is in our own minds and anything else we know we have to construct from that. Those are two quite different sorts of foundationalism, though they often appear together for various reasons. For example, Quine is a foundationalist in the general sense of the British empiricists, although his brand of foundationalism is clearly not the same as the positivists or indeed anybody really who went before him. I have departed from foundationalism completely, and this departure is one of the biggest differences between my views and Quine's. I think I never went for foundationalism; that is, I was never taken by any version of it. It always seemed to me to be a mistake, and I can remember, in fact, arguing with Quine—in my amateurish way—about this even back when I was a first-year graduate student. It's been a topic of pleasant debate between us through the years.

Q. In terms of large conceptual categories, your work has been tagged with the label "externalism" in opposition to "internalism." I know that a response to this next question requires more discussion than you can give it here, but can you describe the primary differences between an externalist conception of language and an internalist conception, and what hangs on these differences?

A. The internalist says that the contents of our thoughts—our beliefs, our desires, our intentions, and what we mean by what we say—are determined wholly by what is in the head. Generally speaking, this is a Cartesian position, and there are lots of internalists around. The externalist, however, maintains that there are factors external to the person which are determinants of the contents of our thoughts, and not just causal determinants—because that's obvious—but, so to speak, logical determinants, too. For example, from an externalist perspective, you can't have a thought about an apple if you haven't had at some point in your life some contact—indirect or direct—with apples. So, externalism has to do with your history and things that exist outside of you that make a difference to what you can think or what you are thinking at a given moment. Now, beyond this description, externalism takes a number of forms, but unlike Saul Kripke, Hilary Putnam, or Tyler Burge, I don't limit the extent to which the contents of our thoughts are fixed by external objects. I think externalism applies universally; there are connections everywhere between the world and the contents of our thoughts. It's not limited to a few words but is true of a very large number of them. So, I am an all-out externalist.

Q. Some of your terminology is now beginning to appear in both the areas of rhetorical and literary theory. I would like to ask you to discuss a few of these concepts. Would you explain first what you mean by "radical interpretation"?

A. Radical interpretation is a way of studying interpretation by purifying the situation in an artificial way. Imagine trying to understand somebody else when you have no head start: there is no translator around; there's no dictionary available; you have to work it out from scratch. It would beg the question, in trying to study the nature of interpretation, to assume that you know in advance what a person's intentions, beliefs, and desires are. I hold that you never could get a detailed picture of any of those things unless you could communicate with the person first. There is no master key or framework theory that you can have prior to a communicative interaction or situation. You've got to work your way into the whole system at the same time.

Q. In your formulation of communicative interaction, you employ what you've termed the principle of charity. What do you mean by this idea? Is it correct to say that radical interpretation relies on the principle of charity?

A. The principle of charity says that in interpreting others you've got to make their thoughts hold together to a certain extent if you're going to see them as thoughts at all, because that's what thoughts are like. They have logical relations to one another. Although people can certainly be irrational—they can have thoughts that don't go together—we can only recognize them as irrational because their thoughts lack rational coherence. You can't make sense of total irrationality. For example, if you believe everything is green, then you have to believe that this table is green, for if you don't, you temporarily depart from standards that you have to have if you're to have the thought that this is green or that everything is green. You can't have those thoughts without those thoughts being related to others, and those relations are logical. The principle of charity really just formulates the recognition of the necessary element of rationality in thought. Thoughts have propositional contents, and propositional contents are in part identified by their relations to each other.

Q. I think I wanted to make more out of the principle of charity. I thought the principle of charity in relation to radical interpretation constituted the very hinge on which swings the notion of comprehensibility. That is, in order to understand that we don't understand something, we already must share a great body of common experience about language and about our being in the world.

A. That's not wrong. An account of anybody's thoughts will no doubt uncover some inconsistencies, but in order to uncover inconsistencies, you must first identify the thoughts that are inconsistent to each other, and to identify them, you have to embed them in a complex of thoughts with which they fit. Otherwise, you have no way of identifying them as what they are. So, I'm not disagreeing with you about that. I also didn't mention the other aspect of charity, which is how thoughts are related to the world. Externalism says there's a connection between the contents of people's thoughts and their causal relations with the world itself. In fact, I would say if it weren't for that, we wouldn't be able to interpret anyone else. It's only because we share a world with others that we can get the hang of what they're talking about. So again, the word *charity* is a misnomer because it's not a matter of being kind to people; it's the condition for understanding them at all. Thus, charity has two features: one is that you can't understand people if you don't see them as sharing a world with you; the other is that you can't understand people if you don't see them as logical in the way that you are—up to a point, of course.

Q. In several of your papers, you talk about triangulation. I think of triangulation as a way around the problem of correspondence and language as mediation. Would you discuss triangulation? What do language users do when they triangulate?

A. Well, the idea of triangulation is partly metaphorical, but not wholly. The basic idea is that our concept of objectivity—our idea that our thoughts may or may not correspond to the truth—is an idea that we would not have if it weren't for interpersonal relations. In other words, the source of objectivity is intersubjectivity: the triangle consists of two people and the world. Part of the idea is this: if you were alone in the world—that is, not in communication with anybody else—things would be impinging on you, coming in through your senses, and you would react in differential ways. Now, here's where the metaphor comes in. If you were to ask, "Well, when you're reacting a certain way, let's say to some pleasant taste, what is it that pleases you?" We would say, "It's the peach." However, in the case of the person who has no one with whom to share his thoughts, on what grounds could you say, "It's the peach that pleases" rather than the taste of the peach, or the stimulation of the taste buds, or, for that matter, something that happened a thousand years ago which set all these forces in motion which eventually impinged on the taste buds. How far out are the objects that he is responding to? There would be no answer to that question at all: nothing for him to check up on, no way to raise the question, much less to answer it. So, the idea of triangulation is this: if you have two people both reacting to stimuli in the world and to each other—that is, to each other's reactions to the stimuli—you've completed a triangle which locates the common stimulus. It doesn't locate it in one person's mouth; it doesn't locate it in one person's eyes; it doesn't locate it five thousand years ago. It locates it just at the distance of the shared stimulus which, in turn, causes each of the two creatures to react to each other's reactions. It's a way of saying why it is that communication is essential to the concept of an objective world.

Q. Speaking of communication and how communication is "essential to the concept of an objective world," would you distinguish between what you call a prior theory and a passing theory?

A. The distinction between prior and passing theories is just the difference between what one anticipates that somebody will mean by something he or she says and what one decides was meant after one is exposed to an utterance. Whenever you talk to somebody, you have an unformulated theory of what that person would mean if he or she were to utter certain words. For example, you would know roughly what you yourself would mean if you were to utter these same words. However, plenty of things may tip you off that your interpretation is not the right interpretation. On occasion, someone's words don't mean what you would have meant by those words. They don't necessarily mean what they've meant in the past. You discover that this might be a slip of the tongue, or it might be a clever invention on the spur of the moment; it might be a joke; there are a thousand possibilities many of which we are so good at catching that we don't even notice we're doing it.

Q. So, theories don't actually need to match?

A. No, no. That's right. They just are nearer to or further away from being correct. Luckily, we can make lots of adjustments as we go along. Communication is always incomplete. It's not as though anybody ever gets everything right; it's a matter of degree.

Q. Some rhetoricians and composition specialists balk at the idea that communicative interaction cannot be codified in some way. They want what I think of as a "big theory" that can do some serious work for us and that actually can model successful communicative interaction. The notion of a passing theory denies this possibility, doesn't it? A passing theory can't be predicted in advance of a communicative situation, and in ordinary communicative interaction—in day-to-day utterances—the passing theory is still always there. It doesn't disappear. It's just that we have become so habituated to using linguistic crutches—conventions of language—that passing theories become, to some extent, transparent.

A. We share an enormous amount of linguistic lore. In fact, we don't ever share it exactly. Each of us has our own ideas, and each of us adjusts how we speak according to the audience. We have ideas about what words somebody else is apt to understand, or what concepts they're apt to control. Now, the passing theory, on the part of the speaker, is what the speaker thinks that somebody else will make of what he or she is saying. The passing theory on the part of the interpreter is that person's best bet as to how to understand what is being said.

Q. Let me tell you why I am pressing this point. Some rhetoricians and linguists claim that language mastery is enough to ensure successful communication. Once you master something—language conventions, rules of syntax, a grammar, a schema, a script, a model of cognitive processes—you have all you need to communicate. This notion disturbs me because I wonder what it is that one masters when one masters a language.

A. Obviously, if you get everything right, you've mastered something. However, what should be considered part of knowing a language? I myself think that it's quite easy to see that to understand even a single utterance you have to know something that cannot be a rule of language in any way at all. You have to know what language the person is speaking more or less. These sounds might mean something completely different in another language, and the rules of the language can't tell you when somebody is speaking that language. So, that's something you have to bring in from outside. That's just a very simple case. I think it's a much broader point than that, but this example is enough to make the point; mastery of the language cannot be restricted in any way at all.

Q. If "mastery" means anything.

A. Exactly.

Q. This point ties in with my next question. In an oft-quoted passage from "A Nice Derangement of Epitaphs," you write that "linguistic ability is the ability to converge on a passing theory from time to time. If we do say this, then we should realize that we have abandoned not only the ordinary notion of a language, but we have erased the boundary between knowing a language and knowing our way around in the world generally. I conclude that there is no such thing as a language—not if a language is anything like what many philosophers and linguists have supposed." Now, this kind of talk strikes some rhetoricians as clearly counter-intuitive and others as downright crazy. Would you help us better understand your meaning when you say that there is no such thing as a language?

A. Of course, you've got to add the proviso, "if a language is anything like what many philosophers and linguists have supposed." In fact, elsewhere in that essay, I say in a fairly sharp way what those assumptions are that I think are wrong. They include such things as the idea that there is a single repertoire of expressions—with their meanings and their semantic interpretation—which everybody shares. That, I say, is just wrong. There is no such thing that's shared. People differ. Every person has got his or her own language in that sense. But to say that every person has his or her own language is to say that there is no such thing as what philosophers have supposed a language to be. Interestingly enough, this is a view that I apparently share with Chomsky, because he said exactly the same thing: everybody's got his or her own way of doing it. Of course, there is a tremendous amount of overlap from person to person in linguistic knowledge. If there weren't, talking would be much more a chore than it is. That the overlap is never complete is not a very shocking view if you understand it. What is much more shocking to some people is my view that it's not essential to linguistic communication that any two people who are talking to each other speak anything like the same language. In fact, it's inconvenient if they don't, but it can happen. I sometimes carry on conversations with people who are speaking French while I speak English. When I read papers in Europe, I'm constantly asked questions in German, French, and Spanish, and I answer them in English. They understand me, and I understand them. Of course, you might say that we have a background that allows us to translate back and forth; that's true. But, we could do it from scratch; it just would be very hard.

Q. And that's another way of saying that language is not convention-bound.

A. Yes, that's exactly right. This is something you probably know, but "A Nice Derangement of Epitaphs" was published along with two attacks, one by Ian Hacking and one by Michael Dummett. I recently attended a conference in Sicily with Dummett, and I finally produced my answer to his concerns. He is about to produce his answer to my answer, so this will go on, no doubt. He is strongly opposed to the idea that conventions are crutches. He thinks speaking as others do is not just a convenience but absolutely essential. He, like Tyler Burge, thinks that what we mean depends very much on what other people mean by the same words. There's a big issue here, for philosophers anyway, because we're on the edge of

Wittgenstein's private language discussion. You know Saul Kripke's book? Kripke attributes the following argument to Wittgenstein and seems to endorse it himself, although he doesn't absolutely commit himself. The idea is that a certain element of objectivity—which is essential to meaning something by what you say—is injected only by there being a social custom or a habit. The question whether you, for example, are meaning the same thing from moment to moment by some given word depends upon whether I use that word in a certain way. And, in fact, it's only that confluence or convergence on a usage, custom, or habit that provides an objective test of whether somebody is going on in the same way or not. This is not my account of objectivity; my doctrine of triangulation is an alternative account that doesn't depend upon people doing the same thing.

Q. Perhaps we might pursue this point. In the discipline of composition and rhetoric, we are fond of saying that knowledge is socially constructed. Following Kuhn, or what they imagine to be Kuhn's position, some rhetoricians desire to push this claim in order to argue the more forceful point that knowledge is communal in the sense that knowledge can be recognized as knowledge only within a community that shares a common discourse. It seems to me that this communitarian formulation buys into the idea that knowledge is relative to a conceptual scheme, a formulation that you roundly criticize. What are some of the problems we encounter when we insist that a framework of social conventions guides or structures what we can know or can say about the world?

A. Well, I shouldn't pretend any kind of expertise on what Kuhn has said, but if he says, as he seems to, that there is no objective standard against which to measure the correctness of a view except its acceptance, then this view seems to me to have all of the obvious flaws of various kinds of relativism about truth and the like. It sort of sounds attractive, but I don't know how one cashes it out.

Q. Let me approach this question from another angle. When social constructionists say that knowledge is relative to a discourse community, it seems to me that they posit a kind of conceptual scheme—made up of social norms or language conventions—to which propositional attitudes must be relative. Although social constructionists see their communitarianism as a break with cognitivism and the internalism inherent in it, I've been arguing that this position is not a break at all, but it's just simply a displacement of the same old Cartesian problem. Instead of meaning being located in mental categories, it now becomes located in a communal scheme of one kind or another, and you run into the old problems of skepticism and relativism.

A. It seems to me that it can be more complicated than that. I also think that there is an irreducibly social element in determining what it is that we mean. After all, the triangulation idea brings in a social element, but it doesn't say that something is right if it coheres with what everybody else is saying at the moment or something like that. It's not relativistic at all. It doesn't lead to a relativistic idea of truth. When people try to formulate this issue, they often get into the most obvious kind of trouble. You see, there are obviously some things that you can say that are true. As time goes on, what we mean by certain words changes, and, therefore, a sentence that might have been true at one time is no longer true because it doesn't mean what it meant before. That change in meaning is a social change and has to do with the development of theory, belief, and all sorts of things of that kind—but that's not relativism about truth. The truth of a sentence is relative to the circumstances of its use, but the intelligibility of this claim requires a non-relative concept of truth.

Q. You emphasize the importance of social change. How do you see your work in relation to social issues, such as institutional power, authority, and ethnocentrism? That is, do you see political or ideological implications embedded in your conceptions of belief and truth?

A. Well, it's not something I would want to push, but I do think that the rejection of certain kinds of relativism does make a difference about how we deal with people from different cultures, backgrounds, and periods. Instead of thinking of these things as sort of blocks that are fixed one way or another, we might think of them as just variance which we understand in terms of what we share and see ourselves as sharing. Understanding other cultures is no different from understanding our next door neighbor, except in degree. It's not a difference of kind. In both cases—understanding a different culture or understanding a neighbor—the principle of charity is essential to yielding the best interpretation. Of course, the more different we perceive people as being, the greater the strain becomes on using the principle of charity. So, when we are faced with these differences among people, we may think what's required to understand them is an entirely different kind of act—namely, a leap of the imagination of some sort. That's a rather common idea. However, I think it's a dangerous idea, because it leads us away from simply doing our best to accommodate somebody else's view of the world. If we think of understanding as needing some magical leap of the imagination, we're no longer calling on ourselves to discover the common ground on which we can make whatever sense we can make of one another.

Q. Yes, I think of triangulation, for example, as a way around the problem of ethnocentricism, so we don't have to throw up our hands and say, as Rorty seems to say, "Ah, yes, we're ethnocentric; we might as well admit it, and learn to live with it."

A. There's a related issue that has always been a lively one in philosophy and that has taken on a new life in recent years. It has to do with the question of the objectivity of values—whether values are either relative and just plain subjective in some sense or whether some values are objective in some way. It is interesting in a way that this dispute is as alive now as it was in Plato's day. It's quite wonderful.

Q. More so, in some ways.

A. That's right. In this matter, I'm on the side of objectivity. I think we have no principled way of making a distinction between evaluative and other kinds of judgments. Intersubjectivity is the only source for understanding other people's values, just as it is for understanding their other beliefs. Certainly, there is a difference of degree in the sense that it may be harder to resolve disagreements—harder than it may be about some scientific matters, for example—but I think about such differences as matters of degree and not as matters of absolute distinction.

Q. Do you think, therefore, that there's no principled difference between our ability to resolve a problem in science and our ability to resolve a problem dealing with value?

A. That's right. People like Bernard Williams, with whom I argue about this issue, say, "Look, there's an absolute difference between moral and scientific views. In science, we have ways of resolving things, and even when we don't resolve them, we have methods of resolution, like performing an experiment. When it comes to ethical matters, there is no such methodology in important cases." I'm not convinced by this line of thinking. For one thing, if we do an experiment, the experiment doesn't tell us what to think. We *decide* what to think. It's foundationalism again. The foundationalist thinks that sense data are going to decide the thing and that certain of our beliefs are tied so directly to sensation that they are forced upon us. I don't think that's right. We interpret the experiment, just as we do anything else. In the same way, we experiment all the time in moral matters. Just by acting, we express our values and often find out how things work out.

Q. So the authorization of a value or a belief derives primarily from meaning holism, our appeal to other values and beliefs?

A. This is a pretty long story to get into in any depth. Let's just say that a very close connection exists between what we actually value and our value judgments, and our value judgments are not different in kind from our factual judgments. There's no principal distinction to be made. There's not a distinction that allows us to say that in one case truth has an application and in the other case it doesn't.

Q. Given these issues of value, how might a feminist employ your work? For example, how might your conception of language contribute to a feminist critique of political issues or social institutions?

A. I don't know. It's not that I don't have any view about feminism, but I don't see that my philosophical views have any special bearing or application here.

Q. Would you say that language is so marked by gender that women think differently about the world than men do?

A. Well, I certainly think that some people have concepts that other people don't. This just means there are classifications that they have at their disposal and words that reflect these differences, just as a chemist has concepts that I don't have. So, I'm perfectly willing to believe that there are societies in which women have some concepts that are not widely shared or even shared at all by men. We know that there are cultures in which women speak a different language, but I take it that this is not really the basic question about whether or not a different language can or can't be translated. If you're asking me how widespread language differences are in our culture, I just have to say that such differences don't seem to me to be a major barrier to communication between the sexes. I think that the real barriers are economic and political questions of power.

Q. You mentioned previously that you've taught a wide variety of philosophy courses during your long and distinguished career. How do you view writing in your courses? Do you see a relation between your philosophy of language—or your theory of communicative interaction—and your teaching?

A. Regarding your second question, I'm not quite sure, but there's a sense in which I don't think of myself primarily as instructing or, at least, passing along information. I tend to tell students what I think, and I try to tell them in such a way that they feel free to disagree with me. I welcome live exchanges, and I prize these exchanges over just straight lecturing. At the beginning of our discussion, you touched on the topic of writing, and it's something that I have some thoughts about. I do think there is a big difference between communication by writing and by speech. In what I think of as the best kind of teaching, this difference comes very much to the fore. As it seems to me, words which are extremely important to us—especially the big words that philosophers are fond of like truth, good, right, courage, sincerity—really do change in force according to the situation in which they're used. There are cases where we're apt to agree whether these words apply or don't, and then there's a huge shadowy area which often concerns cases that don't come up all the time or even cases that we just imagine for the sake of exploring the concepts. In the course of talking, we temporarily sharpen concepts through dialogue. That can't happen in writing, at least in the same way. So, I think that in conversation itself, we give words shapes, especially these big words which are important but vague. Perhaps these shapes will be ones that will remain with us after the discussion. A whole lot of philosophy is like that and teaching, too, if it's done right. It's a matter of people discovering what they think. It's not a matter of people bringing sharp ideas into conflict and then deciding who's right. That can happen, too, but much more important is the situation in which ideas are taking shape as the conversation goes on.

Q. I'd like to pursue this topic. How would writing fit into your triangulation metaphor? Let's distinguish between the production of discourse and the reception of it. Now, we can see pretty clearly how the reception of discourse would work; a text would be an object in the world, and we would triangulate with it and formulate different passing theories about its meaning. However, what about the production of discourse—the actual production of an object in the world? How is that going to fit into your metaphor?

A. First of all, it seems to me that a lot of different cases exist. If you have two people who are dumb sitting next to each other and writing notes, then the fact that the note is written hardly makes any difference. It's the same thing as talking. If they're writing each other letters, well now a difference has occurred. For example, certain kinds of indexical gestures are lost. You can't point to something in a letter. Temporal references slip and so on. If you're writing a proclamation to a group, then further indexical elements drop out, because you're not sharing your ideas just with one person but with a lot of them. If you're writing a will, you're not going to be there to interpret it. So, I envision a whole continuum. A novel, for example, is an especially interesting case, because typically the author does not expect interaction with the readers. It doesn't mean that there is no feedback; it's just not relevant in any very important way, unless you happen to be Rushdie. This lack of interaction surely does make a big difference with the triangulation idea, and you have to ask how to apply the idea. I think the only way to do this is to say that something like novel writing absolutely depends upon the prior existence of conversational exchange. People have to have been in the triangular situation before they could make anything out of a novel.

Q. So, the principle of charity exists here in full force. The novelist must presuppose a large body of shared understanding about rationality and the world in general in order to be able to produce the text in the first place.

A. Absolutely. The normal way in which language gets related to the world is mostly lacking in a novel, or, let's say, it's deferred. It's established through indirect connections rather than direct ones. You can't learn what the proper names refer to from reading the book itself, and, of course, in a novel they normally don't refer to anything. You have to have learned it in some other situation. If someone were to talk about Paris and London or something like that, you can't learn from the book where they are, because the book can't point. The causal connections are lost to you; there's a lot of dependence upon the kind of case that I think of as basic. So, what is radical interpretation like when it comes to interpreting a book? I think that's a very tricky question and to tell you the truth, reading the essays in Dasenbrock's volume [*Literary Theory after Davidson*] has made me think about this. I'm surprised I didn't think of it before, since I began with a great interest in literature. I see that it's an extremely interesting question, and with all the discussion nowadays about the relevance of intention in interpretation, I need to think about some things

I haven't thought about very hard. On the other hand, reading various things has made me realize that people who are talking about literary criticism need to make a lot of distinctions that they haven't been bothering about, at least the critics that I've been reading. They say either that intention matters or that it doesn't. Well, you really can't put it that way, because certain intentions on the part of the author must be known or assumed in order to make anything of the text at all. This is so outrageous an example that it may sound silly, but if we were to discover that the *Iliad* isn't in ancient Greek, that it's in an unknown language we just now learned to decipher and it doesn't mean anything of the sort that we thought it meant, would we go on reading it as being Greek? Some people say, "Yeah, read it any old way you please," but that seems wild. If we want to understand what's there, we need to know what the language is more or less. So, the intentions can't be totally irrelevant. There's no way that a book can say on its cover "understand this book as being in ancient Greek," because those very words may mean something else in the language it's written in.

Q. But clearly you can't go the other route either and say that it is only intention that authorizes interpretation.

A. No, no. All I'm saying is that you can't say that intention has nothing to do with it. On the other hand, it seems to me that when we're reading something as literature, some of the author's intentions in writing it are indeed irrelevant. The thing is that any act at all has many intentions. There's not some one intention that either counts or it doesn't. Some of the intentions are relevant to our interests and some are not. The problem is to distinguish the various intentions, and it seems to me that here there are some very important and interesting things to argue about.

Q. How do you do that? How can you claim that you have discovered the relevant intentions as opposed to other kinds of intention?

A. Well, at the moment—and I may change my mind about this in the next couple of weeks—but at the moment, when it comes to aesthetic matters, I tend to say there's no point in telling other people what they should be interested in. Anything that you learn about a piece of literature may change its value to you—its interest, its informative content, whatever. Reading biographies of the author may be considered very low class, but, in fact, it may alert you to things that are in the work that you wouldn't have noticed before. I don't have some theory about what the right thing to look for is, but I could still make a lot of interesting distinctions. It's just that the discussions I've been reading in literary criticism about intention just seem to me to miss the fact that there are endless intentions involved in every single action.

Q. Let's go back for a second. Correct me if I'm mistaken here, but it seems that one of the implications of your triangulation metaphor concerns the relation of composition studies and literary studies. When we write or produce discourse, we're interpreting, just as when we receive discourse, and in both cases there is nothing that helps us in advance to ensure that we have things right. Because writers and readers engage in a very similar activity, your conception of communicative interaction gives us a way of talking about a connection between discourse reception—what we mostly do in literature courses—as opposed to the production of discourse, which has been traditionally segregated in composition courses.

A. I completely agree with you. Anybody who is writing or speaking is constantly, if not consciously, asking him or herself, how will a reader understand this? What will the reader make of it?

Q. Your conception of communicative interaction, which we've been discussing, and your causal theory of action have created a great deal of controversy. What do you take to be the primary criticism leveled against your ideas? I think especially of someone like Charles Taylor, who has complained about some aspects of your work.

A. That's an interesting question. There are a lot of things that I've maintained that people have criticized a great deal. I find it hard to pick out just one issue. I could think of five or six theses that have attracted hundreds of articles and books, almost always critical. My causal theory of action, for example, rather won the day for a decade or so, and now it's under attack increasingly. In fact, it's absolutely true that in my concentration on what seemed to me to be the bigger issues, I neglected lots of fine points which have come to the fore, and I have to recognize as perfectly good complaints people's objections to this fact. If I think of it chronologically, my theory of causal theory of action was the very first place where I stuck my neck out; next came my claim that a theory of truth for a language, more or less in the style of Tarski, could serve as a theory of meaning. Over the years this position has been criticized from many points of view; in fact, in light of the criticisms, I had to change the doctrine. I've made numerous adjustments so that now people are accusing me of being inconsistent, which is certainly true. Compare what I wrote ten years ago with what I write now; it's clearly different.

Concerning Charles Taylor, I've been the target of Chuck's attacks a number of times. I remember two cases when I was present: one was in London, when he gave a talk on philosophy and language, and then two summers ago in Santa Cruz, when there was a six-week institute on Heidegger and me. The idea of the institute was that Heidegger and I were both anti-Cartesians but obviously came to that position by very different routes. The central question had to do with the way these two such different ways of thinking about things could lead to a common conclusion. The ecumenical position was sort of the official one, but Taylor, who was there for a week to give lectures on the subject, said, "Look, Davidson and Heidegger couldn't be more completely different." For me, the curious part of Taylor's position was his claim that I was the one who was supposed to think that language is something that you can isolate and treat by itself apart from social context. This seems to me altogether wrong. Consider the passage where I say that there is no distinction between knowing a language—being an interpreter of a language—and knowing your way around in the world, a view which I take very seriously indeed. I think I would say that Taylor has not understood my work very well, but lots of people, of course, get something wrong here or there. However, in general, I don't complain that I haven't been understood. I would like to say this: one has one's relatively limited points, and then one also has a big picture. I would say nobody seems to me to have done as well in seeing what my overall picture is than Rorty. Even though Rorty and I think of things in quite a different way, he has made an effort to follow what I was up to, and it seems to me he gets the main thing right. It's extremely reassuring and pleasing.

Q. So, you validate Rorty's readings of your work?

A. He usually gets the biggest things. He sees what I'm up to and sees things I haven't seen or said as plainly. Sometimes he changes his mind, too. At the Santa Cruz institute, for example, Rorty had just read my Dewey lectures, which are three lectures on the concept of truth, and at that time he was rather scolding me for taking the notion of truth too seriously. He thought I'd gone off the track that I should be on. But then we met again about a month ago at a conference at Santa Clara, and he said that he's been rereading those lectures, and he now sees what I'm up to and thinks it's all right.

Q. How would you distinguish your work from Rorty's? In one way—and again correct me if I'm wrong—you seem to suggest that answers exist to enduring philosophical problems like skepticism. Rorty maintains that we should just change the topic since we can't answer the skeptic without accepting the skeptic's presuppositions. Is this a significant difference between you and Rorty? Or is it a difference at all?

A. I don't know. We certainly have a somewhat different approach to philosophy, a fact which I think we both appreciate. To say, as Rorty does, that the skeptic should get lost, or to try to answer the skeptic as I do, seems to me to be more a difference in style and attitude than a sharp distinction. I think each of us has teased the other about this. I say to him, "You just want to tell the skeptic to change the subject; why then do you refer to my *arguments*?" And, at least on one occasion, I think he said, "I'm not really interested in your arguments, it's your conclusion I like." I see this as a temperamental difference rather than anything else. My view about doing philosophy has always been that people should do it in whatever way they most enjoy doing it, and that there isn't one correct way. Rorty has given philosophy a big boost because so many people who are not in philosophy are interested in his work and are reading it. I think that this is all to the good, although not everyone shares my view. On the other hand, I don't think I could do what he does, though he might be able to do what I do.

Q. Yet, your influence on Rorty has been profound, as he acknowledges. In fact, most of his current views about language may be traced directly to your writings.

A. I think I'm right in saying that the piece that marked the point at which Rorty changed was something that was called "The World Well Lost." He wrote it after he read two lectures that I gave at the University of London attacking the idea of conceptual relativism, and he kindly gives me full credit. At that point, I hadn't published this material. I did subsequently, but I knew him through that formative period. We were colleagues at Princeton and, in fact, during the year or two that I was chairman there, he was the assistant chairman. We talked a lot, and we always got along extremely well.

Q. That you two teamed up to direct a department suggests a question about the role you see philosophy playing within the structure of the university. Rorty seems to think that philosophy has done its work. Do you?

A. Well, there are two questions there. One is just sort of social history—what has actually happened—and the other one is what do I think happened? Rorty's idea that philosophy has talked itself out of a job seems to me wrong. I think what he has in mind mainly is a certain way of doing epistemology which was a central part of philosophy through a period of a few centuries. I don't think of analytic philosophy quite in the same way that Rorty does. He thinks of analytic philosophy as being almost entirely concerned with epistemology, with producing one or another response to skepticism; however, I think of analytic philosophy as a method. The method is one which tries to state problems and arguments as clearly as possible and respects the pursuit of truth. So far as the place of philosophy in the university is concerned, my own views are not very sharp. I don't think there is some one thing that philosophy ought to do. Philosophy usefully overlaps a lot of other fields; literary criticism is one; artificial intelligence—cognitive psychology—quite generally is another; mathematics is another; the law is yet another. This is all to the good. Historically, philosophy has been like that. In fact, Plato and Aristotle made no distinction between psychology, mathematics, biology, philosophy; they were all part of the same thing. Some subjects like physics, when they became serious, went their own way, though there's plenty of overlap still. I prize those philosophers who really are competent in other fields. There are a handful of people who really know physics or really know certain branches of mathematics, or really know the theory of evolution. So, I'm against trying to draw lines somewhere and say, "This is philosophy and this isn't."

Q. It seems that these disciplinary boundaries within institutions are growing indistinct, if they're not being erased entirely. I believe that attempts to blur these distinctions are worthwhile.

A. I do, too, but it's probably not something that in general you can do much directly to promote. I think it just happens. Cognitive psychology was given a huge artificial boost, but the most successful cooperation I know about in which philosophy was involved really started before there was the injection of money. Linguistics and philosophy came into serious contact largely as a result of Chomsky's work which changed the way linguistics looked to philosophers. That's an area of cooperation that continues in a big way. There are a lot of people who are in both camps; you don't have to decide whether they are linguists or philosophers: they are both.

Q. However, some people get unnerved by this kind of talk. They don't desire to relinquish the master narratives that have held us together—or kept us apart—for so long. What do you say to calm those people?

A. Well, I guess I don't know how to calm them until I know exactly what it is that they are worried about. As I said earlier, there are two branches to foundationalism. One depends on the certainty that we're supposed to have about the contents of our own mind and the idea that this certainty is the basis of knowledge. I don't question that we know what's in our own mind. There's a presumption that we're right about what we think we think; first person authority is not something I would call into question. What I do call into question is the view that we can construct a world solely on the basis of what we know about the contents of our own minds. I substitute for that idea the triangulation situation which gives objectivity three legs to stand on. The other element in foundationalism stresses the dependence of knowledge on the senses. The senses also play a role for me because the triangulation argument has us reacting to the world and to other people. So, I don't see that anything is lost, but if someone has a reason to think that I'm undermining something valuable without replacing it, I need to be told what it is.

Q. I was thinking more along the lines of social philosophers or even theologians who think that something outside of our own beliefs must exist in order to authorize those beliefs.

A. If the argument is that I don't see anything to correspond with the truth, then that is certainly right, but no one has ever been able to make good sense of correspondence theories to begin with or to show how they would be any use. On the other hand, I've never said anything against God, but if He ever spoke to me, I guess I would have to raise the question on my own whether He was right.

Q. So, you would have to triangulate?

A. [Laughter] Yes.

The Malaprop in Spite of Herself: A Desperate Reading of Donald Davidson

Susan Wells

A month after Gary Olson asked me to respond to Thomas Kent's interview with Donald Davidson, I packed my xeroxes from Davidson's *Essays on Actions and Events* and *Inquiries into Truth and Interpretation* and mailed them to Tokyo, where I would be teaching for a year. By the time my envelopes came, Davidson's principle of charity was for me no longer a remote procedural maxim; without the interpretive patience of someone willing to believe, against the available evidence, that I was a rational agent, I could not open a bank account, do dry cleaning, buy groceries. Davidson was quite clear, in this interview and elsewhere, that charity was not a matter of being kind to people, but, helpless as I was, I had become deeply grateful to anyone who was willing to see me as a logical agent. It was (and is) nothing to take for granted.

I would like to use this desperation to shape my response to Davidson's interview with Kent. Since, like many readers of *JAC*, I encountered Davidson for the first time in Kent's provocative interview, perhaps the projects of reading Japan, being read by Japan, reading Davidson, and allowing oneself to "be read by" Davidson can form a series of mutually illuminating metaphors.[1] Let me open that series with a story.

Rationality and "Passing Rules"

I had gone with my daughter to buy a birthday present for one of her friends at the gift section of our local department store, the "personal gift selections department, full of dream and joy." They had a broad assortment of ceramic birds, bath salts, handkerchiefs, and joke items—latex false breasts, something that might have been sneezing powder. After the gift was wrapped, the salesperson gave me a card, a "cardo," with the price of the item blocked out in thousands of yen. She pointed to some numbers, and said "sen en," or "a thousand yen." Ah, a charge for giftwrapping—and a rather steep charge, I thought. I gave her a thousand-yen bill, which she refused. Instead, she put a red box in front of me and invited me to pick something out of it. I reached in, drew out a yellow candy, and thanked her. But the salesperson—now accompanied by two colleagues—applauded, explained that I had a "lucky candy," and showed me two sets of matching plastic bathroom accessories, white and blue. Since this was one of the few times in my life when a plastic soap dish would be both an addition to the household economy and a substantial purchase, I was pleased, picked the white set, tried out the word for *white*, had my pronunciation corrected, and went home happy. My daughter wanted the candy.

This story demonstrates, besides a traveller's obsession with ordinary confusions, the truth of Davidson's epigram that knowing a language is indistinguishable from "knowing our way around in the world generally." The world of Japanese retailing was new to me; that ignorance generated as much confusion as my bad Japanese. In fact, I probably misunderstood the English signs and slogans in the department store: surely they couldn't have really meant "dream and joy." Both parties in this transaction, buyer and sellers, formed "passing rules" at higher and higher levels of adequacy: we tested ways of explaining procedures, expanded our scanty common vocabulary, found ways of correcting error. But, as Davidson says, our communication was incomplete; we don't get everything right. I might have left the store with a soap dish, but I never did figure out the one-thousand-yen part; I still don't understand why they marked my card, or what the card was for; and I can only guess what embarrassment my clumsiness caused the salespeople.

While it seems true that both parties in this exchange practiced a principle of charity, it is difficult to locate our mutual assumptions of rationality semantically, and one of Davidson's central projects is to connect semantic issues with issues of truth. I made assumptions about buying: that after this confusing business with cards and giftwrap and drawings from boxes, I would be allowed to leave with my purchases. The salespeople made assumptions about selling: that someone approaching a counter with merchandise wants to buy. But these are not arguments, not connected propositions; to dispute them is not to contest a belief. These assumptions are predictions based on schemes of action. If somebody were to dispute one of these assumptions, the correct response would not be to argue for a proposition—to show its plausibility—but to demonstrate an action—to show the efficacy of a prediction, the coherence of an action schema. What we took for granted was not rationality as a mental state or intention of the subject, even the intention to get out of this scene without humiliation. The issues of interpretation would have been much the same if, in some howling lapse of taste, I were buying sneezing powder for an asthmatic grandmother. In this context, rationality implies nothing more than a plausible correspondence between means and ends. The principle of charity, therefore, does not signify that either party considers the other rational, only that each party expects the other to act in a way that is appropriate to the setting—a much less significant assumption, and one without semantic force.

Further, our formulation of "passing rules" was neither a matter of extending our linguistic competence nor of learning the world in general.

The interaction was quite specifically framed: both our good guesses and our mistakes were formed within the model of retail exchange, specifically the action of giving a customer a gift. It was within these frames, or routines, of institutional expectations that we made guesses about which meanings were likely. The salesperson assumed that I offered a thousand-yen note as payment, rather than as a personal gift; I assumed that whatever I picked out of the box would be mine to keep. None of these guesses is itself rational: they are not propositions that can be tested by argument; they do not depend on a belief that either speaker is capable of argument, or accountable for giving reasons. There is, thank goodness, no system of values or beliefs in which it is more rational to offer customers plastic soap dishes than it is to offer them hard candies.

Finally, in this setting, the principle of charity does not imply judgments about individual speakers of a language. The salesperson and I do not encounter each other as innocent speakers, testing the limits of our powers of interpretation. We encounter each other within a series of institutional contexts: this department store, with its particular *ethos*; the system of gift giving, the system of retail exchange in Japan, with its lavish expenditure of young women's labor. We encounter each other, mutually, as strangers representing cultural stereotypes: the store girl meets the foreign humanities expert. Like the action scenarios through which we interpret specific utterances, these frames are not propositional. They can be represented as a series of assertions about gifts, or retail trade, or women's labor, but they are not identical to those assertions. Relations among speakers are not exhausted by the propositions with which we might describe them. This is especially the case when such relations are embedded in such complex contexts as the cultural relation between Japan and the United States that exchanges a certain number of academic workers between the two countries, a relation that neither I nor the salesperson fully understand, although we understand each other only within its boundaries. Actions take place within institutional and historical frames, and they are represented, rather than reproduced, in language.

Davidson and "Truth"

To read my story of retail desperation through Davidson, then, is to be struck both by the analytic power with which he frames the communicative situation and by the limits of his emphasis on the truth of propositions. Since, as rhetoricians, we are mortgaged to anti-foundationalism—what rhetorical theory could make peace with any guarantee of truth outside discourse?—we are also constantly fending off relativism. Davidson's theory provides us with a challenging and useful model of an anti-foundationalism that is not at all relativist. He works out a theory of truth from the relations and assertions implicit in language and communication. But there is more, in any communicative situation, for us to worry about. While it may be that nothing distinguishes knowing a language from knowing how to get along in the world, perhaps there is more involved in getting along in the world than knowing a language.

We experience this distance in our classrooms daily. Control of the propositional content of a discipline is only the first of the problems that a student writer faces; he or she must also undertake the action of writing a particular kind of academic text that takes this propositional content as its theme. Such a text is defined, at least in part, by the agency of the writer, specifically by the writer's skill at demonstrating compliance, at reproducing what has been offered in the classroom, varying its emphasis slightly, offering a new arrangement of details that might be called "her own." A student writer is taken up in an exchange much more complicated, and considerably more arbitrary, than my retail ballet of the soap dish. It may be that in walking a writer through this dance, we are not teaching language. And we are not teaching the world in general, only the discursive actions peculiar to a corner of it, to a specific institutional setting. But we are surely teaching *something*.

About that project, Davidson has important things to say. It is salutary, even emancipatory, to assume that most of what our students think is probably right and that our job is to find the explanatory devices that show us why and how it is right. It is even more praiseworthy to assume that, if we identify a real difference of opinion, we cannot judge in advance, outside the context of a particular discourse, whose opinion is true. Such a notion of truth invites us to ask our students hard questions—how else could we understand what they mean?—but it denies us any indifference to the truth of what student writers assert. It is a guard against the limits of a technical understanding of rhetoric. And, finally, Davidson's understanding of truth forestalls any assumption that we have much to gain from hiding our own ideas from students: it is not as if our ideas are so likely to be right that it would be unfair of us to argue for them.

When we move from questions of truth to the issues raised by the institutional situation of discourse, however, Davidson is much less helpful to us. And this limit proceeds from the strength, rather than the weakness, of his method. Davidson refrains from any easy speculation about the political implications of his theory. In the interview, we see him withdrawing from general questions, complicating issues, making questions more specific and more interesting. Such a discursive tactic is entirely coherent with a notion of truth that reasons from the intentions of speakers. It is difficult to relocate it in the more sedimented and obstructed terrain of institutionally and ideologically bound discourse.

Let me take as an example Davidson's response to the question about whether women might think differently from men, not because I think that Davidson is particularly wrong in his answer (although I do disagree with him), but as a way of getting at the kind of disagreement that a theory of truth based on intentions and on interpretive charity cannot mediate. Davidson rephrases the question about women thinking differently from men as a question about the possibility that specific women might have languages specifically divergent from those of men. Such rephrasing of central political questions keeps us from easy generalizations: it also keeps us from hard and potentially useful ones. I would want to argue against the notion of women having a distinct rationality by uncoupling a description of gender differences in language from any assertion about the ways that men and women generally think. The theory that gender differences in language imply serious and fundamental distinctions in the forms of rationality available to men and women must either deny the connections among forms of rationality, or deny that both genders are rational. To assert a different mode of thought for men and women—even when the motive for this assertion is to proclaim the value of a peculiarly feminine "way of knowing"—is to deny those bonds of language that are our only stay against real irrationality, and to confine women to those discursive forms that traditionally define "their place."

What would a Davidsonian interpreter do, faced with two groups of feminist theorists, one group believing that women think differently than men, and the other holding the position I just outlined: that all speakers have access to the same forms of rationality? Such a position poses both propositional and procedural problems. If indeed women think differently than men—a larger question than simply having some concepts that men don't have—then all interpretations become deeply problematic in their performance of gender. Davidson has written in "Psychology as Philosophy" that "if translation succeeds, we have shown there is no need to speak of two conceptual schemes, while if translation fails, there is no ground for speaking of two." If men and women think differently, then a translation that did not reproduce that difference would fail in its fidelity, while a translation that did reproduce the difference would not be understandable. The interpreter, then, cannot be indifferent to the truth of the propositions advanced in this argument and cannot undertake a radical interpretation without deciding the argument in advance.

On the level of procedure, a Davidsonian interpreter (of whatever gender) faces a second problem. If the interpreter extends the principle of charity to both the parties in this debate, then he or she must do so in accordance with some definition of rationality—and it is exactly that definition that is in question here. If the interpreter assumes that both speakers are rational, and defines rationality in a way that is gender specific, then the speaker who argues that rationality is the same for men and for women is self-contradictory, since the argument for a common rationality has been phrased in a gendered language. A complementary contradiction emerges if the interpreter assumes that rationality is gender neutral. In both cases, the interpreter has produced a contradiction that is extraneous to the argument: it is the rule of charity, ironically, that produced contradictions in the discourse.

Context and Communicative Action

The argument about gender and rationality is an argument about language, and still more an argument about the frames of action suitable for the understanding of language. I discuss it as an instance of the kind of ideologically framed and politically inflected language that it seems to me Davidson's theory can situate and contextualize, but not resolve.

To take my argument a step further, I would hold that Davidson's understanding of rationality cannot support our interventions into such complex contexts because it provides for only one form of rationality and for one means of understanding rationality: the reflection upon what is assumed and asserted in discourse. I would argue that it is characteristic of the discourses of modernity to follow quite distinct practices of rationality and to locate those practices within frameworks of communicative action, so that a good reason within the context of public policy is quite different from a good reason in scientific controversy. Further, such frameworks are not sustained by assumptions of rationality—and sincerity, appropriateness, and other forms of discursive good faith—so much as they are interrupted when such assumptions are violated. Some readers will recognize in these two arguments two of the central assertions in the theory of Jürgen Habermas: the differentiation of reason and the counterfactual force of the truth claims implicit in communication. Both of these arguments allow us to gain a stronger, more rhetorically situated purchase on the difficult issues that Davidson's interview raises.

Davidson's work shows us that issues of communication are issues of truth: while he might interpret this connection to mean that writing cannot be taught, we might interpret it to mean that writing cannot be taught without attending to what counts as truth. In this case, "attending to" means "talking about," a demanding and exacting discussion to be carried out in our classrooms and in our dealings with one another. In that discussion, all of us—feminists, critical theorists, analytic philosophers—will need all the philosophic tools we can lay our hands on, and we can all be grateful to Davidson for those that he has provided us.

Temple University
Philadelphia, Pennsylvania

Note

[1] I was helped in this initial encounter by my colleague Steven E. Cole, whose essay "The Scrutable Subject: Davidson, Literary Theory, and the Claims of Knowledge," is forthcoming in Reed Way Dasenbrock's *Literary Theory after Davidson* (Penn State UP). Cole's argument, commentary, and generous guidance through the body of Davidson's work have been invaluable.

A Response to "Language Philosophy, Writing, and Reading: A Conversation with Donald Davidson"

REED WAY DASENBROCK

Anyone looking for a predominantly critical analysis of Donald Davidson's views on language or of their applicability to composition theory won't find such an analysis here. I think Davidson's work in philosophy of language and in interpretation theory is the most important scholarship being done in those fields today, and it has complex and multiple implications for the teaching and study of writing. Thomas Kent has done an excellent job of drawing out Davidson's views, and "Language Philosophy, Writing, and Reading" works well as an introduction to Davidson's work for those unfamiliar with it. I'd like to think that as composition theorists become more acquainted with Davidson's work, they will realize the relevance of it to their concerns and that Davidsonian scholarship in composition will become less isolated than it is now.

But, of course, for this to happen, it will take much more than proclaiming from the treetops that Davidson is right about everything. Of course, he isn't, and as one studies his writings in context, one realizes what a complex interplay exists between his work and that of others in the analytic tradition. Moreover, even if he *were* always right, that would leave completely open the question of what consequences or implications a Davidsonian position in philosophy would have for composition—the question of application, and the question I would like to focus on here.

The Question of Application

If we accept the general adequacy of Davidson's work in philosophy of language, what remains for us to do? A number of things, but most pressing among them is to develop a theory of *writing*. Surely, one of the things that should strike any reader of analytic philosophy is that its models of language-use are oral and its models of interpretation are based primarily on the interpretation of speech, not writing. I don't take this to be an insuperable obstacle or problem; after all, classical rhetoric began as the study of public speech, not writing, and that hasn't prevented its successful application to writing over the millennia. But Jacques Derrida usefully reminds us that the choice of speaking as a model for the understanding of writing is not a choice without consequences, and his work should remind us to ask of any speech-based theory of language whether there are assumptions in the theory that work better for speech than for writing.

Derrida shows no sign of any acquaintance with Davidson's writings, but he uses the work of the analytic philosopher J.L. Austin as one of his central examples of a theory of language gone astray by its privileging of speech over writing. Austin's theories gave birth to a movement known as "speech-act theory," and it seems no accident that it was not called writing-act theory. Classic speech-act theory postulates "uptake" or a full understanding of the "conversational implicature" as essential to communication. That seems much less easy to posit as a norm for writing than for conversation. The reader may be much further away from the author in time, space and values than any audience, and there is obviously no way for the writer to reformulate the text if understanding isn't reached, no immediate feedback mechanism of the kind that face-to-face conversation is rich in. These are, of course, precisely the differences between speech and writing Derrida has in mind, and he emphasizes in his critique of Austin and Searle how quick such a speech-based model of communication, with what in Derrida's parlance we can call its assumptions of presence, breaks down in writing.

In my judgment (though I don't have the space to go into this issue in adequate detail here), speech-act theory, despite the richness of many of its concepts, does not and cannot meet Derrida's challenge. It does make assumptions which hamper its extension from speech into writing. In contrast, Davidson's work allows us to meet Derrida's challenge. Although most of his examples of communicative interaction may come from speech, his theory isn't speech-based in the way speech-act theory can be said to be. The key to Davidson's position can be found in the passage in the interview when he says to Kent, "Communication is always incomplete. It's not as though anybody ever gets anything right; it's a matter of degree." This is not an admission on Davidson's part that theories of communication don't work perfectly; this is the essence of his theory. If speech-act theory seems to envision a conversation between people who share an idiolect and therefore can grasp every nuance, Davidson's norm for communication is just the opposite: "It's not essential to linguistic communication that any two people who are talking to each other speak anything like the same language. . . . When I read papers in Europe, I'm constantly asked questions in German, French, and Spanish, and I answer them in English."

Davidson insists that understanding is possible in such a situation because we have the capability of developing a "passing theory" to make sense of the other. This is a model well suited to the reality of the world's communicative situation since most people live in multilingual societies; it is also—more to the point here—far more suitable to writing. An author's understanding of what the words he or she uses mean is never perfectly matched by a reader's, and, therefore, theories that posit such a shared understanding as necessary for communication aren't going to work for writing. But since Davidson doesn't have to assign a concurrence of what he calls "prior theories" for communication to take place, his models of communication won't break down in the same way speech-act theory does when applied to writing. What Davidson posits instead is a far more fluid world in which every communicative situation—some only slightly, others more radically—provokes in the interpreter a new passing theory, a provisional understanding (or heuristic assumption) of what the speaker or writer means by his or her words. Looking at this the other way around, no speaker or writer can ever be completely certain of how his or her words will be taken, and writers particularly need as rich an understanding as possible of the multiple ways their words may be understood. Writers need to remember as they write that "communication is always incomplete" and that the illusion of full understanding—full presence—is just that, an illusion.

There is another side to this which makes Davidson's ideas work better for the teaching of writing than many other theories. In emphasizing the mutability of our prior understanding, Davidson establishes creativity and innovation at the very heart of communication. It is not just that the interpreter's theory never matches the writer's and that we need to resign ourselves to this state of affairs; we can actively take advantage of it by challenging the reader's prior theory, by confronting and overturning received conventions. Davidson thus introduces a new twist to the long argument between those who emphasize a mastery of received usage ("current traditionalists" in the currently traditional jargon) and those who see such an emphasis as preventing the development of the individual's own voice. We attain our own voice, a Davidsonian approach to usage suggests, not by slavishly following nor by desperately avoiding received conventions, but by playing off against them. The more radical our departure from received conventions, the more we risk unintelligibility; but the more we respect and follow received usage, the more we risk boredom. And it is in writing that we can most thoroughly utilize the resources of language, risk unintelligibility but "get away with it" and successfully communicate, because we can give the reader more clues about the passing theory needed to decipher the writing.

How we do that is, of course, a very complex question, and not one Davidson has spent a lot of time on. As a philosopher of language, he is more interested in the fact that we can understand the anomalous and the unconventional than he is in detailing how we do this. Such a detailed understanding of understanding is in any case more properly the province of *our* discipline than his. However, I think Davidson's work in philosophy of language gives us a solid base for such an understanding, and his recent work in particular has suggested some of the directions a Davidsonian understanding of writing might take. (I might note in passing that Davidson's uncollected work, the papers he has published after *Essays on Actions and Events* [1980] and *Inquiries into Truth and Interpretation* [1984], is an incredibly rich body of work; see my *Literary Theory after Davidson* for a partial bibliography.) For Kent, Davidson's idea of triangulation seems to be the most helpful pointer, and I would refer any reader intrigued by what Kent and Davidson say about triangulation in the interview to a forthcoming essay by Davidson, "Locating Literary Language," in which he spends some time thinking about the different forms triangulation takes in the interpretation of writing. And I think the remarks on triangulation and those on indexicals and deictic elements in writing in "Locating Literary Language" as well as in the interview are well worth the attention of scholars of writing. But we may not be reading Davidson to his (and our) best advantage if we read him looking primarily for particular ideas and concepts that we can use in building our own system. To reverse Lévi-Strauss' celebrated distinction, Davidson is an engineer, not a bricoleur. The relevant contrast here among analytic philosophers is again to Austin and Grice (and Wittgenstein, for that matter), whose work is continuously stimulating through an accretion of local insights even when the concepts may not add up to a coherent system. There are readers who will find this lack of system a virtue, as clearly at least (the later) Wittgenstein did, and such readers aren't going to find much to like in Davidson, I'm afraid, since he aims at precisely a systematic philosophy in a sense now widely challenged. He breaks with many of philosophy's traditional concepts but not with its traditional ambition. His aim is always to arrive at a systematic understanding of the field under investigation.

Interpretation and Intention
What I find to be most valuable in Davidson's recent work in philosophy of language is his emerging concentration on what it is that lies behind and drives the process of textual creation and interpretation: intentions. To interpret is to try to ascertain intentions. Since words themselves cannot declare their own meaning and since conventions do not successfully stabilize meaning, we as interpreters are always left with the question, "What do you mean by that?" Intention drives the process of interpretation not because there is any method for ascertaining intentions but because unless we consider the process to be one of ascertaining someone else's intentions, interpretation has no point. Only the effort to understand another (which is to understand another's intentions) draws us out of the prisonhouse of our own beliefs and prior theories and leads us to a new understanding or passing theory. If interpretation is intentionalist, so too is writing, as they are two sides of the same coin. To write is to write with the expectation and intention of being understood and having one's intentions understood.

This stress on writing as an intentional act is less likely to be news for scholars of rhetoric and composition—who have generally held onto an intentionalist vision of language and writing—than to literary theorists—who have generally wanted to ban intentions in favor of a textuality without intentions. In this, of course, they have been indebted not just to Derrida but to the general anti-humanism and anti-individualism of French poststructuralist thought. That cast of mind is so broadly diffused that Davidson's insistence on intention may seem startling, and it certainly is to Kent, as their discussion of intention is one of the few moments in the interview when Kent steps out of his role of elucidator and questions Davidson's assumptions. This reluctance on Kent's part to accept Davidson's intentionalism is a significant moment, I think, because Kent's general reading of Davidson's work is to assimilate it to a considerable extent with other currents of contemporary thinking under such labels as anti-foundationalism and externalism. One of the subtexts in the interview I found fascinating is the way Kent kept providing such descriptions for Davidson's work, some but not all of which Davidson seemed willing to accept. For example, Davidson was perfectly willing to join Kent in criticizing "foundationalism," but he did not use the term anti-foundationalism to describe his own position. Davidson is too careful a thinker to use a term like anti-foundationalism, since anti-foundationalism is a self-contradictory notion of just the kind Davidson has exposed elsewhere. But Davidson was willing, in contrast, to accept Kent's label of externalism for his work in opposition to a Cartesian internalism.

I don't find externalism the contradiction in terms that anti-foundationalism is, but I must confess to a general suspicion of this kind of labelling. This is one of the places where I would differentiate my interpretation of Davidson's work from Kent's, and I don't think this is just a quibble over terminology. I understand his desire to make Davidson's work more intelligible by relating it to broader intellectual currents, but such an approach can also mute potentially important distinctions and differences. After all, a lot of different people get gathered under one tent in such rubrics. Kent's recent essay, "Externalism and the Production of Discourse," lists Nietzsche, Dewey, Heidegger, Wittgenstein, Quine, Foucault, Lyotard, Rorty, Derrida, and Davidson as externalist philosophers (70), and I have to say that I find the differences among these thinkers at least as salient as any similarity suggested by the term externalism.

Richard Rorty is, of course, the foremost figure in America who has connected work in analytic philosophy with other intellectual currents, and one of the underlying themes in Rorty's recent work has been the emergence of Davidson as his central point of reference in analytic philosophy, indeed his central point of reference. Kent's use of labels such as anti-foundationalism and, more importantly, the general strategy of linking Davidson to varieties of "post" European thought is very much "school of Rorty." Having reservations about this way of approaching Davidson, I must confess to being surprised by Davidson's unwillingness in the interview to contest Rorty's reading of his work. What emerges from this discussion is a sense of personal respect for Rorty rather than assent to his views, however, so I think the question remains open whether Rorty and Kent's assimilation of Davidson to broader currents in contemporary thought is fully adequate to the specificity of Davidson's work. In the interview, Davidson himself reports some resistance from Rorty concerning Davidson's insistence on the concept of truth, and I think I am right in perceiving resistance from Kent concerning Davidson's insistence on the concept of intention. Thus, Rorty, Kent and I agree on the importance of Davidson's work, but we position him differently in relation to other currents of contemporary thought, and, in accordance with this, we emphasize different tendencies in his work. Specifically, I am more apt than either Rorty or Kent to find in him a useful dissenter from some of the dominant tendencies they assimilate him to. Davidson's work, in my reading, often sharply challenges the orthodoxy of poststructuralism and is valuable for that challenge.

Now, as Davidson's own theories would tell us, there is no "fact of the matter" about this. A great deal depends on what kind of triangulation one is engaged in, or, as I would prefer to put it, on what are the relevant intentions of the interpreters. All of the disciplines in the humanities outside philosophy owe a good deal to Rorty because of his efforts in informing us about Davidson's work, even if we may go on to disagree with his interpretation of Davidson. The field of rhetoric and composition now owes a comparable debt to Thomas Kent for his efforts connecting Davidson to issues in composition. If rhetoric and composition is, as I hope, to engage in an extended conversation with the work of Donald Davidson (and, more generally, with the analytic tradition in philosophy), this interview is a good model of what we stand to gain from such a conversation.

New Mexico State University
Las Cruces, New Mexico

Works Cited

Dasenbrock, Reed Way, ed. *Literary Theory after Davidson*. University Park: Penn State UP, 1993.

Davidson, Donald. *Essays on Actions and Events*. Oxford: Clarendon, 1980.

——. *Inquiries into Truth and Interpretation*. Oxford: Clarendon, 1984.

——. "Locating Literary Language." Dasenbrock 298-311.

Kent, Thomas. "Externalism and the Production of Discourse." *Journal of Advanced Composition* 12 (1992): 57-74.

Stanley

Fish

Fish Tales: A Conversation with "The Contemporary Sophist"

GARY A. OLSON

Perhaps one reason why Stanley Fish influences so many of us in rhetoric and composition is that he has always insisted that rhetoric is *central*, that it's the "necessary center," that "substantial realities are products of rhetorical, persuasive, political efforts." As Fish says in the interview that follows, once you "begin with a sense of the constructed nature of human reality," then rhetoric is "reconceived as the medium in which certainties become established." It's no wonder, then, that Fish feels comfortable being called a social constructionist. Nor is it surprising that he finds "perfectly appropriate" Roger Kimball's label for him: "the contemporary sophist." In fact, Fish sees an affinity between sophism and the anti-foundationalist project he has so long championed. He credits his work with Milton, his first love and still a driving passion in his intellectual life, as the genesis of his struggle against essentialist, foundationalist philosophies: as an antinomian Christian and an "absolutely severe anti-formalist," Milton was "rather far down the anti-foundationalist road."

Another reason for Fish's influence in rhetoric and composition is his continued interest in and support of composition. He remains conversant with the discipline's intellectual developments, and he even goes so far as to say that much of his thinking about theory and anti-foundationalism was formed in the early 1960s when he taught composition classes using Walker Gibson's *The Limits of Language*: "The essays in that book were perhaps the most powerful influence on me." As always, Fish is outspoken about intellectual trends he disapproves of, and certain developments in composition are no exception. He is skeptical of attempts to "teach people that situational experience is in fact always primary" because he believes this "theoretical" lesson will not produce any generalizable result. On the other hand, he favors training in which composition students are placed in realistic scenarios and are asked to write to the scenario. The difference, in Fish's view, is that the first is an attempt to teach students a "theoretical" perspective in the hopes that they can then apply that perspective to particular situations—something that just cannot happen, according to Fish. The second, however, is experience or practice in specific contexts—for Fish the only "real" kind of knowledge. He repeats, "The practice of training students to be able to adjust their verbal performances to different registers of social life requires no theoretical assumptions whatsoever."

Clearly, this position is consistent with his larger campaign over the years "against theory." Says Fish, "I'm a localist. . . . I believe in rules of thumb." That is, he believes intensely in here-and-now situationality; to believe otherwise would be to subscribe to "the fetishization of the unified self and a whole lot of other things that as 'postmodernists' we are supposedly abandoning." Thus, he discounts attempts to cultivate critical self-consciousness, another type of *theoretical* capacity: "Insofar as critical self-consciousness is a possible human achievement, it requires no special ability and cannot be cultivated as an independent value apart from particular situations."

Fish also comments on other issues in composition scholarship. Retreating somewhat from his earlier criticism of Kenneth Bruffee, Fish acknowledges that collaborative learning *can* be productive. But we must not assume, he cautions, that somehow it is inherently superior to other modes of instruction; it is simply "different," each pedagogical strategy having its own "gains and losses." And while he refuses to embrace radical pedagogy, he sees it as "*a* wave of the future." He himself prefers a more traditional arrangement: perceiving the classroom as "a performance occasion," he enjoys "orchestrating the class," noting that no one would ever mistake one of his classes for "a participatory democracy." He quips that he would never adopt liberatory techniques for two very good reasons: "too much egocentrism, too much of a long career as a professional theatrical academic."

In addition, Fish expresses genuine respect for feminism and the influence it has exerted on the intellectual life of society because, for Fish, it has passed the key test that indicates the "true power of a form of inquiry": when "the assumptions encoded in the vocabulary of a form of thought become inescapable in the larger society." He believes that the questions raised by feminism "have energized more thought and social action than any other 'ism' in the past twenty or thirty years." Nevertheless, he does not support feminists "who rely in their arguments on a distinction between male and female epistemologies." Such feminists, he feels, fall prey to the same epistemological difficulties as those who champion critical self-consciousness: a belief that "you can in some way step back from, rise above, get to the side of your beliefs and convictions so that they will have less of a hold on you."

Fish addresses numerous other issues, such as the nature of "intentional structures" and "forceful interpretive acts," the bankruptcy of the liberal intellectual agenda, and the obligation of academics to engage in what Noam Chomsky has called "more socially useful activities." He is particularly concerned about how the larger societal turn toward conservatism is affecting higher education, and he predicts a period of curtailment and purges so long as the well-financed neo-conservative political agenda continues to be "backed by huge amounts of right-wing foundation money." The solution is for academics to speak out to audiences beyond the academy, to help explain intellectual developments to the general public in order to counter narrow conservative perspectives: "I think we *must* talk back."

It may seem something of a paradox that Stanley Fish, who argues so vociferously *against* theory, is becoming more influential in composition studies precisely at a time when the field, or at least part of it, is busily engaged in *theory building*. Yet while the role of theory in rhetoric and composition may still be uncertain, it *is* clear that Fish is in many ways an ally. Especially as more compositionists explore social construction and the role of rhetoric in epistemology, Fish's work becomes increasingly relevant. Responding to criticism from both the intellectual right and left, Fish insists that harkening to him will not "lead to the decay of civilization," nor will it "lead to the canonization of the status quo." Harkening to Fish, however, *may* well lead to productive avenues of inquiry for many of us in composition.

Q. In *Doing What Comes Naturally*, you speak of this as the age of rhetoric and the "world of *homo rhetoricus*." You yourself are frequently called a rhetorician *par excellence*. But do you consider yourself a writer?

A. I do in some ways. Last night at the Milton Society of America banquet I spoke of the influence on me of C.S. Lewis. I think of C.S. Lewis and J.L. Austin as the two stylists I've tried to imitate in a variety of ways, and so I'm very self-conscious about the way I craft sentences. I always feel that once I get a particular sentence right I can go on to the next, and I don't go on to the next until I think it's right. In the sense that this is not just superficially but centrally a concern, I consider myself a writer. In other senses—for example, whether I expect people to be studying my works long after my demise—the answer is that I do *not* consider myself a writer. But the craft I think of myself as practicing is the craft of writing, and my obsession there is a very old-fashioned one, a canonical one, a traditional one—and that is clarity.

Q. What you describe is exactly how Clifford Geertz described *his* writing process recently in *JAC*. Would you tell us more about your writing process? Do you revise frequently? Use a computer?

A. I do not use a computer and I do not revise. I now use one of those small electronic typewriters that you can move around and take on so-called vacations. That's about as far as I've advanced in the age of mechanical reproduction. Since my writing practices are as I just described, I don't tend to revise. I go back occasionally and reposition an adverb, and I often go through my manuscripts and cross out what I know to be some of my tics. For example, I use the phrase *of course* too much, I often double nouns and verbs for no particular reason, and I have other little favorite mannerisms that I've learned to recognize and eliminate. But very rarely do I ever restructure an essay or even a paragraph.

Q. That's surprising considering your polished style. I should have thought you spent countless hours revising.

A. Well, I write slowly. My pace is two pages a day when I'm writing well, when I have a sense of where the particular essay is or should be going. That's often when I sit for six to eight hours and am continually engaged in the process of thinking through the essay. Also, I do this often (not always, but often) while watching television. This is a very old habit. Actually, this is a talent (if it is a talent) that more people of the younger generation have today than people of my generation. But I've always been able to do it. To this day when I reread something I've written I can remember what television program I was watching when I wrote it. I remember once when I was in Madrid and went to the bullfights, I wrote a passage about Book Six of *Paradise Lost*; every time I look at it I remember that I was watching the bullfights when I wrote it.

Q. As an English department chair, what are your thoughts about the future of rhetoric and composition as a discipline? What role will it (or should it) play in the modern English department?

A. I don't know because I don't know whether there will be something called "the modern English department" in the next twenty years. I had thought, in fact, that there would be a more accelerated transformation of the traditional English department than there has yet been. My prediction ten years ago had been that by the year 2000 the English department in which we were all educated would be a thing of the past, a museum piece, represented certainly in some places but supplanted in most others by departments of literature, departments of cultural studies, departments of humanistic interrogation, or departments of literacy. That hasn't happened in the rapid way I thought it would; there are *some* places, like the Syracuse University, and earlier modes of experimentation, like the University of California at San Diego, Rensselaer Polytech, and others, but not as many as I thought there would be. If the change, when it comes, goes in the same direction that Syracuse has pioneered, then it might be just as accurate to call the department "the department of rhetoric," with a new understanding of the old scope of the subject and province of rhetoric. That's a possibility, but I'm less confident now than I was ten years ago about such predictions. For one thing, the economic difficulties we've been experiencing lately have had a great effect on the academy. Two years ago the job market looked extraordinarily promising, and certain kinds of pressures that departments had always felt seemed to be lessening. There would therefore have been an atmosphere in which experimentation and transformation might have been more possible. But now that we have had a return of a sense of constricted economy and constricted possibilities and everybody is talking retrenchment (an awful word, but one that you hear more and more), it may be that the current departmental sense of the university structure may continue because the protection of interests that are now in place becomes a strong motive once a threat to the entire structure is perceived. And certainly many people are now perceiving a threat to the entire structure.

Q. So for progress, we need prosperity.

A. Absolutely, and especially in the humanities. Two or five or ten years ago, none of us would have predicted the current *political* assault on humanities education and the attempt to—and this is perhaps the least plausible scapegoating effort in the history of scapegoating, which is a very long history—blame all the country's ills on what is being done in a few classrooms by teachers of English and French. It is truly incredible that this story of why the moral fiber of the United States has been weakened has found such acceptance, but it has and now these consequences are ones we have to deal with in some way.

Q. During a talk at the University of South Florida, you repeated on several occasions that you are a "very traditional" teacher who uses "very traditional methods." In *JAC*, Derrida characterized his own teaching in much the same way. Yet in English studies now, especially in rhetoric and composition, there's a movement toward "liberatory learning," radicalizing the classroom and breaking down its traditional power structures by attempting to disperse authority among all participants. What are your thoughts about radical pedagogy in general and its altering of the teacher-student hierarchy specifically?

A. Well, my thoughts about radical pedagogy are complicated by the fact that my wife, Jane Tompkins, is a radical pedagogue and moves more and more in that direction; she writes essays and gives talks that command what I would almost call a cult following. I've seen some of these performances. *That* at least tells me that there's something out there to which she and others are appealing. I have *some* sense—which one might call an anthropological sense—of what that something is. But I'm simply too deeply embedded in and too much a product of my own education and practices to make or even to want to make that turn. I would first have to feel some dissatisfaction with my current mode of teaching or with the experiences of my classroom, and I don't feel that. For me the classroom is still what she has formally renounced: a performance occasion. And I enjoy the performances; I enjoy orchestrating the class in ways that involve students in the performances, but no one is under any illusion that this is a participatory (or any other kind) of democracy in a class of mine. However, having said this I should hasten to add that my own disinclination to turn in that direction does not lead me to label that direction as evil, wayward, irresponsible, unsound, or any of the usual adjectives that follow. It seems to me quite clear that this is, if not *the* wave of the future, *a* wave of the future. In fact, I listened to some of the interviews for our assistant director of composition position yesterday, and every one of the interviewees I talked to identified himself or herself as a person interested in just this new kind of liberatory, new age, holistic, collaborative teaching. So I think it is the wave of the future, and I would certainly welcome those who are dedicated. But I'm sure that I would never do it myself—too much egocentrism, too much of a long career as a professional theatrical academic.

Q. You disagree with Patricia Bizzell and those who encourage us to teach students the "discourse conventions" of their disciplines, arguing that "being told that you are in a situation will help you neither to dwell in it more perfectly nor to *write* within it more successfully." Surely, though, you don't really advise compositionists *not* to teach students that there are numerous discourse communities, each with characteristic discourse conventions? Wouldn't we be remiss to ignore such considerations in our pedagogies?

A. Of course, I quite agree. My objection in that essay—an objection I make in other essays in slightly different terms—is to the assumption that if we teach people that situational experience is in fact always primary and that one never reasons from a set of portable and invariant theses or propositions to specific situations (that is, one is always within a situation in relation to which some propositions seem relevant and others seem out in left field), if you just teach that as a theoretical lesson and walk away from the class and expect something to happen, the only thing that will happen is that the next time you ask that particular question, you'll get that particular answer. However, I do believe in training of a kind familiar to students of classical and medieval rhetoric—training, let's say, of the Senecan kind, in which one is placed by one's instructor in a situation: you are attempting to cross a river; there is only one ferry; you have to persuade the ferryman to do this or that, and he is disinclined to do so for a number of given reasons—what do you then do? That kind of training, transposed into a modern mode, is essential. I don't think it need be accompanied by any epistemological rap. What I was objecting to in Pat's essay—and I was to some extent being captious because in general I am an admirer of her work—was the suggestion that the theoretical perspective on situationality itself could do work if transmitted to a group of students. I think that one could teach that way, and many have—that is, they've taught situational performance and the pressures and obligations that go with being in situations—without ever having been within a thousand miles of a theoretical thought.

Q. But isn't this inconsistent with everything you say about rhetoric in the larger sense, that to be a good rhetorician is to know situatedness?

A. It depends on what you mean by "to know situatedness." There's one sense in which to know situatedness is to be on one side of a debate about the origins of knowledge, to be on the side that locates knowledge or finds the location of knowledge in the temporal structure of particular situations. That's to know situatedness in the sense that one might call either theoretical or philosophical. Now to know situatedness in the sense of being able to code switch, to operate successfully in different registers, is something else, and you don't even have to use the vocabulary that accompanies most theoretical discussions of these points. I was a teacher of composition long ago (relatively—thirty years ago) before any of us in the world of literary studies knew the word *theory* (Ah, for those days! Bliss was it in those times to be alive!), and many people taught what we would now call situational performance; and there were many routes to that teaching. So again, my point always is that the practice of training students to be able to adjust their verbal performances to different registers of social life requires no theoretical assumptions whatsoever. They are required neither of the instructor, and certainly not of the student.

Q. Kenneth Bruffee draws heavily on you and Richard Rorty to formulate his version of collaborative learning theory. Rorty has already distanced himself from Bruffee's project, and you criticize it because it "becomes a new and fashionable version of democratic liberalism, a political vision that has at its center the goal of disinterestedly viewing contending partisan perspectives which are then either reconciled or subsumed in some higher or more general synthesis, in a larger and larger *consensus*." Given one of the major (and typical) alternatives—a teacher-dominated classroom and an information-transfer model of education—and given the fact that much of your own life's work has been devoted to illustrating how interpretive communities work, wouldn't you agree that Bruffee's collaborative learning is productive despite his own naive liberalism?

A. Yes, it could be. I think that's an excellent point. I don't know whether it is, but there's nothing to prevent it from being productive. That is, collaborative learning is a mode of knowledge production *different* from other modes of knowledge production. In my view, differences are always real; however, differences should never be ranked on a scale of more or less real. So to refine what might be a point of contest between Bruffee and me, I would agree with him that if we move into a mode of collaborative learning, *different* things will happen, things which probably would not have been available under other modes. Also, *some* possibilities will be lost. I tend to think of pedagogical strategies as strategies each of which has its gains and losses. I also believe that there are times in the history of a culture or a discipline when it's time to switch strategies, not because a teleology pulls us in the direction of this or that one, but because the one in which we've been operating has at the moment taken us about as far as we can go and so perhaps we ought to try something else—which, as you will have recognized, has a kind of Rortian ring to it.

Q. Yes, it does. In fact, let me ask you a related question. Your essay "Change" is a detailed discussion of how interpretive communities change their beliefs and assumptions, and in making the argument that "no theory can compel change" you say that we should think of the community not as an "object" of change but as "an engine of change." Although you don't use Rorty's vocabulary of "normal" and "abnormal discourse," like Rorty you seem to be arguing against the notion that substantive disciplinary or intellectual change transpires as a result of persuasive abnormal discourse. What are your thoughts on the role of abnormal discourse as a catalyst of change?

A. I think that abnormal discourse *can* be a catalyst of change, and that's because I think that *anything* can be a catalyst of change. This goes back to a series of points I've been making "against theory" for a number of years now. One of my arguments is that strong-theory proponents attribute to theory a unique capacity for producing change and often believe (and this is perhaps a parody) that if we can only get our epistemology straight, or get straight our account of the subject, then important political and material things will follow. It's that sense of the kind of change that will follow from a new theoretical argument that I reject. However, theory—or as I sometimes say tendentiously in these essays, "theory talk"—can like anything else be the catalyst of change, but it's a contingent and historical matter; it depends on the history of the particular community, the kinds of talk or vocabularies that have prestige or cachet or are likely to trump other kinds of talk. And if in a certain community the sense of what is at stake is highly intermixed with a history of theoretical discourse, then in *that* community at *that* time a change in practices may be produced by a change in theory.

Of course, "abnormal" discourse comes in a variety of forms. For example, if one takes the term "discourse" in its larger senses, one can think that a recession is an abnormal form of discourse, that suddenly one's ordinary ways of conceiving of one's situation are complicated by facts that a year or two ago would have seemed to belong in another realm. Abnormal discourse can always erupt into the routine structures of an interpretive community, but there's no way to predict in advance which ones will in fact erupt and with what effects.

Q. Well, Rorty claimed in *JAC* that abnormal discourse is "a gift of God," while Geertz prefers a less grandiose notion he calls "nonstandard discourse." For Rorty this happens rarely; for Geertz it occurs all the time. Obviously, these are two different conceptions of abnormal discourse. Does either one seem more useful than the other?

A. Not really. I'm not sure whether Rorty and Geertz are making this assumption, but it could be that one or both of them is assuming that abnormal discourse is itself a stable category, and it seems to me that what is or is not abnormal in relation to a discourse history will itself be contingent. For example, in some literary communities that I know about and that I'm a participant in, it now becomes "abnormal" to begin a class by saying, "Today we will explicate Donne's 'The Good-Morrow.'" *That* would be, at least in some classrooms at Duke, a *dazzling* move—not, I hasten to add, in *mine*, because that's a practice I've never ceased to engage in.

Q. Both you and Rorty have been cited as two of the principal intellectual sources of social construction; however, when I asked Rorty in an earlier interview if he considered himself a social constructionist he seemed baffled by the appellation. Despite your understandable resistance to limiting categories, and given your continual insistence that everything is rhetorical and situated, would you consider *yourself* a social constructionist?

A. In a certain sense I would say, "Sure." If I were to be asked a series of questions relevant to a tradition of inquiry in which several accounts of the origin of knowledge or facticity were given, I would come out on the side that could reasonably be labeled "social constructionism." I myself have not made elaborate arguments for a social constructionist view—though I've used such arguments at points in my writing—but I have no problem being identified as someone who would support that view.

Q. In the essay "Rhetoric" you examine the history of anti-rhetorical thought and the unchanging "status of rhetoric in relation to a foundational vision of truth and meaning." You state, "Whether the center of that vision is a personalized deity or an abstract geometric reason, rhetoric is the force that pulls us away from the center and into its own world of ever-shifting shapes and shimmering surfaces." You contrast this mainstream tradition with a counter tradition, represented in classical times by the sophists and today by the anti-foundationalists, whom you credit with helping to move "rhetoric from the disreputable periphery to the necessary center." First, in establishing rhetoric as a kind of master category, don't you run the risk of what Derrida has warned of in *JAC* and elsewhere: rhetoricism, "thinking that everything depends on rhetoric"?

A. What is his point? What's the risk?

Q. He claims that rhetoricism leads us down an essentialist path. His definition is literally that rhetoricism is "thinking that everything depends on rhetoric." It seems to me very different from what *you* say.

A. I'm surprised to hear that answer from Derrida because it seems to buy back into a view of the rhetorical that would oppose it to something more substantial, whereas in my view substantial realities are products of rhetorical, persuasive, political efforts. When discussing these matters with committed foundationalists, of whom there are still huge numbers, one always is aware that for them the notion of rhetoric only makes sense as a category of inferiority in relation to something more substantial. For someone who listens with a certain set of ears, the assertion of the primacy of rhetoric can only be heard either as an evil gesture in which "the real" is being overwhelmed, or as a gesture of despair in which either a hedonistic amorality or paralysis must follow. All of these responses to the notion of the persuasiveness of rhetoric are, of course, holding on for dear life to a paradigm in which the rhetorical only enters as the evil shadow of the real. If, on the other hand, you begin with a sense of the constructed nature of human reality (one leaves the ontological question aside if one has half a brain), then the notion of the rhetorical is no longer identified with the ephemeral, the outside, but is reconceived as the medium in which certainties become established, in which formidable traditions emerge, are solidified, and become obstacles (not insurmountable ones, but nevertheless obstacles) to the force of counter-rhetorical movements. So I would give an answer like that to what might seem to be one reading of Derrida's warning, though I am loathe to put *him* anywhere near the camp of those whose thoughts I was describing, since he's a man, as everyone knows, of extraordinary power of intelligence.

Q. Then do you conceive of the project of the anti-foundationalists as an extension or resurgence of sophism?

A. I think that's one helpful way of conceiving of it, and it's helpful in a rhetorical sense. Roger Kimball, in *The New Criterion*, wrote an essay that I think later became part of *Tenured Radicals: How Politics Has Corrupted Our Higher Education*. I don't know what the title of the essay is in *Tenured Radicals*, but in *The New Criterion* the essay on me was entitled "The Contemporary Sophist." He meant that as a derogatory label, but I thought it was perfectly appropriate. To call oneself a sophist is rhetorically effective at the moment because you seem to be confessing to a crime. If you begin by saying, "I am a sophist," and then begin unashamedly to explain why for you this is not a declaration of moral guilt, it's a nice effective move; it catches your audience's attention. So I think that right now there's some mileage (although it's mileage that's attended by danger, too) in identifying the new emphasis on rhetoric with the older tradition of the sophists.

Q. Recently in *JAC* Clifford Geertz said that Kenneth Burke was one of two thinkers who had the most influence on him intellectually, the other being Wittgenstein. You yourself have referred to Burke's work from time to time. What is your assessment of Burke's contribution to our ways of thinking about language and rhetoric?

A. I don't have a strong assessment. I've read Burke only sporadically and only occasionally and have never made a sustained study of his work and therefore could not say that I have been influenced by it directly. I'm sure that I've been influenced by it in all kinds of ways of which I am unaware because of the persons that I've read or talked to who have themselves been strong Burkeans. I can think of two such people that I've talked to and read a great deal: my old friend Richard Lanham at UCLA and Frank

Lentricchia, my colleague at Duke, both of whom are committed Burkeans. No doubt lots of things that they have said to me over the years have passed on a heritage of Burke to me, but I've never myself studied him in an intensive way.

Q. Who *has* had a major influence on you?

A. Well, that's difficult to say. Of course, Milton has been a major influence on me. That would be inescapable having spent thirty years studying his work.

Q. Milton, the anti-foundationalist?

A. Yes, in a way. Milton is an antinomian Christian. That is, he's an absolutely severe anti-formalist. Everyone has always known that about Milton. He is continually rejecting the authority of external forms and even the shape of external forms independently of the spirit or intentional orientation of the believer. In his prose tract called *The Christian Doctrine*, which was only discovered many years after his death, Milton begins the second book, which is devoted to daily life, to works in the world, by asking the obvious question, "What is a good work?" He comes up with the answer that a good work is one that is informed by the working of the Holy Spirit in you. That definition, which I've given you imperfectly, does several things. It takes away the possibility of answering the question "What is a good work?" by producing a list of good works, such as founding hospitals or helping old ladies cross the street. It also takes away the possibility of identifying from the outside whether or not the work a person is doing is good or bad, since goodness or badness would be a function of the Holy Spirit's operation, which is internal and invisible. Milton then seals the point by saying a paragraph or so later that in answer to the question "What is a good work?" some people would say the ten commandments, and therefore give a list. Milton then says, "However, I read in the Bible that *faith* is the obligation of the true Christian, not the ten commandments; therefore, if any one of the commandments is contradictory to my inner sense of what is required, then my obedience to the ten commandments becomes an act of sin." Now, if within two or three paragraphs of your discussion of ethics, which is what the second book of *The Christian Doctrine* is, you have dislodged the ten commandments as the repository of ethical obligation, you are rather far down the anti-foundationalist road. And Milton is a strong antinomian, by which I mean he refuses to flinch in the face of the extraordinary existential anxiety produced by antinomianism. So, much of my thinking about a great many things stems from my study of Milton.

Also, I've been strongly influenced as a prose stylist, as I've already mentioned, by C.S. Lewis and J.L. Austin. In fact, I've been very much influenced by J.L. Austin in my thinking about a great many things in addition to my thinking about how to write certain kinds of English sentences. I've also been influenced by Augustine. It's a curious question to answer because many of the people whom I now regularly cite in essays are people that I read *after* most of the views that found my work were already formed. That is, I hadn't read Kuhn before 1979. I'm fond of citing Kuhn, as a great many other people are. I have found support again and again in the pages of Wittgenstein, but I cannot say that it was a study of Wittgenstein that led me to certain questions or answers.

Let me say one more thing. When I was first starting out as a teacher, I gave the same exam in every course, no matter what the subject matter. The exam was very simple: I asked the students to relate two sentences to each other and to the materials of the course. The first sentence was from J. Robert Oppenheimer: "Style is the deference that action pays to uncertainty." I took that to mean that in a world without certain foundations for action you avoid the Scylla of prideful self-assertion, on the one hand, and the Charybdis of paralysis, on the other hand, by stepping out provisionally, with a sense of limitation, with a sense of style. The other quotation, which I matched and asked the students to consider, is from the first verse of Hebrews Eleven: "Now faith is the substance of things hoped for, the evidence of things not seen." I take that to be the classically theological version of Oppenheimer's statement, and so the question of the relationship between style and faith, or between interpretation and action and certainty, has been the obsessive concern of my thinking since the first time I gave this test back in 1962 or 1963. I think there is *nothing* in my work that couldn't be generated from those two assertions and their interactions. They came from a book I used in my composition teaching from the very beginning, and I don't even know how I came to use it. The essays in that book were perhaps the most powerful influence on me. It's a book edited by Walker Gibson, and it's called *The Limits of Language*. It had this essay by Oppenheimer; essays by Whitehead, Conant, and Percy Bridgman, the Nobel Prize winning physicist; Gertrude Stein's essay on punctuation (which is fantastic); and several others that I used in my classes and that informed my early questionings and giving of answers. That book was an extraordinarily powerful influence. Of course, the quotation from Hebrews Eleven came in from my Milton work.

Q. You just mentioned finding support in the pages of Wittgenstein. In "Accounting for the Changing Certainties of Interpretive Communities," Reed Way Dasenbrock suggests that your debt to Wittgenstein is far greater than you have yet acknowledged. Do you think Wittgenstein was a major influence on your work?

A. No I don't, because I don't know him well enough. Reed was a student of mine. I have a bunch of students out in the world who make what I hope is a very good living writing essays that point out my limitations and flaws, and he's one of them. He no doubt knows Wittgenstein much better than I do and has learned a great deal from him; he therefore probably assumes that I *must* have been influenced by him. Now it *is* true that back in about

1977 or 1978 I was for a semester in a reading group with two or three philosophers from Johns Hopkins: David Sachs, George Wilson, and my friend the art historian, Michael Fried. We read Wittgenstein and talked about him for a period of months. Somewhat earlier—and here's another influence that I'd forgotten to acknowledge but should have acknowledged—there's probably a larger influence from Heidegger as transmitted to me in a series of courses I attended given by Hubert Dreyfus, a philosopher at Berkeley whose notes on *Being and Time* have just been published and have been long awaited, and whose early book *What Computers Can't Do* was another strong and powerful influence on me. That's a great book, both in its first and second editions. Through my friendship with Dreyfus, who is a magnificent teacher, and because of the pleasure and illumination I gained from his courses, there is probably some kind of Heidegger-Wittgensteinian circuit (there *is* a relationship, though a tortured one, between Heidegger and Wittgenstein) that has had more power in my work than I consciously acknowledge. Therefore, I guess I end up saying that in a way Reed may be right.

Q. Last October, over dinner, you and I discussed various issues with Dinesh D'Souza, and I remember your eloquent and impassioned plea for him to believe that feminism is "the real thing," that significant and substantial developments are occurring within and because of feminism. Exactly what of importance is happening in feminism?

A. I couldn't answer that question because feminism has become as a discipline and a series of disciplines so complicated, such a map with so many different city-states or nation-states, that it would be foolish of me to start pronouncing. What I was trying to convey to Dinesh (the question of whether or not one conveys *anything* to Dinesh is an interesting one) is that the questions raised by feminism, because they were questions raised not in the academy but in the larger world and that then made their way into the academy, have energized more thought and social action than any other "ism" in the past twenty or thirty years, including Marxism, which may have been in that position in an earlier period but is in our present culture no longer in that position. Now what is that position? It is the position that in my view marks the true power of a form of inquiry or thought: when the assumptions encoded in the vocabulary of a form of thought become inescapable in the larger society. For example, people who have never read a feminist tract and would be alarmed at the thought of reading one are nevertheless being influenced by feminist thinking in ways of which they are unaware or are to some extent uncomfortably aware. Such influence often exhibits itself in the form of resistance: "*I'm* not going to fall in with any of that feminist crap," thereby falling in headfirst as it were. My benchmark comparison here is with Freudianism. Freudianism's influence on our society is absolutely enormous and in the same way. People who have never read Freud, and who would not think of reading Freud, nevertheless have a ready store of Freudian concepts about the unconscious, repression, slips of the tongue, a vague sense that there's something called the "Oedipus Complex," and so on. *That's* when a form of thought has genuine power; it becomes unavoidable in our society. Feminism, I think, has that status and will continue to have that status (especially if there are more things like the Clarence Thomas/Anita Hill hearings).

Q. You have argued that "feminists who rely in their arguments on a distinction between male and female epistemologies are wrong, but, nevertheless, it may not be wrong (in the sense of unproductive) for them to rely on it." Currently, the most influential version of feminism in composition is concerned primarily with such a distinction. Would you explain, first, why such a distinction is problematic, and also how it nonetheless might be productive?

A. Well, it's problematic in relation to my own notion of the way belief and conviction work. My stricture on that particular piece of feminist theory follows from my general position on critical self-consciousness. Critical self-consciousness, which was my main object of attack for a number of years (now I see that the true object of attack all along was liberalism in general), is the idea that you can in some way step back from, rise above, get to the side of your beliefs and convictions so that they will have less of a hold on you than they would had you not performed this distancing action, thereby enabling you to survey the field of possibilities relatively unencumbered by the beliefs and convictions whose hold has been relaxed. This seems to me to be *zany* because it simply assumes but never explains an ability to perform that distancing act, never pausing to identify that ability and to link the possession of that ability with the thesis that usually begins discussions that lead to this point—the thesis of the general historicity of all human efforts. That is, most people who come to the point of talking about critical self-consciousness or reflective equilibrium or being aware of the status of one's own discourse are also persons who believe strongly in the historical and socially constructed nature of reality; but somehow, at a certain moment in the argument, they are able to marry this belief in social constructedness with a belief in the possibility of stepping back from what has been socially constructed or stepping back from one's own self. I don't know how they manage this. I think, in fact, that they manage it by not recognizing the contradiction.

The feminist version of this, at least in the strain of feminism to which you were referring, is to identify the ability to step back and not be gripped in a strong and almost military way by one's convictions, to identify that softer relationship to one's beliefs as "feminine" while perceiving the aggressive assertion of one's beliefs as "masculine." Well, if I'm right about the impossibility in a strong sense of that stepping back, then there could not be such a distinction between ways of knowing. There could be, however, as I do go on to say in that essay, different *styles* in relation to which one's beliefs are held and urged and introduced to others. And those different styles will have different effects, although, again, contingent on particular situations. It's not always the case that proceeding in a soft and relatively mild way to forward a point of view will produce effect *X* while a brusk and peremptory declaration of one's point of view will produce effect *Y*. It depends. I like to think of these not so much as a difference in female and male ways of knowing but a difference in modes of aggression. So, finally, it's whether or not you favor or at the moment find useful garden-variety aggressiveness, or whether you take refuge in passive aggressiveness—which can often be the most aggressive form of aggressiveness. This is the difference often at the root of these discussions, and it also gets into discussions of collaborative learning and of attempts to decenter classroom authority.

Q. You just mentioned your distaste for liberalism . . .

A. Yes, I never tire of it.

Q. I remember your saying not long ago that you see conservatives today as behaving "like a bunch of thugs" and liberals as "foolish and silly," but given a choice between the two, you'd side with silliness over thuggishness. You've been openly contemptuous of liberals, both within the field and in society at large. What is it about the liberal intellectual agenda that you find so repugnant?

A. What distresses me about liberalism is that it is basically a brief against belief and conviction. I understand its historical origins in a weariness with theological battles that were in the sixteenth and seventeenth centuries and earlier (and still today in parts of the world) real battles: people bled, died, mutilated one another, and so on. As every historian has told us for many years, the passions of seventeenth-century sectarian wars, especially in England, led to a sense of weariness, to a lack of faith in the ability of persons ever to be reconciled on these points, and therefore to a desire to diminish their centrality to one's life. That's one of the sources, not the only source, of liberalism's appeal. Liberalism takes the inescapable reality of contending agendas or of points of view or, as we would now say in a shorthand way, of "difference" and tries to find an overarching procedural structure which will accommodate difference and will at least defer the pressure to decide in a final way between strongly differing points of view. Liberalism is a way not so much to avoid conflict (because liberalism is born out of the unhappy insight that conflict cannot be avoided) but to contain it, to manage it, and therefore to find some form of human association in which difference can be accommodated and persons can be allowed the practice and even cultivation of their points of view, but in which the machinery of the state will not prefer one point of view to another but will in fact produce structures that will ensure that contending points of view can coexist in the same space without coming to a final conflict.

The difficulty with this view is that it assumes that structures of a kind that are neutral between contending agendas can in fact be fashioned. What I wish to say, and I'm certainly not the only one or by any means the first one to say it, is that *any* structure put in place is *necessarily* one that favors some agendas, usually by acts of recognition or nonrecognition, at the expense of others. That is, any organization that one sets up already is based on some implicit ordering of possible courses of action that have been identified or recognized as being within the pale. Then there are other kinds of actions that are simply not recognized and are therefore, as it were, written out of the program before the beginning. Now, this has not been a *conscious* act because for it to have been a conscious act it would have to have been produced in the very realm of reflective self-consciousness that I am always denying. Nevertheless, it is an inescapable fact about organization, from my point of view. So what liberalism does in the *guise* of devising structures that are neutral between contending agendas is to produce a structure that is far from neutral but then, by virtue of a political success, has claimed the right to think of itself as neutral. What this then means is that in the vocabulary of liberalism certain kinds of words mark the zone of suspicion—words like *conviction, belief, passion*, all of which are for the liberal mentality very close to fanaticism.

You could have noted a nice instance of this in the Gulf War frenzy of 1990 and 1991 when the charge that was made again and again about Saddam Hussein and his followers was that they *believed* something so strongly that they wouldn't "listen to reason." The February 1991 issue of *The New Republic* was devoted largely to the situation on campus but had three or four essays on the still-evolving Gulf War situation, and it became quite clear that for the editors and writers of *The New Republic* the danger represented by Saddam Hussein and the danger represented by multiculturalism or ethnic studies were exactly the same danger. This was the danger of persons passionately committed to an agenda, a set of assumptions—on the one hand a bunch of nutty Iraqis and on the other hand a bunch of nutty English teachers. In both cases, the obvious and compelling power of reason and rationality somehow had been overwhelmed by passion and conviction. In a way, liberalism, under this description, could be seen as a post-eighteenth-century variation of an old Judeo-Christian account of the nature of man in which man is composed of two parts: willful, irrational passion on the one hand and on the other hand something still residing in the breast, that spark of true intuition left us after the fall. So in many Christian homiletic traditions, human life is imagined as a battleground between the carnal self controlled by its appetites and something else, often called "conscience" or the "word of God," within. Now what happens in the Enlightenment is that the theological moorings of this view are detached, and in place of things like the conscience or the memory of God or the image of God's love, one has Reason. But in the older tradition (and here's the big difference), that which was contending with the carnal, because it was identified with the divine, had an obvious teleological valance to it. You take away that and substitute for it Reason and then you have something as your supposed lodestar which, by the Enlightenment's definition of Reason, is independent of value. It seems to me that out of this many of the problems of liberalism, as described by a great many people, arise. So I think that liberalism is an incoherent notion born out of a correct insight that we'll never see an end to these squabbles and that therefore we must do something, and the doing something is somehow to find a way to rise above the world of conviction, belief, passion. I simply don't think that's possible.

Q. What would be an intellectual agenda that is *not* silly or thuggish?

A. I'm a localist, which is already almost a dangerous thing to say. By that I mean I don't have an intellectual agenda in any strong sense, or to put it in deliberately provocative terms: I don't have any principles. If I believe in anything, I believe in rules of thumb, in the sense that in any tradition there are certain kinds of aphorisms or axioms which encode that tradition's values, purposes, and goals; and people who are deeply embedded in that tradition are in some sense, often below the threshold of self-consciousness, committed to those values, purposes, and goals which, however, *can* in the course of the history of a tradition or profession, change. Therefore, as I say quite often (and it's true) my forward time span is generally two hours. By that I mean I tend not to think about or worry about anything more in the future than two hours hence. From a negative point of view, one might characterize my vision, therefore, as severely constrained and limited. I walk into a situation and there's something wrong sometimes, but my sense of what is wrong is very much attached to the local moment, the resources within that moment that might be available to remedy the wrong, and the possibility that my own actions might in some way contribute to that remedy. Then if someone starts commenting, "You act this way in situation *A* and three weeks ago in situation *B* I saw you act in ways that would under a general philosophical description be thought of as a contradiction," I answer, "Don't bother me. Give me a break. I am not in the business of organizing my successive actions so that they all conform to or are available to a coherent philosophical account." A lot of people assume that this is what action in the world should be: you strive from some mode of action that, if viewed from outside over a period of time, would be seen as consistent in philosophical terms. Again, I don't see that. That seems to me to go along with the fetishization of the unified self and a whole lot of other things that as "postmodernists" we are supposedly abandoning but that keep returning with a vengeance.

Q. In *Doing What Comes Naturally*, you discuss at length the role of "intention" in the production and reception of discourse. As a check on both those who "ignore" authorial intention as well as those who defer to it, you explain that "there is only one way to read or interpret, and that is the way of intention. But to read intentionally is not to be constrained relative to some other (nonexistent) way of reading." You say this is so because any meaning is "thinkable only in the light of an intentional structure already assumed." Would you elaborate on the nature and role of "intentional structure"?

A. Sure. I would back off for a moment and consider what the alternative picture would be. The alternative picture would be intention as something added on to a meaningful structure. In other words, those people who wish either to avoid or ignore intention believe that it is possible to speak of the meaning of something independently of a purposeful human action. I do not so believe. Another way to put this is that linguists (some linguists, not all) often talk about what words mean "in the language" as opposed to what they might mean in particular situations. I don't believe that the category "in the language" has any content whatsoever. I do believe, of course, in dictionaries and in grammars or accounts of grammar, but I always assume that dictionaries and accounts of grammar are being written from within the assumption of a range of possible human intentions as realized in particular situations, and that the fact that this range of possible human intentions as realized in particular situations is not on the surface, is not a part of the surface accounts of words given in a dictionary or in a grammar, is simply to be explained by the deep assumption of intentionality which is so deeply assumed that some people think they can in some particular situations get along without it. I always say to my students, "Just try to imagine uttering a sentence that is meaningful and, not as an afterthought but already in the act of thinking up such a sentence, imagine some intentional situation—that is, a situation with an agent with a purpose in relation to the configurations of the world that he or she wishes in some way to alter or announce—imagine doing without that and I say that you won't be able to." It's always the case that when you're attempting to determine what something means, what you are attempting to do is to penetrate to, to identify the intention of, some purposeful agent.

Now having said that, what methodological consequences follow? The answer is "none whatsoever," because (this is usually my favorite answer to almost any question) having now been persuaded that to construe meaning is also to identify intentional behavior, you are in no better position to go forward than you were before because all the problems remain. You must yourself decide what you mean by an "agent." Are you talking about the "liberal individual" formulating thoughts in his or her mind? Are you talking about the agency of a "community," of a group in *my* sense, or of a paradigm member, in Kuhn's sense? Are you talking, in an older intellectual tradition of the history of ideas, of the *Zeitgeist*—the spirit of an age within whose intentional structure everyone writes? Or in theological terms are you talking of a tradition in which my hand held the pen but it was the spirit of the Lord that moved me—a tradition I myself in no way denigrate? These are not decisions to which you will be helped by having decided that the construal of meaning is inseparable from the stipulation of intention. You then will also have to decide what is evidence for the intention that you finally stipulate, and that too is a question that was as wide open and as difficult before you came upon the gospel of intentionalism as it is now that you *have* come upon the gospel of intentionalism. So for shorthand purposes and in terms that most of your readers and mine would recognize, E.D. Hirsch was right when he asserted the primacy of intention back in 1960 and 1967, and he was simply wrong to think that having done so he had provided a methodological key or any kind of method whatsoever. This is also the argument, made brilliantly in my view, of Knapp and Michaels' essay "Against Theory."

Q. In "Going Down the Anti-Formalist Road" you write, "There is no such thing as literal meaning, if by literal meaning one means a meaning that is perspicuous no matter what the context and no matter what is in the speaker's or hearer's mind, a meaning that because it is prior to interpretation can serve as a constraint on interpretation." You conclude, "Meanings that seem perspicuous and literal are rendered so by forceful interpretive acts and not by the properties of language." Exactly what is a "forceful interpretive act"? What lends it its "force"?

A. A forceful interpretive act needn't be committed or performed by any one person; in fact, usually it is not, except in extraordinary cases. The forceful interpretive act takes place over time, and the agencies involved in it are multiple. Its effects are more easily identified than the process that leads to them. The effects are the production of a situation in which for all competent members of a community the utterance of certain words will be understood in an absolutely uniform way. That *does* happen. It is a possible historical contingent experience. When that happens you have, as far as I'm concerned, a linguistic condition that it might be perfectly appropriate to characterize as the condition of literalism. That is, at that moment you can with some justice say that these words, when uttered in this community, will mean only this one thing. The mistake is to think that it is the property of the words that produces this rather than a set of uniform interpretive assumptions that so fill the minds and consciousness of members that they will, upon receiving a certain set of words, immediately hear them in a certain way. Of course, that can always be upset by a variety of mechanisms, but it need not be upset; this condition can last a long, long, long time.

I'll tell you a story I've told many times. When my daughter was six years old, we were sitting at the dinner table one evening. We then had two small black dachshunds. My daughter Susan was doing something with the dachshunds under the table, and it was experienced at least by me as disruptive. So I said to her, "Susan, stop playing with the dachshunds." She held up her hands in a kind of "Look, Dad, no hands" gesture and said, "I'm not *playing* with the dachshunds." So I said, "Susan, stop *kicking* the dachshunds." She turned my attention to the soft motions of her feet and said, "I'm not *kicking* the dachshunds." So I said, forgetting every lesson I had ever learned as a so-called philosopher of language, "Susan don't do *anything* with the dachshunds!" She replied, "You mean I don't have to feed them anymore?" At that moment I knew several things. First, I knew I was in a drama called "the philosopher and the dupe" and that she was the philosopher and I was the dupe. I also knew that this was a game that she could continue to play indefinitely because she could always recontextualize what she understood to be the context of my question in such a way as to destabilize the literalness on which I had been depending, which she too—within the situation of the dinner table, our relationship, our house—recognized in as literal a way as I did. That story, which can be unfolded endlessly, encapsulates for me this set of issues that you were asking about.

Q. In your essay on critical self-consciousness, you take issue first with Stephen Toulmin because he "advocates self-conscious reflection on one's own beliefs as a way to neutralize bias immediately after having asserted the unavailability of the 'objective standpoint' that would make such reflection a possible achievement." Then you criticize the tradition of critical self-consciousness on the left as being "frankly political," as "rigorously and relentlessly negative, intent always on exposing or unmasking those arrangements of power that present themselves in reason's garb." Finally, you pronounce the critical project "a failure." Granting your argument that we are never free of constraints and therefore there never are truly free actions, would you not agree that the project of critical self-consciousness—whether conservative or radical—is nonetheless productive and beneficial, that we'd be poorer without it?

A. No. I do not agree because I sense you venturing into the regulative ideal territory—that is, we can never do this but it's a good thing to try. The bad poetic version of this is given in a line (that's even bad for him) by Browning (in my view the worst major poet): "A man's reach should exceed his grasp or what's a heaven for?" That is really the philosophy or point of view behind regulative ideal arguments, whether they're Kantian or Habermasian or any other "ian." I have no truck with them; I just don't see their point. It's just a form of idealism.

Q. Sure, it's idealistic to think that we can be truly self-conscious in a critical way, but doesn't the process of trying to get there turn out to be productive?

A. It depends on what you mean by "the process of trying to get there." You may be surprised or even distressed to hear this, but there is about to be published another Fish/Dworkin debate. I participated last year in a conference at Virginia, Pragmatism in Law and Society, which was in some ways appropriately centered on the work of Richard Rorty. The organizer, a professor of political science, assembled a really interesting cast of characters to speak about these questions. A few weeks before the conference, I received what I thought was a strange call from the convener of the conference who said that Ronald Dworkin wished to know which of the participants in the conference were going to write about him and what they were going to say. I said *I* wasn't going to write about him, that I was writing about Posner and Rorty, which I did. What I didn't know at the time is that for some reason Dworkin had been asked to be a commentator on the proceedings. His idea of being a commentator was to find out what essays would be directed either wholly or partly at him so that he could in the G.E. Moore tradition write a reply to his critics yet again. I would have seemed to have, at least with respect to me, foiled this intention because I didn't say *anything* about Dworkin. But when Dworkin came to write his commentary on the conference papers, he ignored this small difficulty and simply picked up the threads of earlier quarrels as if I *had* written my paper on him. When I saw that, I became distressed, and so I wrote a reply to Dworkin.

Now, Dworkin was arguing against the "theory has no consequences" position and for critical self-consciousness and for critically reflective stances on one's own assumptions—for a strong relationship, in short, between critical theory and practice. He chose as his example (this was a huge mistake) Ted Williams. Ted Williams was my hero as a boy. I had carried a picture of him around in my wallet for many years until it just fell apart. What Dworkin said was, as a kind of knock-down argument in his view, "The greatest hitter of modern baseball built a theory before every pitch." His source for this was Ted's book, *The Science of Hitting*. I got the latest edition of *The Science of Hitting*, read it carefully, annotated it, and pointed out several things. First of all, in *The Science of Hitting* Ted has an account of Ty Cobb's theory of hitting which he examines in detail—Cobb thought this and thought that in relation to velocity, to the way the foot moved, what you did with the bat, and so forth. Then after doing this, Ted absolutely demolishes it. He says, in effect, that what Cobb was advising is not possible for the human body to perform. Five pages later, Ted describes Cobb quite reasonably as the greatest hitter in baseball history. The conclusion is inescapable: the greatest hitter in baseball history had a theory of how he did it which had no relationship whatsoever, and could not have had any relationship, to what he did. Ted then goes on in another section of the book to describe what he thinks of as the mode of action of a great hitter. He goes on to hypothetical (but not really hypothetical; you have a sense that he's reconstructing moments in his own career) accounts of what a good hitter is doing as he stands up at the plate. What a good hitter is doing, according to Ted, is thinking things like this: "Well, last time he threw me a fast ball and there were two men on base and it was the fourth inning; now it's the eighth inning and there's no one on base but the score is four to three; I know that he doesn't like to rely on his fast ball so much in the later innings, and so forth and so on." Now what can one say about thoughts like that? First, one wants to say that they're highly self-conscious. They're self-conscious in the sense that there is a definite reflection not only on the present moment of activity but on the relationship between the present moment of activity and past moments which are now being "self-consciously" recalled. However, my point is that this self-consciousness really is not another level of practice but in fact is, how shall I describe it, itself a component in practice and that what Ted was saying to the would-be hitter was something like, "Be attentive to all dimensions of the situation." Now, is there a separate capacity called the "being attentive capacity" or what we might call the "critically reflective capacity"? Answer: No. Is it the case that you can develop a muscle or a pineal gland or something such that you could in any variety of different situations involving different forms of action activate that muscle? The answer is no. What you in fact do, when you do it well, is become *attentive* to the situation. The shape of your attentiveness is situation specific and dependent, so that—returning to your question—insofar as one is ever critically reflective, one is critically reflective *within* the routines of a practice. One's critical reflectiveness is in fact a function of, its shape is a function of, the routines of the practice. What most people want from critical reflectiveness is precisely a distance on the practice rather than what we might call a heightened degree of attention while performing in the practice. I haven't given you the argument as elegantly as I gave it in my reply to Dworkin. I guess in the end what I would want to say is that insofar as critical self-consciousness is a possible human achievement, it requires no special ability and cannot be cultivated as an independent value apart from particular situations: it's simply being normally reflective. It's not an abnormal, special—that is, *theoretical*—capacity. Insofar as the demand is for it to be such—that is, special, abnormal—it is a demand that can never be fulfilled.

Q. In "Profession Despise Thyself" you say that we in literary studies have made ourselves "fair game" to criticism "by subscribing to views of our enterprise in relation to which our activities can only be either superfluous or immoral ("How can you study Milton while the Third World starves?")." Noam Chomsky has said in *JAC* that he does not find most academic questions "humanly significant," suggesting that to be humanly useful academics should devote some of their time to social activism. Do you believe we in English studies should turn our attention to more socially useful activities?

A. I think it depends. English studies cannot itself be made into a branch of inquiry that has direct and immediate social and political payoffs, at least not in the way the United States is now structured. In other countries and other traditions, it would have been more possible for there to be a direct connection between literary activity and social and political activity, and perhaps in some transformation of our society that has not yet occurred it could be the case that the kinds of analyses we're performing in class could have an immediate impact on the larger social and economic questions being debated in society. As for the question (which I now will understand in a way that Chomsky would probably find trivial), "Should English teachers devote their energies to social causes?" my answer is, "Why not?" It's like *pro bono* work in the legal world: you decide what it is you're interested in doing, working in political ways, in social ways, and you volunteer. In a way, what Chomsky is saying is very congenial to the academic mentality—a mentality that has a deep interest in diminishing its own value. Just why this is so is worthy of many pages of analysis. The academic generally participates in the devaluation of his or her own activities to a much greater degree than the practitioners in other fields do. It seems to me that academic activity is a human activity. As a human activity, like any other activity, it has its constraints and therefore its areas of possible effectivity as well as many areas in which it will not be effective because it will not touch them. This makes it no better or no worse on some absolute scale (that doesn't exist) than any other human activity. However, at a particular moment in history a legitimate question is, "Do we want to put our energies in this human activity that has this structure of plus and minus in terms of gains and losses and opportunities, or this one?" That's a perfectly reasonable question to ask as long as one doesn't think that one is asking a question that has a Platonic structure, in the old sense, or a surface/deep structure opposition, in the Chomskian sense. I'm temperamentally opposed to those who wish to regard the academic life as an inferior, unauthentic form of human activity. It's *another* form of human activity. It should neither be privileged—as some romantic humanists privilege it so that only those who "live the life of the mind" are really living—nor should it be denigrated as the area of the trivial in relation to which getting one's hands authentically dirty is the true counterweight. I think both of those characterizations are bankrupt.

Q. In *Doing What Comes Naturally*, you speculate that the immense popularity of books like E.D. Hirsch's and Allan Bloom's signal that "the *public* fortunes of rationalist-foundationalist thought have taken a favorable turn": "One can expect administrators and legislators to propose reforms (and perhaps even purges) based on Bloom's arguments (the rhetorical force of anti-rhetoricalism is always being revived)." Do you predict massive (and counterproductive) state intervention in the educational system?

A. The current political situation (by "current" I mean at this moment) suggests that that would be an unhappily canny prediction. Secretary of Education Lamar Alexander is poised to implement some of the ideas he inherited from William Bennett and which are being given continuing vitality in the administration's thinking by Lynne Cheney, as advised by people like Chester Finn and Diane Ravitch, among others. In all of these instances, the tendency is to label as disruptive and subversive—almost in a sense that returns us to the 1950s—all forms of thought that question the availability of transcendental standards and objective lines of measurement so that these forms of thought are regarded by the persons that I have named not as possible contenders in an arena of philosophical discussion but as Trojan horses of evil, decay, destruction of community, and so on. So long as these persons hold important positions in the government, positions connected to the administration of the educational world and the dispensation of funds, I think we do face a period in which there will be (at least on the national level, and in some cases on local levels) moves to curtail and purge. We're already seeing this in the activities of organizations like the National Association of Scholars and in the extensive network of student journalism that began with the *Dartmouth Review* but that has now extended far beyond the confines of Hanover, New Hampshire, allied with a number of prominently placed journalists in the national news media: people like Dorothy Rabinowitz and David Brooks of the *Wall Street Journal*; Jonathan Yardley at the *Post*; Charles Krauthammer and John Leo; political/popular writers like Dinesh D'Souza, Roger Kimball, and Charles Sykes; Nat Hentoff at the *Village Voice*—a whole series of people who can be relied upon to be mouthpieces for this very neo-conservative political agenda which is backed by huge amounts of right-wing foundation money provided by William Simon and others. I think that's a real force at the moment and a force to which many in the academy are only just now waking up.

Q. You said we should be socially active. What measures can we take to prevent such reactionary trends?

A. The MLA panel I'm about to attend is entitled "Answering Back." Though I'm not a member of the panel, I'll be in the audience and I think we *must* talk back. I think that academics too often disdain communication with people outside the academic world and believe that attempting to speak to the public must necessarily be a diminution of our normal mode of discourse and that in order to speak to the public we must gear down and simplify our usual nuanced perspectives. In fact, I know from experience that speaking to the general public is indeed a task equally complex and difficult, but *differently* complex and difficult, as speaking to one's peers in learned journals or at conferences. There is a set of problems of translation and rhetorical accommodation that one comes upon when attempting to talk to audiences outside the academy which is absolutely fascinating and difficult. So unless we set our mind to this task, the capturing of the media pages and airwaves will continue as it has continued in the past year and a half so that up until four or five months ago it was difficult to find a view widely published *other* than the view being put forward by what we might call "Cheney and Company."

Q. Certainly you have had your share of critics and detractors from both the left and the right. Are there any criticisms or misunderstandings of your work that you'd like to take issue with at this time? Anything to set straight?

A. No, not in any sense that hasn't been attempted before. As I say in *Doing What Comes Naturally* and elsewhere, there are basically two criticisms of my work; they come from the right and the left. The criticism from the right is that in arguing for notions like interpretive communities, the inescapability of interpretation, the infinite revisability of interpretive structures, I am undoing the fabric of civilization and opening the way to nihilist anarchy. The objection from the left is that I'm *not* doing that sufficiently. My argument to both is that on the one hand the fear that animates right-wing attacks on me is an unrealizable fear because one can never be divested of certainties and programs for action unless one believed that the mind itself could function as a calculating agent independently of the beliefs and convictions which supposedly we're going to lose; and on the other hand (or on the same hand), therefore, a program in which our first task is to divest ourselves of all our old and hegemonically imposed convictions in order to move forward to some new and braver world is an impossible task. On the one hand, hearkening to me will not lead to the decay of civilization, and on the other hand hearkening to me will not lead to the canonization of the status quo. In fact, on *these* kinds of points—and this is what most of my critics find most difficult to understand—hearkening to me will lead to *nothing*. Hearkening to me, from my point of view, is *supposed to* lead to nothing. As I say in *Doing What Comes Naturally* in answer to the question "What is the point?" the point is that there *is* no point, no yield of a positive programmatic kind to be carried away from these analyses. Nevertheless, *that* point (that there is no point) *is* the point because it's the promise of such a yield—either in the form of some finally successful identification of a foundational set of standards or some program by which we can move away from standards to ever-expanding liberation—it's the unavailability of such a yield that *is* my point, and therefore it would be contradictory for me to have a point beyond *that* point. People absolutely go bonkers when they hear that, but that's the way it is.

A Response to "Fish Tales:
A Conversation with
'The Contemporary Sophist'"

PATRICIA BIZZELL

I think the name "contemporary sophist" is wonderfully appropriate for Stanley Fish. For one thing, his voice fascinates me—the magic brandished by Gorgias when he discusses the power of rhetoric in his "Encomium of Helen." I think my fascination arises in the provocative mixture in Fish's style. It is clear, crisp, logical, bold, and argumentative; as he himself notes in the *JAC* interview, there is a besetting tendency to overuse "of course." At the same time, it is playfully fond of personal display ("For me the classroom is still . . . a performance"), parading failures, triumphs, odd bits of knowledge, and radical changes of mind without embarrassment.

In short, Fish's prose, like the body of Tiresias, seems to contain both masculine and feminine elements, at least as these genders are traditionally constructed (at one point Fish questions such a construction). His style is hard: it argues quite fiercely. It is soft: it changes its mind quite publicly. Something about this style appeals to me, even though it means courting positions that can be easily misunderstood, adopting labels that seem, as Fish says of the sophist tag, to make one a criminal in the eyes of the theoretically pure.

Fish understands his prose style, too, in a fashion that is congenial to sophistic thinking. He says, "In a world without certain foundations for action you avoid the Scylla of prideful self-assertion, on the one hand, and the Charybdis of paralysis, on the other, by stepping out provisionally, with a sense of limitation, with a sense of style." In other words, one enables oneself to act by rhetorically constructing a basis for action that is admittedly temporary, the product of historical and personal contingencies, and yet firm enough on which to take a stand.

As to the morality of so relying on rhetorical scaffolding, Fish links his view of style to faith. That is, as I understand him, we cannot know that what we do is right, but we can hope so. This strikes me as very close to what Mario Untersteiner identifies as the tragic aspect of human knowledge for the Greek sophists. One must submit to persuasion to avoid quietism, and live with the likelihood that what one has accepted may later have to be changed.

I think Fish's views here help to explain his impatience with liberals: he sees them as mounting "a brief against belief and conviction," knocking down foundations, without the nerve to trust in non-foundational, rhetorically constructed bases for action.

Where Fish's thinking most influences me is precisely in his articulation of the powers of rhetoric. Once again in the *JAC* interview, Fish describes rhetoric as neither "the evil shadow of the real" that foundationalists condemn, nor the "gesture of despair" embraced by total relativists (and many postmodern skeptics?). Rather, for Fish, rhetoric is "the medium in which certainties become established, in which formidable traditions emerge," in short, the medium in which human reality is constructed. The practitioner of rhetoric, then, is one who knows how "to adjust [his or her] verbal register to different registers of social life" and thereby to participate in the construction of reality in a variety of localities. This helps to explain what people are doing in interpretive communities, in discourse communities.

Fish's view of rhetoric has been misconstrued as requiring total conformity and lack of change within the communities rhetoric constructs. Such readings may arise from passages such as the one in which Fish gives what could be taken as another characterization of the practitioner of rhetoric, someone who is "critically reflective *within* the routines of a practice." Fish's point here is that all critical reflection must be within a practice, that is, within the terms constructed by the rhetoric that helps to constitute the practice. He denies the possibility of "critical self-consciousness," if that means the ability to "step back from, rise above, get to the side of your beliefs and convictions so that they will have less of a hold on you than they would had you not performed this distancing action." There can be no such distance if you believe that all beliefs are constructed by rhetoric, for if you believe this, then there is no way to get outside rhetoric.

If there can be no such meta-discursive distance, however, it still seems to me that Fish's view of rhetoric permits dissensus and change when discursive practices from different communities overlap, compete, and critique one another. Attentiveness to one practice is rarely so total that a person cannot participate in a number of other practices. Indeed, Fish's account of feminism in the *JAC* interview describes a practice that has interfered with a large number of other practices. Fish suggests that feminist discourse has come to pervade even "the larger society," much like Freudianism. The terminology, assumptions, and so on are employed even by people who would deny they are feminists, or who would hardly have a clear idea of what feminism might be. Feminist discourse, then, is depicted by Fish as a catalyst for change.

The key issue for Fish is that the discourse that causes change—which he is willing to call "abnormal discourse," after Rorty and Kuhn—cannot be seen as a "special" discourse in the sense of being over or outside the discourses it influences. It is simply *different*. To be sure, there are many "different" discourses around at any given time, and not all of them get attended to as "abnormal." But the ones that do get attended to owe their influence not to some inherent superiority in their terminology, assumptions, and so on—not to a greater critical incisiveness or a clearer picture of reality or what have you—but rather to the historical, and I would add personal, contingencies that make a discourse salient for practitioners of another discourse at any given time. For example, in literary studies there is a history of attending to literary theory such that changes in theoretical discourse, "theory talk," will affect literary-critical discourse generally. This ability to influence does *not* come from some inherent superiority of the theoretical discourse.

Hence, then, on change: Fish is not saying that change cannot happen, or that discursive communities, human groups united by rhetoric, must always be univocal and fiercely conformist. That would be a patently absurd position to anyone who has ever been a member of a human group—that is, to anyone. But Fish is saying that change cannot be attributed to the influence of some sort of meta-discourse, because there is no such thing as a meta-discourse. Change happens when discourses that are only different, not superior or inferior, influence one another (and, of course, as Fish points out, change occurs for any number of other reasons as well, many of them non-discursive).

Fish mentions objecting to my "suggestion that the theoretical perspective on situationality itself could do work if transmitted to a group of students." I think what he is referring to here is my advocacy of teaching about academic discourse (the "theoretical perspective on situationality") as a way of demystifying academic discourse and giving students more control over their use or rejection of academic discourse. In other words, Fish sees me as trying to teach a meta-discourse on academic discourse and to foster a critical self-consciousness, about academic discourse, of the kind he has disallowed. Fish is getting his view of my position here, I think, from my 1982 essay "Cognition, Convention, and Certainty." He is right to suggest that I once advocated teaching about academic discourse as a means to achieving critical self-consciousness, or what I would have called, following Paulo Freire, "critical consciousness." I have come to reject this view of teaching about academic discourse, however, as I have argued, for example, in my 1986 essay "Foundationalism and Anti-Foundationalism in Composition Studies," which draws heavily on Fish's work "against theory." I now agree with Fish that talk about academic discourse cannot be meta-discursive (for a more complete account of the changes in my thinking here, see *Academic Discourse and Critical Consciousness*).

What I would now like to say concerning teaching about academic discourse, however, is that it might be a kind of abnormal discourse, functioning in ways similar to the functionings of theory talk in literary studies. Let us say that talk about academic discourse and the social construction of knowledge is only different from, not superior to, talk that stresses the need to learn Standard English as the *sine qua non* of good writing or talk that treats the construction of knowledge as the heaping of facts. What I would like to say is that it might be different in a way that matters now. It might even empower students in some of the ways I had claimed for it in the past, but again, not because it is superior, but rather because given the history of teaching writing in this country, it is startling, and feels liberating, to hear the teacher talking about ideas instead of correctness.

Another way to put this would be to say that we can still talk about the way we talk, in the academy for example, without having to claim that this talk is "meta" in the sense of being above or outside academic discourse. And I think we can say that talking about academic discourse can help students to understand it better, practice it more fluently, and work to change it more creatively, without having to claim that this kind of perspective on the discourse constitutes critical "distance" of the kind Fish disallows.

When Fish insists near the end of the *JAC* interview that there is "no yield" from believing his theories, I think he means that he does not regard his own theories as any more "meta" than any others. But I don't think he can mean that Fish talk might not be abnormal discourse for some people, might not interfere with their usual ways of thinking about things and move them toward change. The first time I was exposed to Fish talk was in the summer of 1977, at the School of Criticism and Theory, then at the University of California at Irvine. My husband, Bruce Herzberg, was taking a course from Fish that summer and telling me endlessly about the interesting things he was learning. As I recall, I resisted it all. This was not the way to talk about language or literature. I argued against Bruce, against the others in his class, and against Stanley all summer—and look, by the end of the summer I was talking Fish talk too.

College of the Holy Cross
Worcester, Massachusetts

Works Cited

Bizzell, Patricia. *Academic Discourse and Critical Consciousness.* Pittsburgh: U of Pittsburgh P, 1993.

——. "Cognition, Convention, and Certainty: What We Need To Know about Writing." *Pre/Text* 3 (1982): 213-43.

——. "Foundationalism and Anti-Foundationalism in Composition Studies." *Pre/Text* 7 (1986): 37-56.

"Fish Tales" and the Politics of Anti-Professionalism

JOHN TRIMBUR

In "Fish Tales: A Conversation with 'The Contemporary Sophist,'" Stanley Fish offers, among other things, an eloquent analysis of liberalism and the modern liberal state. As Marxist-Leninists say, and as Bush's mobilization of federal troops to Los Angeles in May 1992 indicates, the power of the modern state consists, in the final analysis, of "armed bodies of men." But the authority of the state—its discursive ability to author itself and secure widespread consent—is more complexly mediated, and Fish's analysis of liberalism presents one set of reasons why this is so. According to Fish, the "unhappy insight" liberalism brings to the modern world is that "conflict"—and here Fish refers to sixteenth- and seventeenth-century theological and real (and quite bloody) battles—"cannot be avoided." The point of liberalism, therefore, is not "so much to avoid . . . but to control" these conflicts, to design a state apparatus that ostensibly treats contending parties, interests, and points of view equally so that they may coexist within a regime of civil peace.

As Fish makes clear, the actual liberal state is not, and has never been, the neutral arbiter it claims to be. But this fact should not distract us from what I take to be the central point in Fish's analysis: that popular allegiance to the modern state does not result from the account liberalism has classically offered. It does not result from the rational self-interest of individuals who decide to affiliate rather than continue in the anarchic conditions (what Hobbes calls the "inconvenience") of the state of nature; nor does it result from universalist principles of natural right. Instead, it grows out of a particular historical conjuncture marked by weariness with the sectarian and political passions of the day and, significantly, the inability of Englishmen to agree on fundamental principles of belief. The ostensible and self-proclaimed rationality of the modern state emerges from its apparent reasonableness, as a way to deal with forces such as *"conviction, belief, passion,"* which, as Fish notes, have fallen into a "zone of suspicion." It is not so much that an Age of Reason, as we encounter it in its traditional versions, has triumphed over feudalism and medieval superstition as that the threat of its opposite, figured as an uncontrolled fanaticism, has proved to be more than the social order can bear.

There is a telling point here in Fish's portrayal of liberalism as a "brief against belief and conviction": liberalism does not in the first instance deny or suppress what we have come to call "difference" in the name of a general rationality, a transcendental subject, or some other universalized category of understanding, as we might be led to believe by both liberalism's account of itself and current postmodern critiques of liberal ideology. Rather, the structure of feeling that underwrites liberalism is born precisely from a fateful representation of difference as invariably disruptive and always potentially violent, and a desperate effort that follows to design a social machinery capable of keeping social and cultural differences in check and balance.

I mention these points in part because I admire the lucidity of Fish's analysis of liberalism but also because the main outlines of state formation that Fish sketches can be applied, by way of analogy, to the formation of professions and the constitution of professional expertise as we know it. As I will suggest in a moment, the profession of literary studies emerges not only from a codified body of knowledge and a set of institutionalized practices but also from a very real moment of cultural anxiety about the unregulated circulation and consumption of written texts in the late nineteenth and early twentieth century.

Stanley Fish, as most readers of *JAC* will be aware, has written a number of essays on professionalism that delineate its habits and discontents. One of Fish's prime concerns has been with what he calls "anti-professional" currents of thought running from both the right and the left. In essays such as "Profession Despise Thyself: Fear and Loathing in Literary Studies" and "Anti-Professionalism," Fish has countered charges from the right that literary studies has fallen into hopeless careerism and the relentless production of specialized scholarship, thereby abandoning the abiding truths that make literary studies a vocation or calling, free from the market and special interests, capable of articulating general propositions about the human condition. At the same time, according to Fish, anti-professionalism from the left amounts to charges that literary studies, again because of its careerism and specialized scholarship, is no more than an avoidance of real world issues and political struggles. As Fish has it, the right thinks the "world is too much with us" while the left thinks "we are not sufficiently of the world" (*Doing* 213).

In both cases, according to Fish, left and right wing anti-professionals alike have gone transhistorical by locating literature in a realm separate from the beliefs, practices, and professional routines by which literature is constituted in the first place. Anti-professionalism, in other words, has transplanted literature into an arhetorical world, where, once we cast off the roles and jargons imposed on us by professional and institutional contexts, we will be able to see the true meaning of literary works—not as more grist for the academic mill but as either repositories of timeless value, as the right holds, or revolutionary defamiliarizations of common sense, as the left might say. The upshot for Fish is that neither of these positions can be considered coherent; each appeals to standpoints above or outside the ongoing conversational practices by which literature and literary works—whether periods, genres, authors, canons, or critical methods—become objects of inquiry. Anti-professionalism, as Fish says, is "indefensible because it imagines a form of life—free, independent, acontextual—that cannot be lived" (*Doing* 246).

Fish has become well known for this strong version of professionalism, for mounting a case on behalf of professionalism that does not argue so much for the benefits or desirability of professionalism (as people in rhetoric and composition often do) but for its inevitability, as an unavoidable set of conventionalized assumptions, institutions, and understandings without which literary studies would be quite impossible. I find it hard to disagree with Fish's point, despite (or maybe because of) the fact that he makes it so provocatively by casting himself into the apparently scandalous position of holding that the study of literature is "merely another profession" among many, that operates according to the same processes of initiation, credentialing, assigning credit, and evaluating performances that govern, say, engineering or dentistry. Fish's case for professionalism seems to me a bracing and useful corrective to the self-images currently available within literary studies, whether the traditional image of the custodian of culture or the insurgent image of the cultural critic. Casting himself so unapologetically as a "mere" professional, going about the only business a professional can go about—reading and writing, publishing articles, joining professional associations, going to meetings, taking part in the conversation (and the gossip) of the day—Fish makes the very helpful point that "anti-professionalism is basically an up-to-date, twentieth-century form of the traditional hostility to rhetoric" (*Doing* 219). Fish helps us see that institutionalized practices and professional vocabularies are not "iron cages" that channel a genuine love of literature into the distorting grooves of expertise but are themselves enabling fictions, a local rhetoric made up to get some work done.

Still, one does not have to fall into what Fish calls anti-professionalism to want to make the point that the profession of literary studies is inflected decisively not only by its conventionalized practices and procedures but also by its relation to the public. As I mentioned earlier and as I believe the formation of literary studies reveals, the profession emerges historically from and continues to carry the traces of a particular set of cultural anxieties about literacy. Burton Bledstein, one of the leading historians of the "culture of professionalism" in the United States, suggests that the increased availability of printed matter in the late nineteenth century (a "riot of words") was experienced by the mid-Victorian middle classes as an anarchic and unregulated condition (65-79). According to Bledstein, the unprecedented dissemination of the written word isolated individual readers in their own private worlds, apart from such social settings as the audience at the theater, the music hall, the symphony. This isolation not only created a new realm of human experience, it also served to induce "confusion and frustration that gave way to self doubt and mistrust" (78). Such atomized and unregulated acts of reading produced, in effect, cultural anxieties in mid-Victorian America about "who would distinguish the true words from the false ones" (78), and these anxieties were resolved, at least symbolically, by such measures as the tighter postal obscenity law of 1973, the publication of self-help guides such as Noah Porter's *Books and Reading: Or, What Books Shall I Read and How Shall I Read Them?* (1870), and Charles Eliot's fifty-volume plan of self-education, *The Harvard Classics*. Moreover, with the emergence of professional librarians, spokespersons, educators, and English departments, the "citizen," Bledstein suggests, "became a client whose obligation was to trust the professional" (78-79).

There is, of course, as Fish notes (*Doing* 216), an anti-professional edge to Bledstein's account of the cultural authorization of expertise. Nonetheless, to see the formation of professionalized literary studies as part of a larger interaction of the professions with public pressures and popular anxieties does not, it seems to me, necessitate a break with Fish's strong version of professionalism but instead may supplement it in an important respect. That is, literary studies is not and never has been the self-enclosed body of experts talking to each other endlessly in an arcane and publicly incomprehensible language, as some anti-professionals put it, but has always been subject to and is in part the product of popular influence and opinion. Fish makes just this point in the *JAC* interview when he says that "the questions raised by feminism, because they were questions raised not in the academy but in the larger world and then made their way into the academy, have energized more thought and social action than any other 'ism' in the past twenty or thirty years."

Taken at any particular moment, especially to unreconstructed anti-professionals, such popular pressures from below—and one might list here not only feminism but the force of African-American, gay and lesbian, and Third World movements and the current widespread interest in popular culture—might appear from the right to be "merely" ephemeral intrusions into timeless work, or from the left to be liberatory forces coopted by their academic mediations into "mere" business-as-usual, professional behavior and the production of careers. Both views, however, miss the telling point: that the boundaries of the profession are permeable and subject to consequential redefinition and change from internal and external pressures.

On the other hand, and now I want to return to Fish's analysis of the modern liberal state, it is precisely the permeability of these boundaries that can, and certainly has, induced a great deal of anxiety recently about the "conviction, belief, passion" that appear to have suddenly invaded the academy, threatening and, in some instances, actually precipitating civil wars within English departments. You name it, poststructuralism, deconstruction, feminism, the new historicism, minority and postcolonial discourse, rhetoric and composition, postmodernism, and cultural studies have each and all served to disrupt the normal functions and self-images of English departments. In this light, Gerald Graff's injunction to "teach the conflicts" looms as the essentially liberal gesture, formulated in the name of an even-handed reasonableness capable not so much of avoiding conflict as of controlling it—giving it a shape—in pedagogical form.

Fish is right when he says that the issue has to do with the forms professionalism might assume. As may be evident, I do not find it helpful to argue against professionalism in the name of a pure politics or cultural critique. I don't think one can simply dismantle the boundaries between the popular and the academic—to go directly to the people (to turn "clients" back into "citizens") or to get to literature or writing or mass entertainment as it "really" takes place. Nor does it seem altogether satisfactory to argue, as Graff does, that we can just "teach the conflicts," as if from a position above the fray. What seems most interesting and yet somewhat underpredicated in Fish's analysis of professionalism and liberalism is the ongoing interplay of the academic and the popular, the high and the low, the expert and the public.

It is an (un)civil war, what Gramsci referred to as a "war of positions," that marks contemporary American culture. In the midst of these cultural battles—and I'm thinking of the Mapplethorpe controversy and the NEA, the fight about Carol Iannone at NEH, Camille Paglia and the anti-feminist backlash, the emerging debate about funding PBS, the controversies over the canon and multicultural education, Dan Quayle's bashing of *Murphy Brown* and the politicization of popular culture, and the whole "political correctness" phenomenon—the problem, as I see it, is not a matter of learning how better to explain to the public what professionals in literature or rhetoric and composition actually do and what they believe, as Teachers for a Democratic Culture has suggested. The issue to be faced is not just one of public relations, of how to publicize and advertise professional work. Given the permeability of the boundaries between our profession and public politics, the issue I want to address is how can we, without either abandoning or defending professional expertise, rearticulate it in order to redirect current popular anxieties, beliefs, and passions toward the goals of a democratic culture. At a time in our collective history when the media and opinion-makers have identified the university "elite" as scapegoats, I think it is crucial not to concede the opposed term of "populism" to Dinesh D'Souza, Lynne Cheney, and the *Wall Street Journal* (hardly grassroots spokespersons, after all). But as Fish might say, there's no reason to think that professional expertise can or cannot intervene effectively in the culture wars—and no necessary consequence to any particular analysis or theory professionals offer that would entitle them to speak for or to the public. It all depends on what you want and how persuasive you are. It's a matter of rhetoric.

Worcester Polytechnic Institute
Worcester, Massachusetts

Works Cited

Bledstein, Burton J. *The Culture of Professionalism*. New York: Norton, 1976.

Fish, Stanley. *Doing What Comes Naturally*. Durham, NC: Duke UP, 1989.

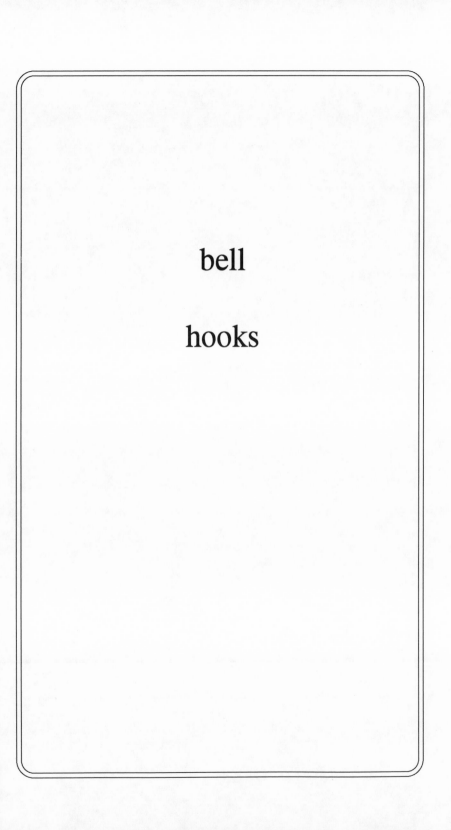

bell

hooks

bell hooks and the Politics of Literacy: A Conversation

GARY A. OLSON

Feminist and cultural critic bell hooks is resolutely committed to promoting literacy. For hooks, literacy is essential to the future of the feminist movement because the lack of reading, writing, and critical skills serves to exclude many women and men from feminist consciousness. Yet, as hooks argues in the interview that follows, "The class standpoint of much feminist theory leads to a depriviledging of and a disrespect for the politics of reading and writing." She makes a cogent case for encouraging "every feminist thinker in the academy" to acknowledge literacy to be "an important feminist agenda," and she expresses "anguish" over the neglect of literacy among feminists: "If we truly want to empower women and men to engage in feminist thinking, we must empower them to read and write, but I really don't see any large group of committed feminists making that a central agenda."

This concern that mainstream feminist theorists have not promoted literacy is in keeping with hooks' oft-repeated charge that white, liberal, middle-class feminists have traditionally set an agenda for feminism that fails to reflect the concerns of feminists who are also women (or men) of color. Since illiteracy is often a concern of the poor and underprivileged, many of whom often are minorities, this issue frequently is not perceived to be a feminist concern by "a lot of privileged women who already read and write, who don't encounter anybody in their life who doesn't read or write, and who therefore don't even think about literacy."

This commitment to critical literacy has made hooks a long-time supporter of Paulo Freire: "I was like a person dying of thirst when I first came to Paulo." And despite the fact that many feminists (including hooks herself) have criticized Freire for being "partially blinded by sexism," hooks feels justified in overlooking these imperfections in order to "take what was nurturing" from his work. Freire's concept of critical consciousness has been particularly important to hooks' own work and not only has strengthened her belief that literacy is necessary to the feminist movement but is apparently one reason why she has chosen to focus her scholarship on feminist theory and cultural criticism rather than literary criticism: "Literary criticism doesn't participate as much as I would like it to in creating a critical readership, in educating people for critical consciousness."

Like Freire, hooks promotes a notion of *praxis* that integrates reflection and action. Thus, she consistently incorporates anecdotes and details of her personal life into her writing in order to illuminate theory: "When you tell a story about how you use an abstract idea or a bit of theory in a concrete situation, it just feels more real to people." This is precisely why, hooks argues, cultural criticism is so exciting: it makes students think, "Wow! there really is something to theory and to thinking about this stuff that I can translate back to my lived reality." In fact, hooks believes that cultural criticism should be an important part of composition pedagogy because engaging in written cultural critique helps student writers become "more deeply engaged in composition."

Undoubtedly, hooks has thought long and deeply about the problems and politics of pedagogy. She argues that preoccupation with audience during the composing process can be "dangerous" because it can lead to self-censorship, but she also believes that a sense of audience can help writers, especially "marginalized people," develop an authentic voice. In addition, she espouses a pedagogy that is not formulaic but that is responsive to the specific situation of each particular group of students. Such a situational pedagogy is especially appropriate for the multicultural classroom, but the transition to a multicultural pedagogy, hooks cautions, is fraught with chaos, and most teachers will need to develop "strategies for dealing with confusion and chaos." Despite the new interventions in curriculum and modes of teaching that have "the power to re-center both composition and the writing process in pedagogy," hooks fears that the conservative backlash may endanger such progressive reforms.

In discussing other issues of concern to compositionists, hooks encourages us to help students become polyvocal, to "talk about how white supremacy is manifested in the way we use language," and to make space in the classroom for "intimacy or passion and desire." She also speaks of the need for feminists to return to the notion of sisterhood, solidarity, but she is "very concerned about certain strands of white lesbian feminist theory that seem to me to be coming out as a kind of policing of other marginal people, especially people of color."

Clearly, bell hooks' commitment to literacy, composition, critical consciousness, and cultural critique makes her an important ally to those of us involved in literacy studies and composition theory. As composition studies increasingly embraces cultural criticism, her work will become even more relevant to our own. Her insistence on turning her critique occasionally even to those who espouse progressive agendas (including certain white feminists, radical pedagogy theorists, and black literary critics) is indicative of her rigor and integrity as a cultural critic always wary of the systems of domination to which we all are so susceptible.[1]

Q. You wrote your first book, *Ain't I a Woman*, at nineteen when you were an undergraduate at Stanford. In *Talking Back* you write, "Although I have wanted writing to be my life-work since childhood, it has been difficult for me to claim 'writer' as part of that which identifies and shapes my everyday reality. Even after publishing books, I would often speak of wanting to be a writer as though these works did not exist." Do you now see yourself as a writer, an author?

A. I do. I think I now see myself more as a writer because it has become so evident that I have an audience, because I now get so much feedback. I found it hard to think of myself as a writer when I felt I was writing in isolation with no clear sense of an audience because for me writing as a writer implied mutuality, that there is both reader and writer.

Q. So the audience made you a writer.

A. Absolutely. I feel that really strongly. Each year of my life, I feel I'm writing with a deeper dedication because it's so clear that the audience grows stronger.

Q. What's your writing process like? Do you plan your works extensively before you begin to write? Do you revise heavily? Use a computer?

A. Well, one dreary thing that I do is handwrite everything; I've handwritten all my books. I like to handwrite because I find that I think differently when I do so. Computers are seductive in that you feel that you don't have to edit and rework as much because the printed text can look so good, and if you have a good printer it looks even better. So for me the stages tend to be that I work something through in my head, and then I start writing it. And I work a lot with question outlines because the question-and-answer format is one I like a lot and use often in writing essays. I think: "What kind of questions do I envision myself and another audience wanting to know, say, about this film or about this issue?"

Q. In your books you experiment with various alternatives to traditional academic prose, including interviews, self-interviews, and dialogues. Do you see such forms as ways to resist traditional, patriarchal discourse, or do you have other reasons for using such forms?

A. Oh, absolutely! I think one of the primary reasons for using these forms is a lesson I learned from the Shahrazad Ali book. When I saw all those poor underclass and lower-middle class people on the subways of New York and in bus stations reading that book, I wondered, "What's so magical about this book? It's not just the content." What I realized was that you could open that book to any page, and any paragraph would make sense; it shared an idea with you. And I realized that conversation books are like that. One of the things I've been thinking a lot about is that I find that lately I read less. I used to pride myself on reading a book a day, because reading was a passion for me. But now I'm lucky if I read a book a week. In busy times I'm lucky if I read a book in two weeks. I wondered how we expect people who work every day to come home and read these ten- and twenty-page essays we are taught to write in the academy. And so I learned from Shahrazad Ali that you can write a kind of book like *Breaking Bread* (which is the conversational book) in which people can come home and open it up to any page and read that page and feel that they got some idea and that they understood it, that they could digest it. Then I got a lot of feedback from readers who said, "I found I could come home from work, open up *Breaking Bread*, and just read maybe a couple of pages." This is a real challenge to us as academics who have been trained to write longer pieces, and I see it as a subversion of the whole sense that there has to be only one monolithic writing style that can be given scholarly legitimation in the academy. Sometimes I write ten pages of something and I think this could have just as well been said in three pages, but most journals aren't going to want to publish three pages. I'd like to see journals become more open to publishing smaller pieces if we can truly say what we have to say in that short space.

Q. In a recent *JAC* interview, Jane Tompkins discusses the need to personalize academic writing, and in *Talking Back* you mention your own attempts to introduce the personal into your writing. In what way is the personal potentially an important component of scholarly writing?

A. If you look at my first two books, you see very little personal anecdote, personal confession. What I began to find was that when you're trying to invite people to shift their paradigms more pragmatically or concretely—for example, I'm trying to get black people to think about feminism and often there's resistance—usually if you just start off from the purely theoretical or the abstract (and I don't think theory and abstraction are one and the same), people don't tend to open up if they already have that resistance. We had a good example of it in a talk I gave today. A young black brother said, "I came here not knowing your work, assuming that you were anti-black-male." If I had not told the kinds of anecdotes that showed my regard for black males, my concern for their well being, I don't think he would have opened up. This is something that has made me think a lot about the personal story as a teaching tool. I gave a lecture recently at the MMLA, and I talked about my concern about everything being personalized. Someone stood up in the question-and-answer period and said that he was sorry to hear me say this because so much of my work has been personal. I replied, "I don't think of *personal* and *personalize* as the same thing. For me, *personalize* means that you see everything as coming back to your ego and to your narcissistic construction of self." I said that I saw my willingness to be more confessional about my life and to share experiences as part of a kind of activism that is about sacrifice for me. I also said that I'd like to spend a year of my life when maybe I *wasn't* sharing in a public arena details of my personal life, but I have found those details often to be what grabs people, and it's what makes theory seem (as it does for me) to have concrete application. When you tell a story about how you use an abstract idea or a bit of theory in a concrete situation, it just feels more real to people.

Q. In *Talking Back*, you write, "To make the liberated voice, one must confront the issue of audience—we must know to whom we speak. . . . When I thought about audience—the way in which the language we choose to use declares who it is we place at the center of our discourse—I confronted my fear of placing myself and other black women at the speaking center." Do you believe writers should "ignore" audience, that awareness of audience can be a *disabling* concern, or do you think writers should develop an ever sharper sense of audience?

A. We need to do both. I've just finished writing a piece on censorship. I was struck by the fact that I was very disturbed by Henry Louis Gates' Op-Ed piece on anti-semitism in the *New York Times*, and I wanted to write a response, but I felt that I shouldn't, that it was inappropriate, that I would be perceived as attacking a black man, and so I thought to myself that I shouldn't write this piece. I thought about other academics who would say I'm trashing Skip, and I was worried that Skip would see me as not supporting him. That's the kind of case where too much recognition of audience can be dangerous. This is a very dangerous phenomenon in academe right now. When intellectuals constitute a rising social class—and I think we see a rising sort of clique in a sense with some black intellectuals—then there's a kind of censorship that says, "Well, maybe I should go out and have a drink with this person and tell him what I don't like about his essay, but I shouldn't write a public response." I really grappled with this question. I said, "My God, if I who have tenure and a clear sense of where I'm going feel that I can't write a critique for fear of how other people might respond, then what must someone who has no job security, who has to fear that this powerful black male academic might have a say in their future, feel?" It stunned me just how dangerous that kind of climate is. In that sense, thinking too much about audience can be dangerous. Yet, thinking about audience can be crucial for marginalized people who haven't had voice but who are trying to come to grips with a voice. In a sense, when I was eighteen and nineteen and was writing the first draft of *Ain't I a Woman*, I had a very artificial academic voice. *Ain't I a Woman* didn't get published until six years or so after I wrote it, and it initially had a lot of stilted language. When I began to imagine myself speaking to other black women, I was able to break out of the jargon that I had learned as the appropriate academic tone. I think that was a way in which thinking of audience was positive and constructive. Sometimes it's good to think about the audience you want to reach because we can reach different audiences in different ways.

Q. One audience you have *not* catered to is the traditional literary-critical establishment. In *Breaking Bread* you say, "I have never focused on publishing my literary criticism to the degree that I have feminist theory or cultural criticism, or even film criticism." What accounts for this decision? Do you believe literary criticism is generally responsive to African-American concerns?

A. We've seen a great welling up of literary criticism about African-American texts. To me, an interesting question is to what extent does literary criticism help create a critical readership? Part of what has made me distance myself from writing literary criticism as much as I write other things is that literary criticism doesn't participate as much as I would like it to in creating a critical readership, in educating people for critical consciousness. That may have had more to do with the *type* of literary criticism we've been writing, but I have not nurtured that aspect of my intellectuality as much because of the fact that so few people read it. Once you have a book that five-thousand people have read (which doesn't seem like a lot, but for academics that's a lot of readers), to think that you will labor over an essay that only ten people might read is really hard. What's great is when we have the luxury of the option to do both. I would never feel happy just to have that limited readership; at the same time, it's also okay when people want to write something that may only be magic for a small audience. I don't want to denigrate that. I think we can have both. It was interesting that at the end of a public lecture I gave today, quite a number of people came up to say that they had, in fact, read the lit-crit articles I've done on Hurston and Walker and which were published in more obscure places and don't have much accessibility. This showed me that people do read those things, but rarely do people write to me about those pieces. It's the whole question of to what extent people feel they can use critical work, critical thinking, in their lives. And I think that cultural criticism seems to excite so many of us right now precisely because it seems to make students think, "Wow! there really is something to theory and to thinking about this stuff that I can translate back to my lived reality." Once you're seduced by the potentiality of a larger audience and a larger critical dialogue, I think it's hard to engage in certain forms of writing that close down the possibility of larger audiences.

Q. You claim in *Breaking Bread* that "when I look at the evolution of my identity as a writer I see it intimately tied to my spiritual evolution." Would you elaborate on this connection?

A. I believe I was thinking about the question of contemplation. A lot of people ask me, "How do you write all these books?" I used to joke, "Oh, it's because I don't have a life." But I think the real answer is that I spend a lot of time alone, and I believe that the act of writing isn't just about spending the time alone writing; it's also the time you spend in contemplation. My development as an intellectual and as a critical thinker is tied to spirituality because growing up as a working-class black woman, the only arena of my life that gave me the sense that I had the right to a space of contemplation was religiosity and spirituality. In fact, it was telling me that everybody needs to go into the desert and to be alone. Given the kind of racist, sexist iconography in our culture that always presumes that black women should serve the interests of others, whether it's black children or black men or the larger society, it's very hard for black women to claim that space that is the precursor to writing, the space where you can think through ideas. This is a way in which those two experiences of spiritual practice and writing converge for me. Also, I'm really engaged with Buddhism. I just did a big interview in *Tricycle*, a marvelous, new Buddhist magazine that covers various cultural issues and tries to relate Buddhist practice in the United States to other aspects of our culture. One of the things I like about Buddhism is its emphasis on practice; when I apply that to writing, writing becomes a form of practice that gives me the energy to spend long hours. I just finished a long piece on Jean-Michel Basquiat, the twenty-seven-year-old black painter who has a retrospective at the Whitney right now. I meditated a great deal because I felt that there was kind of a white supremacist art hegemony that was writing very negative cultural criticism about his work and art criticism. I felt that I really wanted to be able to write something that would illuminate the beauty and power I find in his work. I thought about it, I read a lot of things, and then all of a sudden after months and months that "rush" came. I sat for hours at the computer—I mean serious, say, ten-hour periods. I have evolved into someone who sits in meditation and who values that kind of immersion. When I finished this piece, I felt ecstasy, the ecstasy of being able to make an intervention. I felt that the piece had a lot of power. I called it "Altars of Sacrifice: Remembering Basquiat," alluding to a black church song: "You're all on the altar of sacrifice laid." Again, it's that convergence for me of motifs of spirituality and cultural criticism.

Q. You've often made the point that the margin can be a site of opportunity as well as oppression. Despite the rapid growth of rhetoric and composition as a discipline, it continues to be marginalized within the university. Do you see any advantage in composition's marginalized status? How would you go about exploiting this advantage?

A. Well, I think that those professors who have been most willing to engage cultural criticism and other ways of de-centering the West in writing are finding that their students are more deeply engaged in composition. One of the first areas of my work that I got positive feedback on was from teachers of composition who said, "When my students read *Talking Back*, it really helps them think about having a voice." That was the *last* thing I thought about when I was writing *Talking Back*. I don't think it ever occurred to me that these essays could have power in the composition classroom, opening students up in some ways, because those essays address a lot of the deep fears people have about voice and the act of writing. So, I think that if we really examine the kind of composition work that has done that, I think we would see a new and renewing dimension both to composition and to the art of writing. That's why we're in danger right now with the backlash against those new interventions in curriculum and modes of teaching; those interventions have the power to re-center both composition and the writing process in pedagogy, and it will be a tragedy for us if they get taken out in the interest of people going back to the way it was.

Q. You've pointed out that in a multicultural classroom it's necessary to be aware of the diversity of cultural codes so as to create an inclusive atmosphere. What specific steps can we take to create an effective multicultural pedagogy?

A. The movement toward a multicultural pedagogy was really, to me, tantamount to a revolution; and, like revolutions on all levels in culture, there are times of chaos. Many of us thought we'd make this transition without chaos, and I think partially most of us develop pedagogical practices that don't in any way include strategies for dealing with confusion and chaos. One of the things I said yesterday in talking to an audience at Tufts University was that I find the greater the level of diversity in my classes from a race, ethnicity, gender, sexual-practice standpoint, the harder it is to construct a learning community. It takes longer to create an environment in which people can hold all the differences and allow for harmony and dissent at the same time, and I think that's a challenge to us because when we've had a kind of banking system of education, as Freire says, or a system that focuses so much on quantity ("How much did you get done?"), it becomes harder because the process is slower. I've found in my own teaching experience that the smaller the class, the better. My Toni Morrison seminar has fourteen students in it, and I got to choose those students from a list of fifty after I interviewed them. So the class is diverse: it's ethnically diverse, it has diverse sexual practices, it has tremendous difference. But because we are small, we are able to work through the tensions that those differences create. For example, the other day I was talking about how I felt deeply disturbed by Morrison's eroticization of the scar on Sethe's back in *Beloved*. One of the more traditional, white English majors said, "When I first read Morrison in a traditional English class where we didn't even talk about scars and slavery and woundedness, I just wrote about the imagery of trees in Morrison." This created one of those little moments of uproar and tension and dissent, but we were able to use it as a learning moment. When things like that happen in my course of forty students, they rarely become learning moments in that instant because so much chaos, hostility, or tension arises. So, I think that's a major challenge to us. In what ways does the classroom itself have to change in order to be more conducive to a multicultural perspective? I don't think the classroom can remain the same; I don't think the professor's *place* in the classroom can remain the same, because there are so many areas in which we have gaps in our own knowing. And where is the space in our pedagogical practice to admit, "I can't really be the primary teacher at this moment because I don't know enough"?

Q. But in their attempts to initiate students into the discursive practices of dominant culture, compositionists face a real dilemma. On the one hand, they want to empower students by giving them the tools of traditional literacy in order to help them compete successfully in the world, but, on the other hand, doing so is often asking students from non-privileged backgrounds to reject their own cultural identities and discourses. How can we empower students while preserving cultural difference?

A. One major way is that we can encourage students to be polyvocal and polyphonic, that we don't say, "You've got to give this up to acquire that." You say, "Keep what you've got." For a year when I was teaching at Yale, students had a choice: they could do a paper in black vernacular, in Spanish, in whatever they wanted to, as long as they did that same paper in standard English and followed the required format. I would say to my students, "I would be disempowering you if I did not encourage you to acquire the ways of knowing and the forms of writing that will help you succeed in society as a whole; but to honor and cherish those other ways of speaking and writing, we can do things simultaneously so that you can acquire all of these skills and not be forced to leave the other behind." I feel that a lot of people don't progress in writing because it's actually a deeper psychological issue of language. I just wrote a piece a few months ago for an anthology on language in which I talk about what happens when you feel most familiar in a particular language, patois, or vernacular that isn't affirmed in writing classes, and how diminishing that can be psychologically and how it can turn you off from a process that you don't have to be turned off from if you can find a way to simultaneously hold that language. Once I asked my students in a huge class on black women writers, "Why do we only hear English in this classroom? There are some people here for whom English is not their first language, but they never get carried away and say a sentence in Spanish." A student said, "But if they did, we wouldn't understand them." I answered, "But they're capable of translating; plus, what does it mean for us to learn in a context where we would hear something other than English? Even if we didn't understand a statement, it would remind us of the multicultural nature of our society; it would remind us of the multilingual nature of our society; it might encourage many of us to become bilingual rather than to speak only English; but, also, we can then privilege the translation of the student's statement." I used to have students whose first language was Spanish say, "It's hard for me to do my paragraphs because when I really think passionately, it comes out in Spanish." So I recommend that they write in Spanish and then translate. It's interesting how dualistic thinking operates on so many levels. Why do these students immediately imagine, "I must give up that Spanish," or "It's a negation; I can't express it in

English"? I ask, "Do you have some problems translating?" "Oh, that never occurred to me." It's such a simple strategy, but when we think dualistically all the time, that strategy doesn't come forth.

Q. You say in *Yearning* that when "white critics write about black culture 'cause it's the 'in' subject without interrogating their work to see whether or not it helps perpetuate and maintain racist domination, they participate in the commodification of 'blackness' that is so peculiar to postmodern strategies of colonization." How can white instructors avoid the "commodification" of racial identity while attempting to develop a cultur- ally inclusive curriculum?

A. Well, there again I think that asking questions is really useful. I often do self-interviews. I keep a journal, and I write in it every day to try to get a handle on why I'm doing something or what I hope to accomplish by doing it. Asking such hard questions of ourselves usually compels us to hone our perspective. And I think, too, that when white people ask themselves those hard questions, then they're not pissed off or terrified when a person of color confronts them because they've already dealt with that.

Q. In "Representing Whiteness" you cite Coco Fusco's remark, "To ignore white ethnicity is to redouble its hegemony by naturalizing it. Without specifically addressing white ethnicity, there can be no critical evaluation of the construction of the other." Can you think of ways that interrogation of whiteness can inform pedagogy, especially composition pedagogy?

A. That's an interesting question that I haven't really explored fully. I wonder to what extent we could talk about how white supremacy is manifested in the way we use language. I could see myself teaching a composition class. I work a lot in my courses with the paragraph out of the old-school conviction that if people can write a deep and compelling paragraph, they can usually go on to write a deep and compelling paper. So people in my classes do a lot of paragraphs. I could easily see myself having students write a paragraph about a text or something and saying, "Let's look at this to analyze how this paragraph might be written in such a way as to reaffirm the primacy of whiteness. Does that happen in the manner in which we write, not just in what we say?" That's one way that comes to me immediately, but I haven't really thought about this subject deeply.

Q. You've argued that "To make a revolutionary feminist pedagogy, we must relinquish our ties to traditional ways of teaching that reinforce domina- tion. This is very difficult. . . . We must first focus on the teacher-student relationship and the issue of power. How do we as feminist teachers use power in a way that is not coercive, dominating?" What *is* an appropriate use of authority in the classroom?

A. This issue is really interesting. First, I think it's important for us to distinguish authority from power because authority does not necessarily imply a positionality that can lead to dominance, whereas when we're dealing with questions of power we are talking about how we occupy the space of authority in a way that can reinforce and perpetuate domination. This became clear to me when I read Diana Fuss' book on essentialism. I wrote a critique of that book precisely because I felt that when she critiqued the notion that students are using the politics of experience, identity politics, to assert power over other students in the classroom and to assert a kind of hegemony of experience, I was struck by how so much of the language she used to describe the professor was that of hierarchy, authority, and power. It seems to me that what I have struggled with is that I initially went into this whole question of pedagogy and power not wanting to acknowledge my position of authority, the position that is a power relation that distinguishes me from the students in that I am grading them. I wanted to throw out the idea that there is an authority here, and, of course, that was nonsense. Now what I try to do is to allow myself to acknowledge my authority and the limitations of it and to then think about how we can learn together in a way that no one acquires the kind of power to use the classroom as a space of domination. I think that's one of the things that we have to think about in the diverse classroom, in the multicultural classroom. I think what Diana Fuss was trying to say positively is that it's possible in this diverse context, around these issues of race and gender and sexual practice, for everyone to engage in power struggles and, in fact, for certain students to have potentially the power to coerce, dominate, and silence. What I found sad was that her strategy for dealing with that was to reinforce the authority of the professor as opposed to thinking about what are the ways that we can teach so that students question, "How can I respect your difference, your difference of opinion, without crushing you?" That's a very different sense of power relations. I just finished a piece called "Eros, Eroticism, and the Pedagogical Process" in which I talk about the place of desire and love in the classroom because my students often express great passion for me in their writing, in their journal writings, and I often feel great passion for them. It's an interesting issue since the increased emphasis on sexual harassment has made many of us fear any kind of intimacy or passion and desire in the classroom because it raises these questions of power. We see that, for example, in the recent Exeter Academy case where, when it really comes right down to it, we don't have a lot of proof that the professor who turned out to be gay abused any student. They do know that he liked pornography and pornography with boys in it, but the point is that people immediately felt there had been abuse of power because people think that any time desire is present people will act on desire. So, what I was trying to think about in this piece was to work through a notion of how we might use the place of passion in the classroom to diffuse hierarchy and to create a sense of community. Students would actually come up to me and whine, "There's a way that you hug this student or talk to that student, and I want you to look at me the way you look at Johnny." I kept hearing this sort of sense of diminishing returns that if I have a lot of energy for one student I can't have any energy for others. I said, "Why is it that none of you think that if I look at Johnny this way, I must be willing to look at you this way, too—that it's not like I have this little space of care in me as a teacher and it's doled out for those special students? Why can't you think that I have this space of care that can enlarge to include everyone?" That was a real challenge for them because, again, we were seeing how either/or thinking, hierarchical thinking, was at work: if I really have passion for one student, I can't have passion for another. How can there be passion when students are different?

Q. In *Talking Back* you discuss "the transformative power of teaching, of pedagogy" that you witnessed as a student in segregated black schools: "In particular, those teachers who approached their work as though it was indeed a pedagogy, a science of teaching, requiring diverse strategies, approaches, explorations, experimentation, and risks, demonstrated the value—the political power—of teaching." What do you see as necessary elements of an effective liberatory pedagogy?

A. I've found that we can't have formulaic teaching and we can't have formulaic syllabi, that you have to go into a situation willing to think about what the needs of the people in this situation are. That's very hard, given the way we've been trained. I begin every semester with my syllabi intact and with my strategies in my head, and I think we have to do that because we work within structures. But what does it mean when we have to pull back and try a different strategy? As a person on the lecture circuit, I used to just bring the lecture that I had been told to give, but there were times when I would have an audience that really wasn't open to what I had planned to talk about. Then I thought there's no law that says I can't bring two or three lectures and once I get a sense of who the audience is going to be, of how I feel about them, that I could give the lecture most immediate for those circumstances. Teaching has to be that same way because it always then brings us back to a notion of a subject, a subject encounter. I'm not just imposing onto you a structure I've predesigned; I'm thinking about what this structure will mean to you. Yesterday, for example, I went to Tufts prepared to give a talk that focused mainly on representations of black women. I talked to professors there who said, "We're having such a struggle around cultural diversity. If you have this other lecture, that would be really great." But then I had dinner with students and talked with a lot of them. When I came to the lecture, I sensed that the students really wanted me to talk about black women. I felt I would lose a whole dimension of listening if I switched the topic, especially because the other lecture started with my relationship to a white male. I thought that the students were quite needy (they'd just heard about Audre Lorde's death), and they very much wanted black femaleness to be at the center. And I have to say that the other lecture's more interesting to me because it's raising issues about the academy that are on my mind in a way that a lot of the representation material is old for me, but I made that decision, and I felt it was the wise decision, and then I used the question-and-answer period as a space where I could bring up some of the ideas from the other piece. I think the classroom situation has to function much more like that then we want it to. I came to my Toni Morrison seminar two weeks ago, and it seemed that everybody was sleepy. I didn't feel good. We get a lot of intensely cold grey days, and we are in these hot, hot rooms. When I came to class, several people said, "You know, I really feel that I don't have a lot to give today." So what I said was, "Well, what are some of the ways we might talk about *Beloved* today that might allow us to have not our usual two-and-a-half-hour period but maybe let's just take an hour and a half but to think about how we can be really passionate about that?" So we tossed around and found our ideas. But that is very difficult. I still think, "Are we covering the material? They want to come over to my house for an extra class. Damn, I'm so busy that I don't want to meet with these kids for an extra class." I always think it's the mark of exciting pedagogy when students demand to have extra classes. But as I get older and more busy, I get less interested in those extra classes. That also has always struck me as a potential dimension of teaching that is inspired teaching. I do a lot of lunch meetings with my students where we all bring lunch; we have class but we all eat together. I have a theory that people feel a certain kind of vulnerability while they're eating, that certain things fall away, and so we often move and have class in a different setting; this may bring us closer together as a learning community because people drop their guard in certain ways.

Q. You've mentioned that Paulo Freire has had "a profound liberatory effect on my thinking," and in *Breaking Bread* you call him "one of my major mentors." Yet, in *Feminist Theory*, you point out that Freire's work is partially blinded by sexism. How seriously compromised is Freire's work by sexism?

A. The degree to which it is compromised is overdetermined by the location that one brings to his teaching. When he and I were together discussing this last summer at a conference, I said that I was like a person dying of thirst when I first came to Paulo, and the fact that there was some mud in my water was not important. I thought of his sexism as being like specks of dirt or mud because my need was so great. I was able to take what was nurturing to me and be more compassionate toward the aspect that was threatening, whereas I think many white feminists coming from different locations (not locations of need in the same way, perhaps) felt much more that they couldn't get to those nurturing aspects of the work because of that negative or tarnished dimension. One of the reasons it helps us to think about different positionalities is that perhaps then they could have been more compassionate toward his work by thinking, "Just because the sexism is a barrier to me, maybe there are some other people whose needs are such that it is not the same barrier." I think that it's also dangerous because Paulo has shown himself willing to engage in dialogue about this and is willing to grow. Also, there are limits given his lifetime, where he is now, where he's going, and there are different cultural codes, too. When I did the presentation with Paulo last summer, I had a new boyfriend who came to see me in my academic milieu. All these feminists were there, and Paulo started to introduce me by saying, "Dis is a *beautiful* woman, one no man can forget." I could just see the feminist (mainly white feminist) women in the room shrinking, whereas I think as a woman of color, coming from a different cultural code, I felt totally amused. I felt as if he were my granddad. I recognized it as sexism; I would have preferred a different kind of introduction, maybe one that started with my intellectual brilliance (which he did go on to talk about), but, respecting his code, where he was coming from, I didn't feel denigrated or diminished by what he was saying. But other people there felt that bell hooks is too forgiving of men; she's not angry enough at men; she's too patient. How do we walk that tightrope? Some black women said that to me the other day: "We like certain things about black male culture, but then we feel that maybe if we start tolerating this way of thinking about us or talking to us, it will go too far." I think it's difficult to create that balance.

Q. You've argued that "sisterhood" has been a destructive concept when used to erase differences between women. Yet, you've also argued that sisterhood *can* be a productive concept because "solidarity strengthens resistance struggle." Do you believe sisterhood can be a viable concept for feminist movement in the 1990s? How should it be understood today?

A. If we are to continue our progressive movements for change and to welcome diversity and multiculturalism, solidarity has to become a more central agenda. For me sisterhood always has been a rubric for talking about feminist theoretical and practical construction of solidarity, and it seems to me that we need to return that discussion to our thinking. One thing that was troubling to people at MMLA was that I said I was very concerned about certain strands of white lesbian feminist theory that seem to me to be coming out as a kind of policing of other marginal people, especially people of color. I was thinking particularly about work that has been very negative toward the idea of experience, the use of experience. I'm thinking particularly of a book by Linda Singer published by Routledge. Singer had just died, and in the book's introduction Judith Butler is sharing something about her and says something like, "Linda would be totally unhappy for me to go into a confessional or experiential thing because that is precisely the kind of women's studies she hated." I thought to myself, "Why do we have to engage in this privileging of one thing over another?" I tried to talk about the way in which lesbianism becomes the sign of transgression that then allows certain scholars to put forth analyses that are reactionary along the lines of race but that are not immediately perceived as reactionary because they're coming from what is already identified as a transgressive location. So I think if a straight white man were saying, "These people of color, these gay people, are using experience too much; they're talking about it but not doing the hard theoretical analysis, and so on," we would question that much more than when someone who occupies the cool space of transgression says it. Yet, I see this happening in a way that I think pits us against one another, yet again, and I think that's something that's really dangerous and that we have to look at.

Q. You make the point in *Ain't I a Woman* that feminist rhetoric often deploys an analogy between "women" as an oppressed group and "blacks" and that this analogy "unwittingly" caused people to "suggest that to them the term 'woman' is synonymous with 'white women' and the term 'black' synonymous with 'black men,'" thereby creating a "sexist-racist attitude toward black women." Do you believe that feminist rhetoric has changed since you first wrote this?

A. That kind of piggybacks on what I was just saying. What disturbs me about this new trend is that I do feel we have made major changes in feminist theory and that people were really working to be inclusive, to try to think from different positionalities, but it's very easy for people to undermine those interventions that I do believe were made. Feminist rhetoric *was* changing. It disturbs me a lot that neither Susan Faludi's book nor Naomi Wolf's book shows any awareness of the push to think about differences of race, class, and gender. They both reconstruct the kind of monolithic category of woman even though Wolf has some analysis in the footnotes (that's in *The Beauty Myth*) of differences for black women. I thought to myself, "Why does she put those differences in a footnote?" It's because it then allows her to reinforce *her* thematic construction of woman as a model of the category: woman that responds to beauty in the same way. It also then allows for the reprivileging of experiences that are specific to certain classes of white women, and I think this trend is scary because it has the danger of undermining the profound changes in feminist thinking and feminist rhetoric that have come about.

Q. What do you think accounts for our inability to "think" the concepts of race and gender together?

A. One is the hostility of the old academic guard to that and the increasing scarcity of jobs within the academy in that no matter how transgressive our sexual practice or anything else, many of us are still having to have that older guard evaluate us. That's one major factor that creates a barrier. Another is that many of us simply have not been trained. One thing about the kind of work I do and that I think the way I write belies is that I do a tremendous amount of reading across disciplines. (And I don't have the thousand footnotes that some people do; some people footnote everything, and the footnotes are just as long as the text. I don't tend to do that.) For example, for the piece that I just finished on Basquiat, I read enormous amounts of art criticism, but I also did reading in symbolic anthropology because I wanted to make some connections between what he's doing and the work of people like David Napier in his book *Foreign Bodies*, and I think that we haven't been trained to read that way. Let's face it, we all have time limitations, too. A lot of people just feel, "I can't do this because I can't really get all that background work that would allow me to do it." But rather than acknowledge that, why do we have people writing essays that say, "This essay will only speak from the position of black middle class dah-ti-dah because I didn't feel that I had the knowledge base to extend it," rather than announcing that as though it's okay?

Q. In "Educating Women: A Feminist Agenda," you argue that basic literacy is a necessary ingredient of continued growth of feminist movement, and you say that the lack of basic reading and writing skills excludes many women from feminist consciousness. Besides your recommendation for creating neighborhood literacy programs, how can we further integrate the goals of feminism and the spread of literacy?

A. We can't even begin to talk about that until every feminist thinker in the academy acknowledges literacy to be an important feminist agenda. Again, the class standpoint of much feminist theory leads to a deprivileging of and a disrespect for the politics of reading and writing, and this has become all the more rampant with the privileging of metalinguistic theory over other forms of theory, increasing the sense that it's a waste of time to think about reading and writing. That has been an ongoing cause of anguish to me because I do feel that if we truly want to empower women and men to engage in feminist thinking, we must empower them to read and write, but I really don't see any large group of committed feminists making that a central agenda. For example, look at how much energy women have brought to the issue of sexual harassment in the workplace just since the Anita Hill/Clarence Thomas exchange on national television. If we brought that kind of energy to literacy, the results would be incredible. We would reap the benefits much more quickly than the benefits of trying to raise patriarchal consciousness about sexual harassment. Yet, who decides that sexual harassment is more central than the question of literacy? A lot of privileged women who already read and write, who don't encounter anybody in their life who doesn't read or write, and who therefore don't even think about literacy. They don't even consider that as great a matter as sexual harassment in the workplace is, it's possibly not as great as the growing illiteracy among women, particularly poor women, many of whom in our society are women of color. We don't even say we are setting agendas here for public policy. We weren't saying to Bill Clinton or any of our candidates during the presidential election that literacy is a big issue. A lot of black men and other groups of men who are unemployed are in part unemployed because many of them can't read or write. Even if there is some job available that they might do, they're out of luck if it requires a skill that they don't have. Even the process of voting in this culture necessitates literacy. My class and I did a whole discussion on literacy and voting and how you could enter some space and say, "Look, I can't vote this way because I don't read. The ballots were so overly wordy, so overly packed, it was frightening."

Q. You write in *Yearning*, "Language is also a place of struggle. We are wedded in language, have our being in words. Language is also a place of struggle. Dare I speak to oppressed and oppressor in the same voice? Dare I speak to you in a language that will move beyond the boundaries of domination—a language that will not bind you, fence you in, or hold you? Language is also a place of struggle. The oppressed struggle in language to recover ourselves, to reconcile, to reunite, to renew. Our words are not without meaning, they are an action, a resistance. Language is also a place of struggle." Your language in this passage is suggestive of writing experiments carried on by various French feminists. Do you feel any affinity with French feminists such as Luce Irigaray despite the obvious cultural differences?

A. I feel both affinity and sometimes jealousy because sometimes a lot of regular scholars will read my language as a place of struggle and make fun of it, as I think my ex-colleague at Yale, Sara Suleri, did; yet, they will privilege that writing when it's done by French theorists: writing that plays with language, writing that isn't complete sentences, writing that seems to be convoluted but disjointed thoughts. I find that interesting because I do feel those affinities, but I sometimes feel, "Wouldn't it be nice if I could write a little book like this?" I also feel that I learn a great deal from French feminist thought. I don't evoke it much because of the way it has been privileged to be dismissive of a lot of what goes on in that form of feminist theory-making in this society that wants to be more engaged in theory and practice. I tend not to privilege it in my writing, though I do certainly read and study it.

Q. In *Ain't I a Woman* you say that "Malcolm X was the black Muslim leader that many people saw as an exemplary figure of black manhood, but it is impossible to read his autobiography without becoming aware of the hatred and contempt he felt toward women for much of his life." In light of the recently renewed interest in Malcolm X, are you concerned that this aspect of his identity will be glossed over?

A. Actually, I think just the opposite. I'm concerned that it will be affirmed that Malcolm was right when he told us that black men were experiencing these things because of black women, black women who were in cahoots with white men. I'm concerned that people will focus on *that* dimension of Malcolm's work and life and not the dimensions where he was beginning to rethink gender. Even though we have enough statements and documents to let us know that he *was* rethinking gender, he didn't say enough of those things publicly with the force and the quantity with which he said misogynist things, and so people are much more likely to cling to that version. It's up to feminist scholars to address this issue. I was just interviewed on Pacifica, and I said that I felt that it was the task of feminist thinkers not to allow Malcolm scholarship to be completely done by non-feminist male scholars, that we must take a role in calling attention to the ways he changed his thinking about gender by publicizing those quotes and hard facts. In a piece I wrote about going to the big Malcolm X conference a few years ago, I talked about my own fear of going to that conference, but I felt that I needed to get up and say that if we really take seriously the notion of "by any means necessary," then we have to take seriously the notion that if giving up sexism is essential for the freedom and the liberation of black people, that's one of those necessary means. (I was afraid to go to the conference because I was afraid that I wouldn't be well received by the audience.) Feminist thinkers have to engage this image, this icon and his teachings, if we want to ensure that people recognize the evolutions he was making as a thinker. I deeply feel that he would have been the first major black male leader to wholeheartedly support gender equality and to condemn sexism.

Q. Over the years, your work has generated substantial criticism as well as praise. Are there any criticisms or misunderstandings of your work that you'd like to address?

A. I would like to address why I don't tend to write responses. One of the most recent trashings of my work was by Sara Suleri in an issue of *Critical Inquiry*. Lots of people said that one thing that disturbed them as readers was that she made a scathing critique based on my first two books and pulled out a lot of quotes, misquoting some of them. These people kept asking, "Why don't you write a response?" I didn't write a response because I felt that often women of color are set against one another by people in journals who think they'll have a great journal issue if, for example, they publish a trashing of bell hooks and she responds. I usually tend to withdraw and think about writing something later, reformulating or questioning rather than responding directly. This is also a dimension of Buddhist practice, where rather than feeling that I have to engage in a battle with critics, I tend to think that I have to take on those ideas. For example, in the piece I'm writing on censorship, I talk about things people have said about me. I don't keep confidences because often in my anecdotal sharings, I refer to things that come up in spaces that in the academy are seen as sacred or private. I talk about what I perceive my commitment to ideas to be, that they're not about allegiance to specific people, and that they do have to do with a sense about truth and what it means to push yourself to say something even if you think it will alienate an individual. I try not to feel alienated from individuals because of their critical trashings or constructive critiques of me because I think that's another dilemma of intellectuality in the academy than the personalizing of critiques so that you feel, "That person has shot me down; let me shoot him or her down." Instead, I try to flesh out the ideas and to think how I could write something that might address the issues. For example, consider the homophobic remarks made about me and my work in *Black Collegian*. I thought about what my response should be and decided to incorporate that whole discussion into the article on censorship because I felt that part of the aim of that review was to say to black people at black colleges that they should not read the works of bell hooks. So, I'm not trying to take that person on directly because I feel it's not the person; it's the ideas that he was cultivating, and I'd like to take those ideas on.

Another example was when I referred at the MMLA to "some strands of white lesbian feminism." People immediately stood up in droves and wanted to know who I was talking about. I said, "That's the whole point," and we had that whole discussion of personalizing. It isn't a matter of *who* I was talking about. The real issue was why we as marginal groups allow ourselves to be played off against one another, and I thought it was endemic to how we want to personalize everything. The people immediately wanted to know who I was talking about rather than wanting to deal with the idea I was referring to, which is why we allow this to happen, what mechanisms of power go on that allow one marginal group to receive favors from the dominant group by trashing other marginal groups, and what we have to do to avoid that. In working closely as colleagues with Third World women, many of whom come from different class backgrounds than myself, I find that we often have to have meetings about the ways our white colleagues try to pit us against one another. It seems to me that kind of effort to address ideas and standpoints and alliance is much more productive than focusing on personal responses. So I tend to shy away from them.

Note

[1] I would like to thank my colleague, Elizabeth A. Hirsh, for extensive assistance in preparing for and conducting this interview.

bell hooks on Literacy and Teaching: A Response

JOYCE IRENE MIDDLETON

Reading bell hooks' interview with *JAC* was empowering for me because I am currently exploring and analyzing the ways in which African American feminist perspectives on literacy transform the traditional, lingering conceptions of Western, academic literacy. Hooks' thoughts about audience, about the uses of narrative as a teaching and intellectual tool, her explicit valuing of dialogue (the question-and-answer format), her explorations in teaching, and her advice for contemporary pedagogy (especially a multicultural pedagogy) are strikingly similar to views expressed by African American women writers such as Zora Neale Hurston, Barbara Christian, Elsa Barkley Brown, Toni Morrison, Toni Cade Bambara, Paule Marshall, Audre Lorde, and Alice Walker.

Audience, Teaching, and Authority

Hooks' frequent references to audience, both explicit and implicit, illustrate a major theme in her interview. When she admits that the audience made her a writer—"Absolutely"—she stresses the importance of concrete feedback in her development as a black woman writer. When she talks about the implied mutuality between reader and writer, her need as an isolated writer to have a clear sense of audience, she goes straight to the gut of the experience of most novice or inexperienced writers: knowing that we have something to say is essential to clear writing, but knowing that there are interested readers is a crucial element in developing a voice. This aspect about writing is really important, hooks tells us, "for marginalized people who haven't had voice but who are trying to come to grips with a voice." Hooks' focus on the importance of audience strengthens my interest in the subject of audience as a priority in my teaching. How do I as a teacher of writing and literature create substantial time in my class assignments for real feedback from real audiences for my students?

Despite this strong focus on concreteness, hooks knows—from experience—that "thinking too much about audience can be dangerous." Obviously, one of the gauges here is to determine how much the sense of audience liberates/validates or silences/censors the writer's voice. Another gauge seems to be linked to the writer's own agenda. Hooks aims to create a critical readership. She wants to create some "magic" (I like her word choice) with her readers. In addition, she wants cohesion between ideas and "lived reality." Her interest reminds me of what other African American women writers express in their work. But to specifically address the rhetoric and composition community, hooks' views support a new dimension to our growing sense of schooling and its relationship to "lived reality." The Western tradition of schooling and literacy, with its implicit schemes of hierarchical and either/or thinking, often serves to separate and alienate marginalized students from the roots of their "lived reality." Related to this observation about marginalization is hooks' criticism of white lesbian feminists and feminist agendas. As a woman of color, she observes that these feminist communities continue to be seduced by hierarchical thinking, privileging, and power relations that are implicit in Western patriarchal conceptions of schooling and literacy. Her criticisms are consistent with her interest in bridging theory and practice and in enlarging a critical readership of feminism that must include the growing numbers of illiterate women who are often poor and women of color.

Hooks' conception of audience is not only an abstract, rationalized, or theoretical construction; it is also experienced and felt. Perhaps, more importantly, her concrete sense of audience and feedback is empowering, not only for herself but also for her readers.

Thus, when hooks compares her personal strategies for lecturing with her strategies for teaching, her thoughts, feelings, and experiences about audience contribute to her articulate sense of teacher-student relationships in general and multicultural pedagogies in particular. Teaching, like her lecturing, must be situational; it must not be formulaic. It should also exploit the "question-and-answer" period to incorporate differing agendas or an additional range of inquiry in the classroom. Encouraging such teaching practices, hooks, like other African American feminists, poses a challenging call for change in our conception of literacy and its pedagogy.

In her struggle to create change in her teaching strategies, hooks' references to chaos—a key term, I think—and eros are two largely unexplored subjects for thinking about transitions from a Western, traditional pedagogy to a multicultural pedagogy (although hooks' interest in eros certainly reminds me of Audre Lorde's well-known essay, "Uses of the Erotic, the Erotic as Power"). Transforming our classrooms, venturing into new pedagogical territory, involves strong feelings of vulnerability, a willingness to take risks, and a confrontation with and unlearning of traditional formulaic thinking: "Am I covering the material?" For this kind of search, the chaos seems inevitable. Among her many explorations that she shares, hooks articulates two distinctions that speak directly to my own experiences with students. Defining the personal in relation to teaching is useful to me, and distinguishing it from the act of personalizing is helpful to my thinking about teacher-student relationships. We see immediately that hooks' sense of the personal is audience-based (and activist); to personalize is not.

The second distinction that hooks makes between power and authority is especially timely for me. I've been reading Elsa Barkley Brown's "African-American Women's Quilting" with my students. Brown questions the use of white Western pedagogical strategies—those that are individualistic, competitive, linear, symmetrical, and that equate fairness with uniformity or sameness—to teach African American women's history, a history that is "polyrhythmic, nonsymmetrical, nonlinear, and noncompetitive regarding the individual and the community" (15). Brown describes her own role in the classroom. She decenters, and she "pivots the center." But readers may remain unclear about how Brown views her own authority in the classroom. Admittedly, she relinquishes most of it. Importantly, however, she describes the class as a scene of "chaos" in her efforts to construct a multicultural learning environment: "The structure I create is, by Western norms, a disorganized, chaotic, sporadic, and very unworkable class." But the class evolves so that chaos leads to learning and self-empowerment. Brown continues, "What in fact we get by the end of the semester is a serious improvisation . . . in which people are empowered by their own authority and their right to expect things from others" (16-17). Hooks admits that her own venturing about issues of authority began with a total rejection of it and then led her to redefine her sense of power relations in the classroom. The central issue for hooks, Brown, and myself is shifting the classroom from an either/or, hierarchical paradigm to a "both/and," learning community paradigm, where, as hooks tells us, "no one acquires the kind of power to use the classroom as a space of domination." Although her sharing about experiences with chaos is helpful to me, I would have liked to have heard more from hooks in this interview about how the concept of eros enables her to construct these learning environments.

Multicultural Pedagogy and Language Use
As an African American woman and faculty member who teaches at a predominately white institution, I share similar experiences with hooks. I agree strongly with her views about the transition to a multicultural pedagogy. But I also note that she speaks from a position of privilege. For example, I read with envy that she handpicked the fourteen members of her seminar on Toni Morrison. Yet, it is clear that a commitment to learning environments that empower all members to work through "chaos, hostility, and tension" must include smaller classes in the curriculum. These are the environments out of which significant rereadings of literate culture create powerful implications for future studies and future teacher-student relations. I am reminded, for example, of Toni Morrison, who dedicates her provocative rereadings of American literature in *Playing in the Dark: Whiteness and the Literary Imagination* to her students at Princeton who were

members in an "academic environment, open and demanding."

In addition to pedagogical issues, hooks addresses two significant questions about language. First, she talks about "language as a place of struggle" and "writing that plays with language." Her expression about this issue in *Yearning* is beautiful and poetic. Yet, in this interview she connects her interests to the activity of French feminists. I wanted to hear her link this issue to the uses of the African American oral tradition in writing by black authors, a tradition that is well-known for its complexity of codes and playful representations in oral and written language. I was reminded of classic texts such as Zora Hurston's "Characteristics of Negro Expression," or Paule Marshall's "From the Poets in the Kitchen," or Toni Morrison's "Unspeakable Things Unspoken."

Hooks is admittedly brief in her response to the second question about language—the one about "white supremacist manifestations in language." Perhaps some familiar issues come to mind immediately, such as the connotations of *black* as negative, bad, or evil, and the connotations of *white* as positive or good. Malcolm X's *Autobiography* is a good reference for this issue. Also, in a discussion on black power, Martin Luther King, Jr. wrote that in "Roget's Thesaurus there are some 120 synonyms for 'blackness' and at least 60 of them are offensive—such words as 'blot,' 'soot,' 'grime,' 'devil' and 'foul'" (41). In contrast, King observed, "There are some 134 synonyms for 'whiteness' and all are favorable, expressed in such words as 'purity,' 'cleanliness,' 'chastity' and 'innocence.' A white lie is better than a black lie" (41). He concluded his brief discussion of semantics with a reference to Ossie Davis, who "suggested that maybe the English language should be 'reconstructed so that teachers will not be forced to teach the Negro child 60 ways to despise himself and thereby perpetuate his false sense of inferiority and the white child 134 ways to adore himself and thereby perpetuate his false sense of superiority'" (41).

The issue of white supremacist manifestations in language use appears in many of Toni Morrison's recent publications, such as in her "Introduction: Friday on the Potomac" in *Race-ing Justice, En-gendering Power*. In addition, during a videotaped interview with John Wideman, author of *Philadelphia Fire*, Morrison addresses questions about writing in a racialized society. She notes that critics compare Wideman to Faulkner. One critic in particular hails Wideman as *"the black Faulkner*, the soft cover Shakespeare" (emphasis added). Responding to this description, Morrison suggests to Wideman that "you can't ever have Faulkner, assuming one was living in the same time (both of you writing at the same time) [referred to as], you know, *the white Wideman*. It doesn't quite work that way" (emphasis added). Working with a recent issue that bell hooks addresses in *Black Looks*, I am currently writing an article, "Loving Blackness as Political Resistance: Oral Tradition and Literacy in Hurston, Morrison, and Wideman," in which I critique the powerful gestures these three writers make in order to create blackness and the black voice in written language. These writers demonstrate black language not as inferior compared to standard or intellectual English, especially as historically documented. In these historical texts, for example, we find Edgar Allen Poe's spelling of *nose* for the word *knows* in order to distinguish the voice of a black slave, or the court record of the Salem witch trials in the 1600s that records the voice of a black woman differently in order to mark her racial identity as inferior or infantile. Instead, these writers work to represent black language as irrevocably beautiful and, as Morrison describes it during the interview with Wideman, a sign of modernity. Despite the emotive force of hooks' phrase, "loving blackness" does not mean that only black people do it (which reminds me of a former white male composition student in one of my classes who thought that Martin Luther King, Jr.'s "I Have a Dream" speech was addressed to a black audience). Hooks' introductory poem in *Black Looks* is especially eloquent about her audience and this issue.

This interview with bell hooks enables the rhetoric and composition community to broaden our range of listening so that we may explore the intersections between the varied, but familiar, arguments about literacy and the less familiar arguments that black women writers have voiced. As teachers and students become polyvocal and polyphonic, these explorations will enhance our understanding of literate processes, language use, and human relationships.

University of Rochester
Rochester, New York

Works Cited

Brown, Elsa Barkley. "African-American Women's Quilting: A Framework for Conceptualizing and Teaching African-American Women's History." *Black Women in America: Social Science Perspectives.* Ed. Micheline R. Malson, et al. Chicago: U of Chicago P, 1988. 9-18.

hooks, bell. "Loving Blackness as Political Resistance." *Black Looks: Race and Representation.* Boston: South End, 1992. 9-20.

Hurston, Zora Neale. "Characteristics of Negro Expression." *The Sanctified Church.* Berkeley: Turtle, 1981. 49-68.

Lorde, Audre. "Uses of the Erotic, the Erotic as Power." *Sister Outsider: Essays and Speeches.* Trumansburg, NY: Crossing, 1984.

Marshall, Paule. "From the Poets in the Kitchen." *Merle, a novella, and Other Stories.* New York: Feminist P, 1983.

Morrison, Toni. "Introduction: Friday on the Potomac." *Race-ing Justice, En-Gendering Power: Essays on Anita Hill, Clarence Thomas, and the Construction of Social Reality.* Ed. Toni Morrison. New York: Pantheon, 1992. vii-xxx.

——. *Playing in the Dark: Whiteness and the Literary Imagination.* Cambridge: Harvard UP, 1992.

——. "Unspeakable Things Unspoken: The Afro-American Presence in American Literature." *Michigan Quarterly Review* 28 (Winter 1989): 1-34.

Wideman, John. "The Black Writer and the Magic of the Word." *New York Times Book Review.* 24 Jan. 1988: 28-29.

Literacy and Activism:
A Response to bell hooks

Tom Fox

Most of the issues brought up in bell hooks' interview with Gary Olson should resonate with readers of *JAC*. Issues of audience and power, the pedagogical challenges of multiculturalism, and the difficulties of developing constructive self-critiques are among the topics she raises that are routinely discussed in our journals and conferences. For these reasons, it's not hard to understand why composition studies was one of the first disciplines to respond to hooks' work.

Hooks' scholarship has been important to me and my teaching for several reasons. Like Mike Rose in composition studies, she has sought an audience outside the academy and has conceived of her academic role broadly. She has not been confined by narrow disciplinary boundaries that not only limit audience but limit the voice that academics can have in public matters. For my students, this broadly defined sense of academic writing models one kind of writing that I hope they will strive for: critical, sensitive to audiences and their responses, historically minded and informed, and committed to public intervention. In the spirit of the self-contained short pieces that hooks refers to in the interview, I'd like to concentrate on five discussions that, for me, embody the issues that seem most important to my classrooms and those of my colleagues.

Writing, Audience, and Race
In the interview, hooks comments, "I think I now see myself more as a writer because it has become so evident that I have an audience, because I now get so much feedback. . . . [F]or me writing as a writer implied mutuality." She goes on to say that "thinking about audience can be crucial for marginalized people who haven't had [a] voice but who are trying to come to grips with a voice." If anyone needed more evidence of the importance of dialogue in the teaching of writing, hooks' insightful comments about the relationship between audience and the development of her self-concept as a writer provide it. More interesting, though, is how the sense of audience is complicated by divisions and hierarchies based on gender and race. Hooks' comment about the specific rhetorical situations of marginalized people

presents one of the central pedagogical challenges of teaching composition. The issue of audience, as hooks' anecdote about Gates shows, is an issue of power. Audience in a composition classroom, so long as there are grades and the power that accompanies them, generally means the teacher. Hooks' story about the generative effect of identifying other black women as her audience points to the necessity of creating classroom contexts where marginalized students can feel this power. This is a difficult task in my classroom because positional authority of the teacher is aligned with the socially dominant categories of white and male. Women students of color must feel at best challenged and at worst silenced by this rhetorical situation. They must feel an even stronger version of censorship than hooks felt responding to Gates.

Composition studies has been at work on this issue for many years, seeking pedagogical and institutional practices that reduce the dominating authority of the teacher. For example, in my own classes I try several measures. First, I invite women writers of color into the classroom to talk about writing and authority and to listen to students' concerns about writing. Also, I use collaborative groups and allow, and even suggest, homogeneous grouping. Students of color may feel a sense of authority that emerges from these potential social and political alliances. In addition, I use texts by women of color, not just to be "representative," but also as a force that widens the rhetorical possibilities for students and lessens their sense of isolation. Furthermore, I introduce the history of writing by women of color. Hooks, in the concluding essay in *Breaking Bread,* cites the tradition of black women intellectuals, who, like women students of color in most universities today, had to write against another, more visible tradition in order to write at all. A multicultural tradition of intellectuals and literacy has to be present and obvious in a composition classroom. Finally, I imagine and act on long-term solutions to the virtual lock-out of African Americans from higher education. Affirmative action in hiring is not enough given the scarcity of African Americans in higher education. We need curricular change that will demonstrate the educational system's commitment to the success of students of color. From grade school to graduate school, we need to demonstrate—in all parts of the curriculum—support for African American history, literacy, culture. The end result of these curricular changes must be the entrance of students of color into our schools and universities as teachers, professors, and scholars, ultimately resulting in a significant change in the composition of university faculty. We must disrupt the routine association of "professor" with white and male. Affirmative action is a pedagogical issue.

Also interesting are hooks' views on composition. She says, "Those professors who have been most willing to engage cultural criticism and other ways of de-centering the West in writing are finding that their students are more deeply engaged in composition. One of the first areas of my work that I got positive feedback on was from teachers of composition. . . ." She goes on to comment that "If we really examine the kind of composition work that has done that, I think we would see a new and renewing dimension both to composition and to the art of writing. That's why we're in danger right now with the backlash against those new interventions in curriculum and modes of teaching." This was part of hooks' answer to Olson's question, "Do you see any advantage in composition's marginalized status?" The answer, I take it, is yes and no. Yes, there's an advantage; composition's view of institutions is from the margin and that perspective encourages criticism. This may explain both composition's ability to read and use texts like hooks' and the field's interest in developing, discussing, and researching democratic pedagogies. Our institutional context is inseparable from what hooks calls the production of "new interventions in curriculum and modes of teaching."

The "no" part of the answer is that "we're in danger right now." At my campus, and at many more campuses across the country, budget cuts—year after depressing year—threaten writing programs. The politically neutral term for these cuts, "across the board," masks the real political effect. At my campus, most of our writing courses are taught by part-time instructors. These teachers are politically progressive and committed to the success of students of color. If laid off, which remains a very real threat, they will be replaced by less progressive full-time instructors, most of whom have little training or interest in the teaching of writing. Politically progressive institutional allies of composition programs like the writing center (which serves a large number of students of color) and the writing across the disciplines program (which has conducted workshops on collaborative learning, student diversity, and the politics of education) all are threatened. Budget cuts, handled this way, are politically conservative. There is no advantage to the margin when the center has the power to cut you off the map.

Hooks was probably referring to an ideological backlash which has reared its ugly head on campuses across the country. Popular books like *The Closing of the American Mind*, *Illiberal Education*, and others have emboldened and wrongly legitimated conservative and racist views, including the bizarre (and frighteningly common) view that affirmative action is racist! Despite the quirkiness of the ideological backlash, its effects are anything but eccentric. Newer faculty, hired under more serious affirmative action guidelines, are threatened, silenced, hurt, and discouraged by this backlash. These faculty—the ones "willing to engage cultural criticism," the ones whose students are most "deeply engaged"—are frequently the best teachers of women and students of color.

Multiculturalism and Revolution
Hooks says, "The movement toward a multicultural pedagogy was really, to me, tantamount to a revolution; and, like revolutions on all levels in culture, there are times of chaos. Many of us thought we'd make this transition without chaos, and I think partially most of us develop pedagogical practices

that don't in any way include strategies for dealing with confusion and chaos." This answer, along with the next one, were the two places where I felt a sense of distance between hooks' perspective and mine. For most of the interview, I felt that we were looking at a similar world and thinking similarly about institutional politics, multicultural teaching, writing, and activism; but here I felt there must be a gap somewhere in our experiences. What revolution? I felt like Mark Twain: "Reports of the death of monocultural pedagogy have been vastly exaggerated." Hooks, I know, is probably better aware of the opposition to multiculturalism than I am. But I do think there's a danger in thinking of multiculturalism as a revolution that has already occurred. The small changes toward more inclusiveness and diversity in our curriculum and pedagogy don't seem anything like a revolution. And even those small changes are in danger of backsliding into monoculturalism. Stanford University changed the requirements in only *one* of its required courses and the apoplectic response from conservatives was astonishing; you would have thought it *was* the Death of Western Civilization As We Know It. Actually, there's been minuscule success in hiring people of color in universities across the country, baby steps toward a more inclusive, more constructive curriculum, pedagogical changes only by a tiny few, and only a slight increase in the representation of students of color in higher education (after a *drop* in the 1980s). Yet, the repressive response to these changes is outrageous, like smashing a fly with a hammer.

Of course, we should not be blind to progress. A colleague of mine also recently taught a seminar on Toni Morrison's work, and she would have not received any flack had she not taught it under the title *"Major* American Authors." What worries me is that the success of the revolution will be measured by the addition of a few texts by women and people of color. These additions may signal a more general revolution, but they *may* be simply a way of accommodating the protests of students of color and a few faculty: add some texts; avoid some conflict (see Graff for a sense of the history of this way of accommodating change). What's needed for a revolution is a far more fundamental change in the level of respect that educational institutions confer on women and people of color, their language, their culture, their history, their knowledge. Morrison and Walker can function too easily as literary exceptions while the texts by *students* of color are still treated as deficient. It is certainly progress to be having conversations like this one in major journals, but the material conditions of programs, classrooms, and curricula have got to change.

The other answer that did not correspond with my own perspective is when hooks' comments, "I was trying to think... through a notion of how we might use the place of passion in the classroom to diffuse hierarchy and to create a sense of community. Students would actually come up to me and whine, 'There's a way that you hug this student or talk to that student, and I want you to look at me the way you look at Johnny'.... I said, 'Why is it that none of you think that if I look at Johnny this way, I must be willing to look at you this way, too. . . . Why can't you think that I have this space of care that can enlarge to include everyone?'" This place in the interview created in me "one of those little moments of uproar, tension, and dissent" that hooks referred to as opportunities in her classroom. Hooks has written a great deal about the authority of the teacher; it is a theme that runs throughout this interview, too. She has been one of a number of people who have seen the issue of the teacher's authority as not simply something that you give away, but as a more complex bundle of legitimate and illegitimate power. The source of my discomfort in this particular discussion is both in the students' focus on physical demonstrations of affection and hooks' own sense that what's wrong with the picture is that the students are imagining a scarcity of affection that they have to compete for. Hooks disapproves of the competition, while I'm uncomfortable with the focus on "passion" defined this way. My objection is that this kind of passion is entirely teacher-centered and functions through institutional position, much like grading. It is entirely hers, even if, as she wishes, they would understand that she has enough for all. It isn't the kind of passion that students can take up independently of hooks; it's located in a relationship with her physical presence.

I think that part of the source of my discomfort is that, for me, the history of passion in the classroom has been a history of exploitation. I can't think of it apart from the violence it has caused in the lives of many women, especially. On my campus, there is currently a group of professors who wish to deny the existence of widespread sexual harassment by professors, claiming that it's based on (as one professor put it) "spectral" evidence. So my discomfort about construing passion in this way is located both in my local, institutional politics and in my position as a white male.

Hooks' institutional position and her social location make her perspective on this issue much different from mine and the issue of passion far less charged with dominance. Yet, I still couldn't construct a way of defusing hierarchy and creating a sense of community from this definition of passion without hooks' developing this point further (as she most likely does in her article) and showing how passion defined this way creates a classroom where students become more critical and more responsible.

The Politics of Literacy
Hooks' sense of critical vision does not protect her own field, nor should rhetoric and composition be spared from self-critique. She writes, "The class standpoint of much feminist theory leads to a depriviliging of and a disrespect for the politics of reading and writing, and this has become all the more rampant with the privileging of metalinguistic theory over other forms of theory, increasing the sense that it's a waste of time to think about reading and writing." Almost all English departments and many composition

programs within them also deprivilege the everyday study of reading and writing as it occurs in settings outside the academy. One of the consequences of composition's history as a service course is that the study of writing in social and cultural contexts has not been a major part of our discipline's work. Only recently have studies of literacy outside the academy been taken up by composition scholars, thanks mainly to progressives like Patricia Bizzell, Linda Brodkey, Jacqueline Jones Royster, Beverly Moss, J. Elspeth Stuckey, Judith Rodby, John Trimbur, and others. So while the teaching of college writing has a long history of study, the study of literacy practices outside of the university has not been at the center of composition studies. Because of the separation of "intellectual" from "public," which hooks seeks to unify in this interview and in her publications, college teachers of writing do an especially bad job of educating students whose literacy practices vary from dominant practices. For instance, much of the history of literacy practices by African Americans has taken place outside the academy. One of the reasons for this is that institutional literacy has tended to be used as a weapon against African Americans. The literacy requirements for voting, as hooks points out, continue a practice that has antecedents in Southern efforts to hold on to Jim Crow culture in the 1940s and 50s, including what Manning Marable calls "Kafkaesque" literacy requirements for voting. He cites one white registrar who asked black potential voters the question, "How many bubbles are in a bar of soap?" (26). While we may sneer at such tactics, we ought to look twice at our own placement and proficiency tests, whose questions function essentially in the same way. How different is it to ask a potential university student to write in thirty minutes an answer to an abstract question to an unknown audience? The literacy practices in institutions are not neutral to most marginalized students. They are oppositional and thus pose an additional challenge to radical educators who must not only help students imagine literacy as constructive intervention, but must undo, unteach, the expectation that all literacy in institutions works against their interests.

Our ignorance of everyday literacy practices, because of the elitist history of English department scholarship, also blinds us to the history of literacy practices that have worked to resist domination. Anne Gere's study of women's writing groups in the nineteenth century is one such history; another is Janet Duitsman Cornelius' fascinating look at African American literacy practices in the South before the Civil War. While students, if they're lucky, may have heard about how slave owners used every means available to prevent slaves from reading and writing, and they may have also read Douglass' autobiography, I doubt that they know of the widespread resistance to this oppression. Literacy instruction, especially writing, was common and connected to central values of freedom and education. African Americans have both a long and a powerful history of writing for social action. When "literacy" is separated both from "literature" and from "composition," these progressive examples of uses of literacy outside the academy are lost to us and our students. Bell hooks' insistence on the connection between activism and literacy reconnects the academy with the political world it inhabits and reconnects us with the political work that we have a responsibility to take up.

California State University
Chico, California

Works Cited

Cornelius, Janet Duitsman. *When I Can Read My Title Clear*. Columbia: U of South Carolina P, 1991.

Gere, Anne Ruggles. *Writing Groups*. Carbondale: Southern Illinois UP, 1987.

Graff, Gerald. *Professing Literature: An Institutional History*. Chicago: U of Chicago P, 1987.

hooks, bell, and Cornel West. *Breaking Bread: Insurgent Black Intellectual Life*. Boston: South, 1991.

Marable, Manning. *Race, Reform, and Rebellion*. Jackson: UP of Mississippi, 1991.

J. Hillis

Miller

Rhetoric, Cultural Studies, and the Future of Critical Theory: A Conversation with J. Hillis Miller

Gary A. Olson

Who better to discuss the future of literary studies and of the English department itself than J. Hillis Miller, past president of the Modern Language Association, former department chair at Yale and Johns Hopkins, and distinguished literary critic for four decades? Generally, Miller seems pleased with the radical changes the English department is undergoing and is "optimistic" about the directions in which it is evolving. He applauds the increased attention to multiculturalism, cultural studies, critical theory, and rhetoric and composition; such disciplinary forces have had a positive effect on the field. He predicts the English department will continue to undergo substantial change because "within about five years forty percent of the senior faculty will retire and an entirely new set of people will be in charge, with all the power and responsibility to make changes." Because this wave of new faculty will have been trained with a sensitivity to and understanding of "these new interests," even the powerful conservative right will be unable to halt the inexorable tide of change. The challenge for this new generation, says Miller in the interview that follows, will be "to figure out how to deal with the possibilities of change in a responsible way."

Miller identifies cultural studies as the future of English studies: "That's obviously where we're going." He perceives the current preoccupation with cultural studies as an attempt among young faculty "to make what they do have some importance in our society," and he finds this concern "quite natural" in that those now ascending to power in English departments were the first to be "brought up on the mass media." Miller has "certain anxieties" about these developments, however, saying that such interdisciplinarity necessitates "responsible" academic preparation, be it the mastery of appropriate languages or other cross-disciplinary skills, and arguing that we need to establish the kinds of procedures that will "allow people doing cultural studies to do what they want to do in a responsible way."

Miller has much to say about the influence of various critical movements on English studies. Acknowledging the great debt English studies has to feminist theory, Miller points to the fact that most doctoral exams in English now "have *some* feminist component," and he suggests that it's difficult today to write a critical work that *does not* account for gender issues, "So, I think everybody's work has been transformed." Similarly, deconstructionist theory has been "assimilated" by the academy, and the danger he once saw of "dyed-in-the-wool narrow deconstructionists" turning poststructuralist theory into "dogma" or "a rigid set of prescriptions" has "to a considerable degree been by-passed." And he argues that phenomenology has had such a major influence on poststructuralist criticism that anyone "seriously interested" in understanding deconstruction should "make a serious study" of both Heidegger and Husserl. Also, he takes issue with those who attempt to draw a strong relationship between the sophists and the deconstructionists. While "there's no doubt that certain aspects of sophistic thinking do anticipate deconstruction a bit," Miller is "more willing to say that *Plato* is the founder of deconstruction." Defending this unusual position, Miller says that "the easy reference to Plato as though he were the foundation of Western values" "annoys" him because Plato himself read deconstructively. In addition, Miller argues that the new cultural criticism is a kind of "continuation" of deconstruction in the sense that both share a political and social dimension, seeing a "need to intervene in the institution, the university, and make changes in it" and understanding that you make these changes "by the active work of reading or teaching something." This realization is helping Miller relinquish his earlier antagonism toward new historicism, and he says that "new historicism really owes a tremendous amount to linguistically based procedures like deconstruction, but that we can now learn a lot" from the new historicists.

It was this very need to come to terms with those critical approaches oriented toward culture and society that impelled Miller into his well-known work on the ethics of reading: "For me, the political goes by way of the ethical, and it's easier for me to understand the teaching or writing situation along an ethical model, a model that is of a one-to-one reciprocity of responsibility, than it is to think of it in terms of these larger, more abstract political questions." Miller goes on to imply that we in rhetoric and composition should explore an "ethics of writing."

Hillis Miller has always been interested in rhetoric and composition, even though in the past he hasn't always seemed to understand fully what we in the field do, and this interview reconfirms this commitment. He perceives a "natural alliance" between specialists in critical theory and composition theory. He notes the "real excitement about the methodological and theoretical aspects of the discipline" of composition and maintains, as he has repeatedly in the past, that composition should remain in the English department, not only because such an arrangement is best for the English department but because it is best politically and financially for composition itself. Besides, he argues, the hostility toward composition is fading as he and others join the many voices in support of the discipline.

Miller addresses other aspects of composition theory and pedagogy. He defends writing across the curriculum, and he argues forcefully for combining composition and ESL instruction and for integrating reading and writing pedagogy. Miller is not so receptive to radical pedagogy, however. While he understands that liberatory learning is "an important new direction in teaching," he nonetheless feels that it carries with it a danger: "that it will free the teacher from one of the teacher's major responsibilities: the obligation to display a way to do something."

Regardless of his support for *writing* and for the discipline of rhetoric and composition, J. Hillis Miller is and always has been the supreme champion of *reading*. He has devoted his life's work to careful, close, methodical reading of texts. His numerous essays and books are an impressive collection of detailed explications of major canonical texts. Even his primarily theoretical works are crafted illustrations of theory in praxis: "That's the objection I have to teaching theory as simply a set of postulates or ideas. . . . Theory is of no use unless it's used for something." Perhaps it is in this very integration of theory and praxis that our kinship with Miller lies, for like Miller we in rhetoric and composition have often sought such a balance. In effect, we have supported *his* project just as he has always been a major supporter of *ours*.

Q. You've written about a dozen books and over one-hundred articles on a multitude of literary figures and theoretical concerns. Do you consider yourself a writer?

A. I never thought of myself as a writer, though, like a lot of teachers of literature, I had the idea when I was a teenager that I was going to write poetry or novels or something but soon found I had no aptitude for that at all. My writing is an adjunct to teaching. Though it's something I do seriously, I think *writer* is too big a word for what I do.

Q. Would you describe your writing process?

A. The computer transformed my life. There was a period a long time ago when I wrote on a typewriter and then revised with pen, writing things up and down the margins and on the backs of the pages. Then there was a long period, essentially while I was at Yale, when I wrote longhand in notebooks. That allowed me to revise on the page and on the back of the page. (If you were to see those notebooks, you'd find them totally illegible.) Then I would read the manuscript onto a tape; it would be typed by a secretary; then I would revise it; and it would have to be typed again. With a computer, I shortcut all those procedures. I write a draft on the computer (I use a Macintosh) and revise it myself on the computer very extensively, both as I go along and later on when I come back to it. These revisions are "extensive" in that they're changes in individual sentences: cutting long sentences into two or three short sentences, rearranging phrases, moving them around, and so on. The computer has made my revision process longer and more complicated than it was because I'm not inhibited by the necessity of having it typed over again. Of course, all those stages of revision are completely lost; there's no trace of the earlier stages.

Q. In *Theory Now and Then* you speak of "the myth of the 'Yale School.'" In what way is it a myth?

A. Like all abstractions, it doesn't correspond all that well to reality, and like most abstractions of that sort, like "existentialism" or "deconstruction," it was a product of people talking about it who needed a name for this entity. It's *not* a myth in the sense that there was a group of people at Yale who had a certain role in representing the theoretical side of the faculties there and who were friends and collaborators. By saying it's a "myth" I mean that the differences among those five people are as important as the similarities, and that's easy to see. That's all I mean. To try to say that the Yale School believes such and such is much more difficult or absurd or preposterous than even to say the New Critics all believed such and such; it's much more difficult to find uniformity.

Q. Clifford Geertz mentioned in *JAC* that Kenneth Burke was a great influence on him intellectually, and you often mention Burke, saying that he was one of the "distinguished native grandsires or at least great-uncles" of deconstruction. Was Burke an important influence on you personally? And what is your assessment of Burke's contribution?

A. Yes, Burke was an important influence on me early. When I was in graduate school—I went to Harvard, where theoretical writings were considered to be a waste of time or worse—I somehow found myself interested in theory. I read Burke, William Empson, I.A. Richards, G. Wilson Knight—and all on my own; nobody was teaching those people. I can no longer quite remember how I heard about them. Burke gave one lecture at Harvard, but I'm sure I knew about him before that. I must somehow have been steered in the direction of Burke. My dissertation, which was never published, is very Burkean; it was deeply influenced by Burke. The idea of dramatic action, the notion that a work of literature is a strategy to deal with a situation so that it makes a kind of movement and attempts to move the writer or reader from one place to another, the notion that there's a lot going on under the surface of the language that you can trace in one way or another through implications of the language that are figurative but not just figurative (that is, a tracing that goes beyond simply looking at metaphors or whatever)—all of that I learned first from Burke. I still immensely admire him, and I think he is a major theorist and critic. As I've often said, "If you have Kenneth Burke and can read him wisely, you don't need the French." For me, Burke is still the wisest and subtlest and most intelligent Freudian critic and Marxist critic of his time, certainly among the Americans. At a time when neither Freud nor Marx was being read very intelligently by American academics who claimed to be Marxists or Freudians, Burke was able to read and make use of them in ways that were very productive. And Burke's general conviction that literature ought to matter to individual human life or to society is something I believed in then and still believe in now. So Mr. Burke is one of my heroes. I was very pleased not too many years ago (I guess he was eighty-nine at that point) to be invited to a celebration of Burke at Seton Hall University in New Jersey, and I got to meet him again, though I know him a little bit also in that we've corresponded. For me he's very important, but it's no secret that he's very important generally in many different fields. It didn't surprise me to hear that Clifford Geertz was deeply influenced by Burke because Burke's had a big influence in the social sciences.

Let me add that Burke is very difficult to appropriate or to teach. I've never really tried to teach him. For example, say someone asks, "You say Kenneth Burke is wonderful. What should I read by Burke?" It's very hard to answer that question, to say, "Here is a representative essay." That makes him different from, let's say, Derrida. You can say, "Here are representative examples of Derrida, and you can really learn something about Derrida's assumptions and procedures by reading these three or four or five essays." Burke is not so simple. You have to say, "Well, you've got to read four or five books by Burke before you begin to get the hang of it." That's curious. I'm not quite sure why that is. There are no essays by Burke that you would call landmark essays on particular authors. There are very interesting essays on Keats, let's say, or one that I immensely admire on Hawthorne's *Ethan Brand*, but you wouldn't call them masterpieces of literary criticism. They're very provocative, so that you say, "Well, if Burke can do this, I would like to see whether I could do it over here." That's a little different from saying, "What's William Empson about? Read *Seven Types of Ambiguity* or *The Structure of Complex Words* and you'll see." I've never quite been able to figure out why that is with Burke. His essays are all wonderfully inventive, provocative, and suggestive. And they're likely to go off in all directions, so there'd be something in there for the social scientist, something for the psychologist, something for the literary critic.

Q. In "The Function of Rhetorical Study at the Present Time," you discuss the discipline of rhetoric and composition, saying it has accumulated "an impressive body of theoretical, empirical, and statistical work." You write, "People involved at the frontier of this exciting new branch of the broader discipline of English language and literature have the air of persons doing something justifiable and good, while teachers of literature sometimes seem to me to have a furtive and guilty air, as though they were doing something not altogether justifiable in the present context." What role do you see this field playing in the English department of the next decade and beyond?

A. I'm inclined to agree to some degree with Stanley Fish when he says in the

JAC interview that the English department as we knew it is undergoing changes and that he's surprised it's still as much like it used to be as it is. These changes take awhile, but I think they really have begun to occur. They certainly have in my department at Irvine. The examination given to Ph.D. candidates these days is radically different, not only because philosophy and theory overtly get into the examination but also because works by women and so-called minority writers are now a regular part of the curriculum, and people are examined on it for their Ph.D. So it's really a different department, and I think the role of composition in such a department will also be different. A lot of the changes in composition have gone along with those changes and will reinforce them in one way or another. That joke about the furtive air of the teachers of literature was meant to refer to the fact that whatever admiration we have for literature, you would have to say that it plays a smaller role in the intellectual and personal life of most Americans than it used to, even among graduate students, whereas the need to be able to write clearly and effectively for a given purpose is going to remain. There's going to be a need to teach composition well in any conceivable university. So, composition is more secure.

The other thing I meant was that among the people I know in composition there is a real excitement about the methodological and theoretical aspects of the discipline. There's something really going on there that's not unrelated to these changes in the makeup of English departments. So, I think composition in particular is going to be there. And something that will be even more important than ever before as we begin to enroll (at Duke and my university, for example) more and more people for whom English is a second language is ESL instruction. I see ESL as a frontier of composition. I know they're often thought of as separate operations—they certainly are at my university—but they seem to me really part of the same thing. One of the criticisms I would make of my own composition group, at least in the theoretical way it's set up, is that there's ESL over here and composition over there, each run by different people. It seems to me that ESL is a large part of the challenge in teaching English composition at a place like Irvine, where forty percent of the undergraduates are Asian American and very large numbers of them have English as a second language; the two problems don't seem to me separable. It's not that people who have English as a first language cannot be very bad writers—they often are—but that if you have a mixed university population like ours some very large part of the problems are ESL problems. I would see combining composition and ESL as a very interesting and challenging thing to do. Irvine is a wonderful laboratory for studying composition and ESL because there's such a mix of people in the undergraduate population. You hear five or six different languages just in crossing the campus. You hear Japanese, Chinese, Korean, Thai,

Cambodian—all spoken by the students. Some of my colleagues and some of the administrators tend to say, "This problem is going to go away. We don't have to put a lot of money into ESL." It's not going to go away. It's a problem all right, but a very exciting intellectual problem, not an insuperable kind of obstacle to making people able to write.

Q. You argue in many places, including "Stevens' Rock and Criticism as Cure, II," that the future of literary criticism "involves a return to the explicit study of rhetoric." You define *rhetoric* as "the investigation of figures of speech rather than the study of the art of persuasion, though the notion of persuasion is still present." Stanley Fish recently commented in the *JAC* interview you just mentioned that eventually "the English department in which we were all educated would be a thing of the past, a museum piece" and that given recent developments "it might be just as accurate to call the department 'the department of rhetoric,' with a new understanding of the old scope of the subject and province of rhetoric." Do you agree, then, that the future of both literary criticism and the English department itself lies in rhetoric?

A. I wouldn't be prepared to go quite that far because I think departments of English (or, like my department, departments of English and comparative literature) also have other obligations that could only with difficulty be put under the rubric of rhetoric—obligations such as the teaching of literary history. I'm prepared to say that that's *part* of rhetoric, but it's obviously stretching it a little bit. And there's the obligation to teach an understanding of ethnic communities within the larger community, the teaching of women's literature, African American literature, Native American literature. To call this rhetoric might unnecessarily limit it. Nevertheless, for me all of those things—women's literature, African American literature, Native American literature, Hispanic and all ethnic literatures—are best taught by reading, not by generalizations about history or the study of sociology of those peoples (though that has to be done) but, in an English department or a department of English and comparative literature, by reading texts by those people. That's where rhetoric, a rhetorical approach, is necessary. As I've said before, there's a kind of link between "highfalutin" literary theory which appears to have nothing to do with composition in one direction and composition theory in the other. They often come together, and so there's often a natural alliance in departments between the young people who do literary theory, who are Lacanians or Derrideans or whatever, and the people who are doing composition theory; and there *ought* to be a kind of bridge between them, an alliance or coalition. I see *that* as something a good department would want to enhance. It's one of the reasons why I would be very anxious about separating composition from literature departments in universities. I know this is an issue; it's certainly one that we discussed at length recently at Irvine. I've been on a task force committee to discuss the status of the composition program at Irvine, and one of the issues that came up (it almost always does) was the question of whether composition ought to be taken away from the English department and given to some dean, made a cross-school program that was as much the responsibility of the scientists and social scientists as of the humanists. The English department, when they were presented with this possibility, and I was interested in having people consider it, reacted very powerfully and expectedly. They said, "No, no. We can't do this," partly because they do consider teaching composition their responsibility, but also, I think, because they were appalled at the thought of losing all those graduate fellowships. But I think on principled reasons, composition ought to stay in English departments, not to help composition but to help the English departments. It's good for them to have the composition people.

Q. You've made this very point in several forums, including "Composition and Decomposition" and "On Edge." You note that "independent departments or programs in composition are beginning to overshadow the adjacent departments of English literature in size, strength, and funding," and you make an urgent plea that rhetoric and composition not break away from English. Given the utter contempt that many within traditional English department power structures feel for the new discipline, as well as their reluctance to improve the material conditions under which many of us work, why should we take this plea seriously?

A. One answer would be a pragmatic one: to recognize the losses that would probably follow for composition were it separated. It *might* turn out to be even weaker from the point of view of having clout with the administration, getting money, and so on; it might not, but you would have to make a careful calculation about that. It's a little hard to tell. In other words, composition does gain something from having the strong budgetary support of an English department. That's certainly true at Irvine. On the other hand, we've had conversations about just how this budgetary relationship ought to work. If you had a situation in which the English department chair could move money around, taking it from composition to use, let's say, for other kinds of graduate support or even for other things, I'd be uneasy if I were in composition. We've been talking about the need to have a stated separate budget for composition within the English department to secure the support for composition.

The other thing to say is that in spite of that hostility, I think people in composition with the help of those people like me and my colleague Steve Mailloux (and various other people in my department at Irvine, to speak of that context) do patiently go on trying to explain to the people who have that hostility that they're wrong. I think much is to be gained by that. My own university is an example of how gradually that works. When I first went to Irvine, there were many more of my colleagues who were prepared to say it would be really good if we could get out of composition and who had this contempt for the research in writing that goes on in the field. That voice has gradually faded a little bit because we had a committee that evaluated the program, and the committee was composed of respectable people who strongly argued the other—I strongly argued the other—and we now have Mailloux there as a result of that. We now, believe it or not, have funding for a tenured person in composition (which has never been the case), another appointment of somebody in the department. I think the program in composition is going to be better for that, better than it would have been had it cut itself off and had that hostility allowed itself to get institutionalized. I think that might be the case in other places. It's a battle that goes on needing to be fought.

Q. In "Composition and Decomposition," you insist repeatedly that "reading is itself a kind of writing, or writing is a trope for the act of reading," concluding that "we must make sure we base our rhetoric as reading on the deepest possible knowledge of what good reading would be." How do you respond to those critics who claim that while this may be true enough in the deconstructive sense, it nonetheless is used as a rationale by those in positions of power within English to appropriate the new re-emergent discipline of rhetoric and composition, to resubsume it under English as reading?

A. That's a good question. That academic/political fact doesn't really change the fact that reading and writing are closely related. The problem is to figure out an institutional way to avoid the danger you mention, and the way, it seems to me, is easy enough to see: you persuade the rest of the English department that it's their responsibility to teach reading. You can't say that composition and reading go together over here and we're doing something else over there. It's got to be an across-the-board understanding that the teaching of reading is the major responsibility of the English department as a whole, say rhetoric generally, and it then has a kind of easy transition to teaching which is primarily oriented toward composition. So the composition people have got to depend to some degree on the people in the English department and other language departments to do some, if not most, of the teaching of reading. But the theoretical point I was making (if you want to call it theoretical) is absolutely true—that students taking beginning composition who can't write are also probably unable to read well, and you could demonstrate that; you can do all the teaching of writing you want, but if they haven't somehow learned to read it's not going to stick. So the composition people have a big stake in making sure that somebody is teaching college students how to read in its broadest sense. Insofar as that's a *rhetorical* skill, it goes along with Stanley's suggestion that they ought to be called departments of rhetoric.

Q. In one of your President's Columns in the 1986 *MLA Newsletter*, you argue that "teaching is not primarily an interpersonal transaction oriented toward an interchange between teacher and students. The teacher is, rather, oriented primarily toward the text, primarily responsible to that, obligated in what he or she says to that. . . . Students are not so much partners in an intersubjective relation as the witnesses or overhearers of an activity of reading that is the teacher's interaction with the text at hand." Many teachers interested in liberatory learning or radical pedagogy would sharply disagree with this characterization. They would argue that good teaching is first and always an intensely interpersonal, intersubjective transaction. (You may have read Jane Tompkins' "Pedagogy of the Distressed.") What are your thoughts about radical pedagogy?

A. I don't know very much about it in detail, but I know what it is. The statement you cited was meant to be deliberately provocative, but that doesn't mean I didn't mean it. I think the danger I see in libertarian pedagogy is that it will free the teacher from one of the teacher's major responsibilities: the obligation to display a way to do something. If you have a class in which the students all say what they want and the teacher just facilitates this, that display is missing, and that seems to me too bad. By the way, there's nothing new about it. I was told that Yale graduate teaching traditionally (before I went there, but in recent memory) consisted of the professor—the great William Wimsatt, let's say, or whoever was sitting at the end of the table—each week assigning little papers that students prepared from an assigned topic and read in class. Wimsatt didn't have to say *anything*, and I think that's wrong. I don't see these approaches as absolutely incompatible, but I have some sympathy with Stanley Fish's answer in *JAC* to a similar question: on the one hand, I see this as an important new direction in teaching; I understand the psychological and political reasons for it, and I'm sure it works. Nevertheless, I think there's still room for the other kind of teaching, not because the teacher is necessarily going to be showing the "right" way to do something, but because the teacher has a kind of responsibility to show how he or she does it. You don't teach a beginning carpenter how to build a building by just saying, "Let's all just get together and see if we can learn to drive nails." What you do is drive some nails, and then you let the person try it, and then you say, "Well, you haven't got the hang of it quite yet." On the one hand, the *example* of the master carpenter is a fundamental part of the instruction; on the other hand, the apprentice carpenter would never learn how to do it without doing it him or herself, and I think that combination is what's needed.

Q. I think what the liberatory learning person would say is that in the old model you have the master carpenter simply performing as an example and saying, "Follow my example." In the more libertarian model, the students have the opportunity to help shape their own pedagogy, and, yes, the instructor may very well say, "Okay, we're learning to drive nails today. Try your hand at it. See what you can do and let's work at it from there." The objectives are the same, but the methodologies are different. It's asking students to participate in their own education and to try something right from the beginning rather than simply to mimic someone else.

A. You might do that with the driving of nails, but you might have to intervene after a while. I worked one summer years ago as a carpenter's helper, and I was taught both ways. First, they taught me how to wheel a wheelbarrow full of cement by saying, "Wheel this over there." I dumped it over, and everybody stood around and laughed. Then they gave me a few pointers, like you've got to keep it absolutely level because a wheelbarrow full of wet cement is pretty heavy and once the weight begins to shift it will turn right over. So I think it was a combination of those two. The other wisdom (I don't have any great wisdom about this) is that in my experience in visiting classes of beginning teachers I've noticed that there's a wide variety of teaching methods that work, and it is a deeply personal thing. Also, teaching has ideological and institutional determinants; that is, you teach in a way you've learned that you ought to. I think this move toward radical pedagogy is not an insignificant one, and I might also report that I've begun a little more to experiment with something like it in my own teaching just this year.

Q. Really, what have you done?

A. Well, there's a little more time for free discussion. It isn't *me* asking questions, but I'm trying to have free discussion much more (in graduate courses) than had been my instinctive habit, and I must say it worked to some degree. I found it very interesting.

Q. Long ago you renounced your allegiance to phenomenological criticism and the Geneva School with its emphasis on literature as a form of consciousness. Will there be any role for phenomenological principles in our poststructuralist criticism, or will phenomenology simply be relegated to the status of a historical curiosity?

A. The debt of poststructural criticism to phenomenology, often obscure and devious, is so great that certain aspects of phenomenology are perpetuated already in poststructuralist criticism. Therefore, anybody who is seriously interested in understanding Derrida, just to take one example, sooner or later would have to make a serious study not only of Heidegger, which is obvious enough, but also of Husserl. There are certain aspects of Derrida that remain faithful to some Husserlian assumptions. I've learned this just recently from recent work of Derrida that alludes back to Husserl in a way that's quite surprising because you'd think that Husserl was so far behind him and that the early work was so critical of Husserl that there would be no way that you could speak of Derrida as in any way consequent from phenomenology. That's not true. We have to go not by way of the superficial principles of so-called phenomenological criticism, like the "primacy of the self," and so on—those have been put in question. There is a deeper, you might even say "technical," link with phenomenology that remains very much there. It's most evident in the indebtedness to Heidegger. I was interested to see Stanley Fish asserting the influence on him of Heidegger by way of Hubert Dreyfus' teaching. If you wanted to define Derrida's "field" as a philosopher, Heidegger is the author he keeps coming back to again and again, much more than Hegel, much more than Husserl. In the little essay he wrote when he was being examined for his doctorate, he makes a survey of his intellectual history in which he says, "The question of what is literature was an initial problem for me perhaps even more important than the question of philosophy." The question of what is literature was a Husserlian question. Derrida was on record to be writing a dissertation on the ideality of the literary object, and in some sense you could say that's been his topic all along. So this question has a great deal of import and complexity.

Q. In your 1986 Presidential Address, you commented, "Another example of the triumph of theory is the development of feminist literary studies. This development has had a tremendous and irreversible effect on the way literature is studied and taught, on the curricula and canons of literary studies." Exactly what is the impact of feminist theory on the discipline?

A. There have been many changes. One of them is the larger number of women actually teaching in departments, the larger force that they have, and the fact that women's studies or feminism have liberated women to work in their own ways, to be interested in literature by women and to raise the sorts of questions that women's studies has raised. It's very difficult now for a male member of the English department to ignore this because you're working side by side with women colleagues. I spoke of the difference in the makeup of doctoral examinations lately. There is hardly a one that I participate in that doesn't have *some* feminist component, even when the candidate is a male, and that's a *big* transformation. But I think the transformation is even larger. I would agree with Stanley Fish: it goes along with transformations in our society that feminism has initiated that make the whole contextual situation in which literature is studied different. Fish is right: if you measure the value of a theory by the way it becomes effective outside the academy, that has happened very much with feminism. For example, I'm sure it will be a major factor in the 1992 presidential campaign. That doesn't necessarily mean Clinton will win, but I think pro-choice/pro-life is a fundamental issue in the campaign, and that would not have been the case twenty years ago.

Q. So you think that society at large has moved closer to gender equity?

A. Well, these are now issues that everybody is aware of, and they're very difficult issues. The conflicts within feminism itself—between essential-ism, on the one hand, and a social-constructionist view of gender, and so on—are very lively. The energy of those debates and their sharpness indicates how much is at stake and how serious matters are. So you can't say, "Feminism holds such and such." It doesn't. It's a very diverse movement. But everybody has to take those issues seriously and think about them. For example, the paper I gave recently on ideology in *Absalom, Absalom!* has a section on gender in that novel, and I found myself needing to think out two things: first, where I think Faulkner stands on gender in that novel, what the assumptions are about both male and female gender there; and, secondly, what *I* think about it, what *my* judgment is. It wouldn't have been too long ago that I could have written about *Absalom, Absalom!* without having to think about gender at all, without thinking that I *had* to think about it. So, I think everybody's work has been transformed.

Q. In your well-publicized debate with D.A. Miller in *ADE Bulletin*, you state that perhaps the enterprise of the new historicists is threatened by deconstruction. Would you elaborate on what is problematic about the new historicist project and why deconstruction should be a threat to it?

A. I don't think it needs to be. There's an obvious tension between the apparent focus of the new historicism on the historical context of works of literature and the sort of intrinsic reading that one associates with deconstruction. On the other hand, it's easy to exaggerate those differences. The new historicists are or ought to be interested in the reading of literary works as much as in the context, and deconstructionists have always been interested in history and historical context. So it's a difference of emphasis. I saw a good bit of Stephen Greenblatt about a month ago at Dartmouth's School of Criticism and Theory; we had a conversation about this, and Greenblatt said something that really sticks in my mind: "For me the end point of all I do is the reading of works of literature, Shakespeare especially." There's a kind of statement of allegiance there, and I would agree with Greenblatt on that. So, I think what I meant—I would no longer put it quite the same way—is that it may be that some of the new historicists take a little too much for granted the link between history and the literary work, and that for deconstructionists that relation is extremely problematic and needs itself to be reflected on. Insofar as deconstruction would inhibit the taking for granted that once you've established the historical context you have an explanation of the work, then deconstruction would be threatening to the new historicists' project. But that would certainly not include Stephen Greenblatt or most of the other really sophisticated new historicists. Nevertheless, there's a difference, and the difference appears to me to be the genuine fascination that somebody like Greenblatt has with the historical context itself. He was teaching a seminar at the Dartmouth School of Criticism and Theory this year on witchcraft, and he is really fascinated by those "non-literary" texts that formed the background of Shakespeare and others. Nevertheless, for him the end point is not the historical documents and understanding *them*, but Shakespeare. Moreover, Greenblatt would agree with my predisposition, which would be to say that these so-called historical documents should be read just as carefully and with just as much intelligence and imagination as you would read Shakespeare, and they're going to turn out to be interesting from that point of view. So I'm now changing a little from what I said earlier, not only saying that new historicism really owes a tremendous amount to linguistically based procedures like deconstruction, but that we can now learn a lot from them and that there needn't be any insuperable crevasse between the new historicists and the so-called deconstructionists.

Q. Some theorists in both rhetoric and literary criticism have argued that the sophists were the philosophical precursors to deconstructionists or that they were themselves deconstructionists. For example Howard Felperin writes that "the search for the founder or originator of the discourse of deconstruction" leads to Gorgias and the pre-socratics: "The first work of thoroughgoing (what I shall later term 'hard-core') deconstruction to come down to us, so striking in its wholesale anticipation of the contemporary project as to demand reconsideration of the cultural and philosophical context that could have conditioned it, is the fifth-century BC treatise *On Not Being, or On Nature* by Gorgias, the argument of which was summarized by Sextus Empiricus: 'Firstly . . . nothing exists; secondly . . . even if anything exists, it is inapprehensible by man; thirdly . . . even if anything is apprehensible, yet of a surety it is inexpressible and incommunicable to one's neighbour.'" Do you agree that the sophists were deconstruction's forbears?

A. That's Felpie's own winning way of putting things. He was a colleague of mine at Yale and a friend. I don't think he's got it right. I don't think that passage characterizes deconstruction at all. He's accepting there, for no doubt his own purposes, a rather public notion about deconstruction that doesn't correspond very well to what it is. So, I would disagree with that way of talking about it. On the other hand, the relationship of the so-called deconstructionists to the sophists is a complicated one. There's no doubt that certain aspects of sophistic thinking do anticipate deconstruction a bit. It would take a bit more working out than Felperin does in that particular statement. I would put it a slightly different way: Plato not only gives us a good bit of what we know about the sophists in the dialogue called the *Sophist*, but Plato is a kind of lesson himself in the inextricable relationship between let's say foundationalist and deconstructionist thinking. In other words, Plato's dialogues are for me absolutely fascinating because they contain both of those directions in themselves, not just in the *Sophist* but in a dialogue like the *Protagoras*. I would be more willing to say that *Plato* is the founder of deconstruction than to say the sophists were, partly because we know relatively little about them; we only know about the sophists primarily what the people on the other side have allowed us to learn about them. Moreover, the pre-socratics and the sophists are not at all the same. The relationship of the pre-socratics to modern thought is very complicated. There's a brilliant young scholar at the University of Colorado, a student of mine from Yale named Paul Gordon, who has written a book about rhetoric that goes back to the sophists (he knows Greek) and all the way up to Nietzsche; this book is in a way really about that complicated continuity.

Q. Does he support the lineage?

A. In the sense of a very twisted and circuitous lineage. It's not an unintelligent question to ask if there's a connection, but the answer is a complicated one and it's not correct to say, "Deconstructionists are like the sophists because the sophists said you can't know anything and everything is based on nothing and it's all language." That bears no relation to what deconstructionists say. That's what I meant when I said I would rather say Plato is the father of deconstruction for the kind of paradoxical sound that has; nevertheless, one can learn a great deal from Plato about how to read. It's not a matter of saying that you can read Plato deconstructively but of saying that he himself read that way. It's not an accident that one of Derrida's early fundamental essays is "La Pharmacie de Platon," which is not a deconstruction of Plato but a demonstration of the complexity in Plato's dialogue. One thing that annoys me is the easy reference to Plato as though he were the foundation of Western values. Go back and read Plato and you'll see that he's not what you've been led to expect. Just as Felperin's definition of deconstruction does not correspond to deconstruction, neither does the characterization of Plato as a set of ideas about the one and the good correspond to what's really in Plato when you sit down and try to read his dialogues.

Q. In *Theory Now and Then* you talk about the "negotiations between deconstructionisms and the almost universal turn in the 1980s to forms of literary study oriented toward society, toward history, toward ethical questions and questions of institutional organization, toward questions of race, class, and gender." You go on to say, "Though some of these cultural and historical critics have been unable to recognize the fact, their work would have been impossible without 'deconstructionisms.' . . . These recent forms of 'cultural critique' are more the continuation of deconstruction than its cancellation." We've already discussed the tension between deconstruction and new historicism. What accounts for the tension between deconstruction and those critical approaches oriented toward culture and society? And in what way is cultural critique a "continuation" of deconstruction?

A. I think the tension is to be expected when you have a younger generation that needs to think of itself as doing something new, something that's different from what people that came before did; nevertheless, there really are differences and they shouldn't be minimized. I think the *connection* lies (often these younger critics are not aware of these similarities) both in the political dimension of cultural criticism and of deconstruction (they are only apparently opposed to one another in this area), and also in assumptions about what you'd call in a broad sense "reading" or "interpretation." First, I think that cultural criticism like deconstruction assumes that quite a lot is at stake in the choice of what you study in a course, in what you write about, and in how you do it; so there is a political dimension, a social dimension. Both approaches see the need to intervene in the institution, the university, and make changes in it, not by changing the committee system and so on, but by changing what's actually taught in the classroom. They're alike in that way, and I think they've both succeeded. That is, what is actually taught now is to a considerable degree different, but they agree in seeing the teaching and writing about literature and culture as being an active intervention that goes by way of changing the university. That's why people who want things to remain the same are right to see this as threatening. As a matter of fact, I think those people who see cultural criticism as something assimilable, who say, "Well, this is really something we can make use of," are probably underestimating the degree to which it will change the university. The ease with which departments of ethnic studies and departments of African American studies have been generated in universities suggests to me that some administrators are probably underestimating the power it will have to make things different, just as they probably see deconstruction as just another mode of literary study that won't in the long run make much difference. The other way in which they are similar and one inherits the other is an understanding that the way you make these changes is not by abstract political pronouncements but by the active work of reading or teaching something. Both deconstruction and cultural criticism would agree on that sense of how you do it, which is to say, and it sounds paradoxical, there's an anti-theoretical bias in both of them: both of them see theory itself, abstract theory, as being relatively ineffective. It's like the passage in *As I Lay Dying*: language goes off like smoke and doing goes along the ground. Reading or interpretation of works and passing them on to other people as read is where the real work is effected. Using a speech act distinction, you might distinguish then between theory as being at least apparently knowledge, that is constative, simply giving knowledge—that's what the word sounds like it ought to mean—and reading as being performative, as really making something happen. I think the two approaches are in agreement on that, but maybe part of the reason why there is some tension and hostility between them is that the directions they want to go in are not necessarily the same, or they have to be adjudicated. You can't be sure that just because somebody is a deconstructionist that he or she is going to care about African American literature, so the relationship let's say between theory in African American literature and deconstruction is an uneasy one. One knows about these debates: theory is white, elitist, Eurocentric, and if we use it we're going to be betraying cultural identity; at the same time there's a recognition that these are the best instruments around for doing what we want to do, so we have to transform them rather than repudiate them.

One of the things that interests me is the question of the transformation of theory when it moves from one domain into another, both within the academy and also from one country to another. I've been involved with the translation of Western theory into various languages, especially Chinese. A colleague at the Chinese Academy of Social Sciences, Fengzhen Wang, and I are co-editors of a very ambitious program of translation of Western theory into Chinese for publication in the People's Republic of China. Although Tiananmen Square slowed us down a bit, the project hasn't, to my surprise, been stopped. The idea is ultimately to have as many as fifty volumes (initially about twelve or fourteen) containing ten or twelve essays each—essays by Stanley Fish, Harold Bloom, Georges Poulet, Fred Jameson, and so on—translated into Chinese by good translators. Ask yourself what will happen in mainland China when they read Stanley Fish or Fred Jameson or me or Geoffrey Hartman or Harold Bloom. You can be certain that they will be transformed, that they will be assimilated and used for different purposes, that they will have an effect, but an effect that's unpredictable. In the same way, you can say that though deconstruction was not developed for the use it might be to people doing cultural criticism, it nevertheless will have a use there. Edward Said's work will be included in our series. Said has written a new essay (I don't know whether it's been published yet) which he gave as a lecture at Irvine last year, a follow-up on the traveling theory lecture. In this essay he talks about the influence, according to him, of Lukács' *History and Class Consciousness* on Fanon, the African writer. He makes a double point. On the one hand, Lukács didn't write the *History and Class Consciousness* with any idea that it would be useful to somebody in Algeria in aiding the liberation of Algeria. On the other hand, it could be used by Fanon to aid that and to aid his thinking in writing what according to Said is his most important book, *The Wretched of the Earth*. But that could only happen if Fanon *did* something to Lukács; Lukács is not any longer the same. I think that's the general way to think of theory as being useful, even in a personal way. What I made of Kenneth Burke was something that involved transforming Burke in order to write a dissertation about Charles Dickens. Burke had no idea of helping me do that, and it involved certain changes. This is illustrative of the usefulness of theory. That's the objection I have to teaching theory as simply a set of postulates or ideas that you learn and pass an examination on. Theory is of no use unless it's used for something, and using it means changing it.

Q. In discussing how you yourself have used theory, William Cain writes, "Miller over-rates the degree of innovation that his theory introduces into literary studies, and he fails to perceive the conservative impulses that keep its subversive forces in check. He believes that he is drawing on

Jacques Derrida and translating this French theorist's 'deconstructive' program for an American audience, and this is certainly true up to a point. But Miller safeguards and hedges in the 'radical' theory that he presents, so much so that to connect him with Derrida comes to feel inaccurate and misleading." What is your response to this oft-repeated charge?

A. What I've done with Derrida and other Europeans is an example of what I was talking about: it's a transformation, just as I transformed Burke. There's no doubt that that transformation has been an assimilation into my own American concerns and interests. It would be quite true to say that there are certain issues that are very important to Derrida that are not so important to me, even though I share with Derrida an interest in both Husserl and Heidegger. (Heidegger has always been very interesting to me.) It's a little difficult to answer that question because it's hard for me to get outside myself, but I'd be perfectly willing to admit that my concerns have always been somehow presupposing that literature was a good thing to study, that it could have a positive effect. Derrida, I think, would agree with me on that. A much more uneasy area for me now is to try to think of my relation to Paul de Man on this subject. I have the feeling that I differ more from de Man than from Derrida. There are many places in Derrida, particularly recently, where he, like me, wants to use deconstructive thinking as a way to imagine the possible movement toward a better form of democracy. That aspect of Derrida I find fascinating and much more positive than the normal picture of Derrida as destroying the Western tradition. And that I find much more akin to my thinking. I've only recently begun to realize that there are certain statements of de Man that influenced me greatly but that are very dark; he speaks of the impossibility of reading, of the impossibility of foreseeing what the performative effect will be of what you do, of wanting to shift the notion of responsibility away entirely and say, "What happens happens; it's all a linguistic matter." I find in myself some resistance to that. I feel a little uneasy about it because I have so much respect for the rigor of de Man's thinking, but I draw some comfort from the fact that I think that that's Derrida's direction too. But I would make no claim to having carried all of Derrida over, to be a Derrida purist, nor would I in any way deny that my use of Derrida has been determined and limited by things like the American New Criticism. This is often said. Nevertheless, there are certain principles of the New Criticism that I think my own work is not consonant with—for example, the valuing of organic unity and the political conservatism of the New Critics, which I've always been uneasy about. I would be happy if one would say, "That's the New Criticism all right, but for Miller it was Empson and Burke rather than Brooks and Warren." Long before I'd read any Derrida at all, I had made that choice; that is, the Anglo-Americans that I was spontaneously attracted to were Empson and Richards and Burke and "wild man" G. Wilson Knight. By the way, I was emphasizing the differences among the Yale Critics; that's something I would share with Harold Bloom, for whom G. Wilson Knight and Burke were also very important, though probably not Empson so much. (I found Empson terrific and I still do; he's just wonderful.)

Q. In discussing the future of deconstruction, you've said that now that poststructuralist modes of criticism have been assimilated into college and university curricula, the danger is "that deconstruction might petrify, harden into dogma, or into a rigid set of prescriptions for reading, become some kind of fixed method rather than a set of examples, very different from one another, of good reading." Some believe this is already occurring. Do you agree?

A. Since I said that, things have changed quite a lot, at least at my university, so that it would be hard to find a dyed-in-the-wool narrow deconstructionist who said, "All I do is derived directly from those people." I think the danger I saw has to a considerable degree been by-passed because now the challenges are to do things that are so different—like cultural studies and so on—that if you're going to do them at all, a good bit of nimbleness is required; *that* will keep deconstruction from being petrified in any particular person, and I think that's all to the good. It's been transformed and assimilated. I don't see it any longer as the danger (what *did* happen with Northrop Frye or New Criticism or F.R. Leavis in Australia and other places) of a whole set of people entrenched in departments who are teaching the dogma of deconstruction year after year. It certainly is not happening in my university. People read Derrida or de Man but in connection with a lot of other things, and I don't think there's as much danger of reducing it to a set of recipes as I once thought, certainly not in the students that I see.

Q. You've said that Edward Said's *Beginnings* is "a major work of creative humanistic scholarship, a splendid demonstration of the way it might be possible, after all, to go 'beyond deconstruction,' though without wholly forgetting its insights." What do you predict will be the future of criticism beyond deconstruction?

A. Well, I think it's already happening. I think we're already seeing something that's beyond deconstruction in any kind of narrow sense of a codified dogma; it's been assimilated and transformed, "translated." I happen to feel very positive about the direction cultural studies has now taken and the move in that direction. That's obviously where we're going. The first half of my *Illustration* book is an attempt to talk about cultural studies. I have various things to say about it. Why has this happened? I think one answer would be that especially the young people teaching literature now are anxious to make what they do have some importance in our society, so they've begun to think about how that might happen. Secondly, they are the first generation of people, now taking over departments of English, who were brought up on the mass media, who've been watching television since they were small children and going to the movies and listening to popular music; it's quite natural that they should be interested in this, to try to understand it and figure out ways to talk about it. I see this not only as natural but as all to the good. I live in the city of Irvine, which is essentially an upper middle class part of Orange County, and someone did a little questionnaire in the grade schools (I think among first graders or kindergarten kids) and found that there's something like twenty-six different languages spoken at home—not just five or six but twenty-six different languages. Well, if you live in a culture like that, it's natural that you're going to take an interest in some of these other than purely Anglo-Saxon American cultures as they are active in the United States. So I see this ethnic multiculturalism as natural and good. And as the various forms of communication around the world make it much more difficult to forget that there's an Africa, an India, the Far East, and so on, it's natural that we should begin to think in terms of global history questions, such as Francophone African literature being part of French literature generally. I have certain anxieties about this subject, but I've also got some answers. We were talking about "department of rhetoric" as a name; my feeling as a "comparative literature imperialist" is that what should happen is the disappearance of the separate study of national literatures. More and more the necessity is to study literature in more than one language, even if you're an Americanist. American studies I think is in the midst of a radical transformation. Originally, American studies meant primarily New England and was primarily Perry Miller and that kind of thing. Now a new kind of American studies is emerging that involves literature of ethnic minorities. It involves literature in several languages: you have Chicano literature, and so you have to know Spanish, and then once you start doing that you have to get interested in Latin American Spanish literature, and so on. Pretty soon those who began as American studies specialists, like my colleague John Rowe, have turned into comparatists. There's a natural affinity in my department between the American literature people and the comparative literature people. We tend to have the same ideas about what appointments should be made, and there's an actual overlap. For example, a colleague of mine in comparative literature, Lilian Manzor-Coates, who does Chicano literature is also an Americanist; she's in both fields. I see this as the real direction that literary studies is taking. (And composition then will be part of that; that's why I resist calling it a department of rhetoric.) The major requirement for doing this respectably or honestly or responsibly is knowing the languages. The small anxiety I sometimes have about the cultural studies people is that they undertake very laudable projects without having had the training either in languages or in social science methodology that is necessary for doing this work well. In other words, you still have Ph.D. programs, in spite of all the changes say at Irvine, that are relatively Eurocentric,

English-language centered. You now get people with a Ph.D. from an English department and what they want to do requires training in the protocols of social science research; doing film studies requires the knowledge of several languages, sometimes very exotic, difficult languages. Nobody has really institutionalized the procedures whereby you would know you were capable of doing one of those projects. Say you want to do a great project, a big comparative study of the novel which would involve the English novel, French novel, Arabic fiction, and African works. You can't really do this well without knowing Arabic and one or two African languages. Even if the African novels were written in English, they were written by people whose first language was an African language. Those languages are very difficult. Anthropologists know how to deal with this problem. The last time I ran into Clifford Geertz, he told me how horribly difficult it was for him at the age of forty or forty-five to learn Arabic, but he *had* to learn Arabic. He was in Chicago then and went to an undergraduate class. It's harder to learn languages when you're older. He knew that he had to learn Arabic in order to do the research he wanted to do. I think we need to get in place procedures like those in anthropology and certain other disciplines that allow people doing cultural studies to do what they want to do in a responsible way. I notice, by the way, that Gayatri Spivak is learning Arabic, clearly for just that reason. To do what she wants to do she needs to know Arabic.

Q. This question of intellectual border crossings is a difficult one, especially when it comes to disciplinary borders. Several scholars, such as philosopher Beverly Brown writing in *The Oxford Literary Review* and, more recently, H.P. Rickman in *Philosophy and Literature*, have criticized your "reading" of Kant in *The Ethics of Reading*. In "Making a Mess of Kant," Rickman characterizes your reading as "disastrously misunderstanding a great and frequently discussed philosopher," and he attributes this misreading to "the mistaken assumptions behind the belief that philosophy can be treated as 'just literature.'" Do you agree with the implication that academics should not cross disciplinary boundaries, deferring instead to scholars trained in a particular area; or do you believe that deconstruction allows us to dissolve such borders?

A. I don't think deconstruction particularly allows for dissolving those borders, nor would I want to dissolve them absolutely. Different disciplines have their own traditions and communities (to refer back to Stanley Fish), their own ideas about the kinds of questions it's proper to ask and the things that you can and cannot say. They have their values. There has to be a kind of community that moves forward gradually and so on, so you can't say all these borders ought always to be crossed; there ought to be these communities that develop their own ways of reading and writing. But that doesn't mean a non-philosopher can't read philosophy. Surely, Rickman doesn't mean to say that. I haven't read the Rickman essay and so I can only comment on your citations from him and your characterization of what he says. If he really means that because Kant has been "frequently discussed" it is impossible to do anything more than agree with what the specialists in philosophy have already said about him, he's an idiot, and certain to make a mess of Kant. If he means that it's inappropriate to pay attention to figures of speech, the choice of examples, narrative elements, and other minutiae of language in a philosophical text, he's even more certain to make a mess. Presumably he's not an idiot, so he can't mean either of those things. Certainly, literature is one thing, philosophy another. We have different expectations of the two kinds of texts. Nevertheless, it is as true of philosophy as of literature that a given text often turns out to mean something substantially different from what the secondary authorities have led you to expect. It's the first rule in reading either kind of text, or any other kind, to be prepared for that. It may happen or it may not happen, but it happens pretty often. Figures of speech, choice of examples, and so on are just as important in a philosophical text as in a literary one. Good reading of any text is rhetorical reading. To say that is not to treat philosophy as "just literature." It affirms what is a primary rule in reading any sort of text, however different the protocols of philosophy are from those of literature. Philosophy is by no means "just literature," but it is, one might say, contaminated by literature in never succeeding in being no more than a set of interlocked abstract propositions. The figures of speech and choice of narrative examples tie the philosophical text to time, place, and history. They cannot be eliminated as adventitious. Kant's little story of the man who makes a promise intending not to keep it is an example of that. Since he uses it as a basic proof of one of his propositions about morals, the proposition cannot be detached from the example that is essential to making us understand it and persuading us to accept it.

One of the things we haven't talked about in the area of composition is my strong commitment to the notion that good writing differs not only for different purposes but in different professional areas. The justification for having writing across the curriculum is that assumptions about what constitutes, say, a good and effective engineering report differ from those about a good essay in art history or anthropology. Good writing goes beyond getting the grammar right. Somebody in an English department really doesn't know what the rules are about writing in the different fields; it's hard to learn these because there are built-in conventions and so on. Nevertheless, one could say *that* ought not to prohibit somebody trained in one discipline from, however modestly and tentatively, dealing with texts in another discipline, and often that person will see some things that wouldn't be seen within the conventions of the primary discipline. So the answer to your question about border crossing is yes and no. I think I was a good reader of Kant, but I'm not surprised that somebody trained within the protocols of a certain way of reading Kant would have found what I said to be troubling.

Q. What you're saying relates to the distinction you've made on numerous occasions between "good" and "bad" readings, good and bad readers. In another interview you said, "You can't give the same validity to every act of reading. Some people are better readers than others. Some people are better readers at some times than at others. I find the distinction between good and bad reading pragmatically valid. But the distinction is also polemical in the sense that I want to be able to say that one reading is better than another." Against what standards or criteria can we make such distinctions?

A. The easy answer (and the true answer) is to say "against the standard of the text." This is an area where I differ from Fish. For Fish, if I understand him, the text is absolutely nothing in itself without some community of readers to give it meaning. For me the text contains so strong an inherited way of being read, which is carried from generation to generation in spite of all the changes in the community, that there are certain things that the language allows you to say and other things that you can demonstrate are very implausible. I think I would have to come back on something like that with a full awareness of the difficulties in claiming it. I see that Fish in the *JAC* interview talks about how a certain way of reading a given text can persist for a long long time. For me the time is even longer than it is for him. He sees a more radical possibility of changing the way of reading a text as one generational community substitutes for another than I do. I would say that there are certain readings which are (I'm thinking of how Stanley would respond to this) so unlikely to be useful that you could say that they are bad readings. Or to put this another way, I think that Fish's example of his daughter's ability to substitute one context after another in order to make a given sentence mean something entirely different is a very powerful argument for his position, but for me there are limits to that in a given piece of language. So I would be prepared to say that a good or bad reading is determined in complex ways by the oversaturated, overdetermined context for that particular act of reading, but that one would nevertheless want to be able to appeal back to the text for support. And I'm aware that's a somewhat contradictory answer.

Q. You've applied these same standards to deconstructive reading. You once commented that the only effective way to "attack" you or other deconstructionists would be to demonstrate that details of your readings are "false." As an example, you cite Derrida's reading of Plato and say, "The only way to refute it, I think, is not to say that deconstruction is nonsense, or it's immoral and is going to lead to the end of the western world, but to show that's not what Plato's text means. Now one might be able to do that, but nobody ever really tried." How do you respond to critics who argue that it's incongruous to appeal to what a text "means" and "true" or "false" readings as a defense of deconstructive reading?

A. I don't think it's incongruous. I see the notion of truth and falsehood as absolutely indispensable; there's no way to do without them. The same is true with good and bad readings; I wouldn't be willing to throw those away. These concepts are necessary, but I would see them not as solutions so much as in themselves problems that require a lot of definition and thoughtful consideration. I think that's true in general about so-called deconstructionists, that they would want to claim a kind of authority for their readings as being better than other people's readings, far from saying this is just a reading put forward within a certain circumstance. And I think that has to be somehow recognized and thought through in the same way that I was trying to do by way of thinking of how I differ from Fish. It's not that I feel that Fish's position leads to anarchy or chaos. I think it's very principled in his case. The position he takes is very plausible; one would want to disagree with him only in a thoughtful way. Nevertheless, I find myself feeling that the text gives more as a basis for the reading than Fish is willing to allow. That goes along for me with a sense of the recalcitrance and conservatism of language, so that when you learn a language you learn not only a way to use it or read it but, even more than that, something is carried in the signs themselves that comes down from a long long long time ago (I put in one more "long" than Fish).

Q. You've commented that Harold Bloom is "perhaps the most dazzlingly creative and provocative of critics writing in English today." Similarly, Richard Rorty has said in *JAC* that Bloom is "strikingly original" and one of those few "people whose individual voice is so distinctive that one feels immediately attracted." What do you believe to be Bloom's important contribution?

A. I hadn't encountered Rorty's statement, but he's put his finger on a feature of Bloom's work. It's not any theoretical presuppositions in Bloom that I like; for me it's the wonderful exuberance and enthusiasm and an admiration and love for literature that's very infectious. You might even say it goes along with a—*taste* is an old-fashioned word—remarkable ability he has to show you, persuade you, that you ought to like something and you ought to read it, even when you disagree with what he says about a given work. I owe Bloom a lot. One of the things I owe to him is a better understanding and admiration for the Pre-Raphaelites and for people like Pater and Ruskin. Ruskin had always seemed to me a rather dull, moralistic writer until I read Bloom's preface to the Anchor edition of Ruskin's literary criticism. It's wacky Bloom, and it gives you the idea, a quite correct idea, that Ruskin himself is kind of wacky and wonderful; it makes you want to read Ruskin—and I did. The same thing goes for Meredith and Swinburne and all these out-of-fashion people that Bloom is very good on. We both share an admiration for Pater. "Ah," he says, "the divine Walter." So that's what I would emphasize about Bloom, and it's certainly true of his teaching. He's a remarkably good dissertation director, not because the dissertations are Bloomian in the sense of using Bloomian revisionary ratios and so on, but because he somehow has a remarkable ability to bring out the best in graduate students and to allow them to be themselves. Even though he no longer officially directs dissertations in the English department at Yale, he's kind of a shadow director of a lot of dissertations, and they are among the best dissertations I've had anything to do with.

Q. You argue in *The Ethics of Reading* that "there is a necessary ethical movement in that act of reading as such, a moment neither cognitive, nor political, nor social, nor interpersonal, but properly and independently ethical." Would you elaborate on your notion of the "ethical" and your attempt to shift the focus of literary study from political, historical, and social concerns to ethical considerations?

A. It was, you might say, a political move on my part to try to come to terms with the new interest in politics and society on the part of literary people. I've always been willing to admit that there's a political dimension to teaching; you don't enter a classroom exempt from political responsibility and exempt from actually making political and social changes, however small. Nevertheless, it always seemed to me rather distant and abstract to figure out how that could be, whereas the ethical dimension seemed a little more concrete and specific and a little easier to think about. For me, the political goes by way of the ethical, and it's easier for me to understand the teaching or writing situation along an ethical model, a model that is of a one-to-one reciprocity of responsibility, than it is to think of it in terms of these larger, more abstract political questions. But I think that's less true for me now than it was when I got started. For that reason I was motivated to ask myself initially the question, "Is there an ethical dimension to teaching and writing about literature?" I became interested in trying to work that out. But the ethical was for me defined as a more manageable, face-to-face, person-to-person relation, and one that seemed to me to have a little more to do with what goes on in works of literature, for example, novels. It's not that there are not political novels or that there's not a political dimension in all novels but that the good political novels dramatize that in terms of ethical or even family relations. *Absalom, Absalom!* is a good example; it's a great novel about southern history, but southern history is expressed in that novel in terms of the Sutpen saga, in terms of a very personal story that involves ethical responsibility and decision; one is expressed in terms of the other. Therefore, I asked myself what seem to me not all that transparent questions: "What ethical responsibility, if any, do I have to students when I'm teaching? What's my ethical responsibility to the text? What about the institution I teach for? The institution hired me; don't I have certain responsibilities to it?" Those questions led me to explore literature from that point of view.

Q. Since elsewhere you have argued that writing is a form of reading, would you then argue that there is an ethics of writing?

A. Oh sure. I think that's a way of naming the notion that writing is always "in a situation." That's a very Kenneth Burkean idea that I would fully agree with. The key to teaching writing probably is to convince students that in some way they're in some kind of situation that they've got to write their way out of. That's *ethical*; it involves an ethical dimension. That's not its only dimension, but it has continuously an ethical dimension. I would define the ethical situation now as—this is why I was interested in the side of Kant that appears to be not what Kant is supposed to be saying—one in which in the end you have no real help from ethical norms or preexisting codes of ethics. That is, an ethical decision is not one in which you say, "The Ten Commandments say such and such, and so I'll apply this rule and I'll know how I should act." Far from that. It's a situation in which in some way you have to innovate, and therefore it's very uncomfortable being in a real ethical situation, a situation of ethical responsibility and decision. I think that the novels I study demonstrate that. It's a theme that recurs again and again, not only in radical novels like, let's say, those of Henry James where you might expect that kind of thing, but even in what appear to be more conventional novels like those of Trollope. The lesson about ethical choice that Trollope's novels teach you is that in the end all of the advice of your family and friends and the whole community is of no help; you have to decide for yourself. I think one of the reasons students have difficulty putting pen to paper and writing is that they're confronting a situation in which all the teaching you can give them doesn't really tell them what words to put down on the page; it's a kind of paradigm of the ethical situation. I don't know that saying this, however, will help at all in *teaching* writing.

Q. In *Victorian Subjects*, you discuss "the present state of humanistic studies in America," saying, "The concrete situation of teachers of the humanities is changing at the moment with unusual rapidity. More even than usual it seems as if we stand within the instant of a crisis, a dividing point, a 'parting hour.' Aspects of the change include the increasing emphasis on the teaching of writing (which may be all to the good if it does not involve the imposition of narrow notions of clarity and logic), the decline of enrollments in traditional courses in literature and other humanities, the catastrophic reduction of the number of positions open to younger humanists, and a conservative reaction in the universities." Given this "crisis," what directions do you predict the humanities, particularly English departments, will take in the next few decades?

A. A lot has changed since I wrote that essay. One thing that's changed, at least in my university, is that the enrollments are not going down anymore; they're going up. We still have the conservative reaction, and we have what appears to me to be the possibility of a major change in American higher education. It's an interesting question, but I don't know the answer: Are the current cutbacks all across the country, both in private and public universities, simply part of a temporary recession, or are they part of a larger change that won't really go away? I don't know the answer to that, but it's conceivable that for various complicated reasons it might happen in the United States that there will be a change in the assumption about what percentage of the population ought to get a higher education. The United States is quite unique in the West in this; a much smaller percentage of the population goes to the university in Germany or England. Relatively speaking, you still have to be chosen, and not as many people are chosen. *We've* decided to make higher education almost universally accessible. We think of it as part of democracy, but England, France, and Germany are democratic countries too, and they don't give the same access to the university. It's a democratic access, but not as many people are chosen. Whether that will be the case in this country or not, I don't know. It would be a major change. I hope not. But there's no doubt at the moment that there is both a conservative attack on the universities and a reduction in funding that gives people an opportunity to begin eliminating things, especially in the humanities. It's already being used for that purpose, particularly with the so-called peripheral programs, the ones that are precisely the interdisciplinary ones. You say, "We've got to have an English department, but it's not so clear that we have to have women's studies," and so you just sort of phase women's studies out. Lack of money can always be used as an excuse for making political and ideological decisions, and one is made very uneasy about that; nor can one deny that this might happen. I hope it doesn't happen. Moreover, I think the transformation of the goals and purposes of teaching, particularly in the people who are going to be doing it, will occur especially within a few years when so many older people will have retired. The younger professors, trained as they have been with these new interests, will for better or worse be all there is to hire, and their ideas of what you do with an English department are going to be different enough so that the changes will happen in spite of attacks from the conservative right. I think that's why the right is worried; they see this change as something that's really going to happen and is already happening. So I'm very optimistic. I think there will be a lot of interesting transformations. I'm sorry I'm not going to be around another thirty years or so because I think it's going to be very exciting to try to figure out how to deal with the possibilities of change in a responsible way. That is, in many cases you'll have an English department where within about five years forty percent of the senior faculty will retire and an entirely new set of people will be in charge, with all the power and responsibility to make changes; it's going to be both exciting and interesting but also a challenge to do that responsibly.

Q. Over the years you've certainly had your share of intellectual disagreements with other scholars, and you've even complained of "a phase of irrational polemic, sometimes by distinguished older scholars who apparently feel so threatened by these new directions of literary study that they are willing to abandon all traditions of scholarly accuracy and responsibility in order blindly to attack what they appear to have made no attempt to understand." Are there any misunderstandings of your recent work that you'd like to address now?

A. Sometimes in reviews people have cited things I have said that were intended as ironic or as the miming of somebody else's position as though they were my opinions. Sometimes this is done disingenuously. You take a passage out of context. Miller says this and you quote it. However, if you look back at the context, Miller wasn't really saying this at all; he was saying something like, "People say" or "This is a position"—and that ought to be clear. On the one hand, you point out that this sentence does appear in that essay or in that book; on the other hand, I thought I was making it clear that I was simply saying what my author said: it was Thomas Hardy who was saying this or George Eliot or somebody else, not me. So, I have two exhortations for my readers. First, try to notice whether I might conceivably not be speaking for myself but doing what any literary critic has to do: trying to speak for the author that I'm discussing or even for some imagined position which I'm then going to differ from.

The other exhortation would be to stress again the fact that for me, and I think for my colleagues like Derrida, those theoretical formulations that *can* be detached and are not ironical, that are straight, nevertheless have their meaning only in the context of a reading. The relationship between theory and reading is the really fundamental one, not the detachable theory that you can make into a system. The theoretical statement should always be put back in the context of the reading which—the relationship is a very complicated and uneasy one—both facilitated the theoretical formulation but at the same time isn't quite congruent with it; they're not quite symmetrical, and it's that asymmetry between reading and theory that seems to me fundamental to the nature and function of literary theory. Theory is never fully sponsored or generated or supported or confirmed by the reading; far from it: the reading always does something to the theoretical formulation and at the same time generates new theoretical formulations which have to be modified then in their turn. So a theory is never something that's fixed once and for all, and the thing that alters it is more reading. I think that's often forgotten, perhaps inevitably, in the attempt to reduce my work or somebody else's work to a handy set of theoretical formulations. That's certainly true with Derrida. People will say that Derrida talks about "the free play of language in the void" or something, and you go back and find he's really talking about Lévi-Strauss in that passage and the formulation is only made possible by the reading of the particular author. I think it's often forgotten in what you might call pedagogical accounts of Derrida, accounts used in teaching him, that almost all his work is the reading of some text or other. That's certainly true of my own work.

On Transforming
the English Department:
A Response to J. Hillis Miller

PATRICIA HARKIN

In his introduction to *JAC*'s interview with J. Hillis Miller, Gary Olson writes that "Hillis Miller has always been interested in rhetoric and composition, even though in the past he hasn't always seemed to understand what we in the field do." Perhaps the most useful way of beginning my task as respondent is to comment on Olson's characterization (I agree) and to say whether in this interview Miller demonstrates a different, and somehow more accurate, understanding of "what we in the field do" than the one that informs his earlier writings.

Prior to this interview, Miller's crucial statements had been "Composition and Decomposition: Deconstruction and the Teaching of Writing," and "The Function of Rhetorical Study at the Present Time," both reprinted in *Theory Now and Then*. In both essays, Miller seemed (perhaps strategically, so as to discriminate compositionists' construction of "writing" from his own account of "reading") to understand research in composition as exclusively empirical. "It founds itself," he wrote, "on the most advanced twentieth century scientific or quasi-scientific discoveries about the nature of language and the nature of composition, the processes whereby writing is generated and revised . . . " (227). In composition research as he construed it, "The emphasis can be happily on praxis as opposed to *theoria*. Such theory as there is is immediately testable in praxis" (228). To gather the grounds for this claim, Miller "examined" a collection of composition handbooks (by Elaine Maimon, Susan Miller, Joe Trimmer, Sheridan Baker, Robert Scholes and Nancy Comley) and concluded that composition studies failed to observe that all language is figurative.

What I found problematic then (see my "For Its Own Sake") was the way in which Miller's language constructed composition, and compositionists, as other. The word *nature*, and the undeconstructed theory/praxis binarism (unusual articulations for an author closely associated with deconstruction) implied that compositionists held essentialist notions of writing. Many of us, for important political reasons, did (and still do) *deny* the opposition between theory and praxis, or have worked to blur it, but that is not what Miller said. Instead, he formulated the procedures of composition studies in the most reductive terms of empirical science. Further, he seemed to claim that compositionists understood and attended only to the communicative function of language. Let me try, by analogy, to explain how these characterizations were problematic.

"Naming" and the Service Function
In this interview Miller speaks of the "myth" of the Yale School as "a product of people...who needed a name" for the men whose thinking and writing and teaching had "a certain role in representing the theoretical side of the faculties" in New Haven during the 1970s and 80s. To describe them as "the Yale School" diminishes the differences among them and, by making them all into epigones of Jacques Derrida, contains and reduces their work. I remember in particular a *New York Times Sunday Magazine* feature on the Yale School that included a photograph of Hillis Miller in a New Haven pizza place. Why would the popular and academic press *need* to enact that reduction, to "name" "the Yale School"? Whence any need to contain difference by the political use of the naming function that, along with the communicative function, constructs language's "nature"? We might say that the critique of metaphysics as presence posed a threat to persons who wished to perpetuate certain aspects of metaphysics from which they profited—such aspects, for example, as the power of deciding what's fit to print, what's true, what's valuable. Miller found it unpleasant when people said that deconstruction "is going to lead to the end of the western world," as though his critics construed his only job as maintaining it. I suspect that I speak for many compositionists when I say that I found Miller's early account of what we in the field do as similarly reductive and as much a product of needing to name as those responses to the Yale School. Turning "bad writers" into "good" ones is not all we do. We spend a lot of time deconstructing those categories and using that "deconstructive thinking as a way to imagine . . . movement toward a better form of democracy." Few compositionists—and, I suspect, no compositionist who cares about Hillis Miller—think that language has a "nature" or that practice tests theory or that empirical science can tell us much about what we want to know. We object to being understood in terms of five textbooks just as he resists being conflated with Geoffrey Hartman, Harold Bloom, or even Paul de Man. And we resist especially the strategy of containment that reduces our work to service.

I believed then that Miller's definition reduced composition studies to an "empiricized" freshman composition while reserving humanistic inquiry, for its own sake, for literary studies. The obvious question now is whether Miller's view has changed. In this interview, he speaks enthusiastically of the "methodological and theoretical aspects of the discipline," and he remarks on "a kind of link between 'highfalutin' literary theory which appears to have nothing to do with composition in one direction and composition theory in the other." But when Gary Olson asks how Miller sees the role of composition changing, he replies that "the need to be able to write clearly and effectively for a given purpose is going to remain," and so "there's going to be a need to teach composition well in any conceivable university."

Clearly, Miller is now better informed about what we in the field do, but he evidently sees this research and theorizing as directed toward the improvement of a service (making "people write well"). This perception makes me uneasy. It is not, of course, that I oppose the service function. It is surely well within the rights of states to require the educational systems that they support to provide instruction in the direct and clear communication of the information that makes the society run. Nor would I diminish the important theoretical work of compositionists like Stephen North, Louise Wetherbee Phelps, David Bleich, and James Sosnoski, who seek to blur the conceptual and political boundaries between teaching and research. What makes me uneasy about Miller's positions is that he seems to see composition studies *only* as service. Miller is distanced by enormous social and political structures from most of the people who teach composition on a daily basis. His account of what he thinks we do is, I believe, informed by his interest in our continuing to do it and thereby relieve him and his colleagues from "shouldering the burden of expository writing." I am troubled by the dissociation of service from research, as though composition had no inquiry and literary studies no service. This dissociation, as I see it, is consistent with students' commodification of their education, their disinclination to ponder the workings of language, the heavy responsibilities of writing program administrators, the appalling exploitation of part-time faculty, and state legislators' demands for larger classes, more teaching, less attention to theory, and more "basics."

Responding to this interview has therefore been for me a difficult ethical task—in both senses. What's the right thing to do and how can I find the *ethos* in which to do it? It would be churlish (not to mention stupid) to fail to appreciate the support entailed in Miller's remark that "respectable people" in the Department of English at the University of California at Irvine voted to have a tenure-track position in writing, "believe it or not." But what really is difficult for me to believe is that there is only one tenure-track position, that it has taken this long to get it, and that he thinks composition studies still needs such respectability as professors of literary studies can give. My ethical problem is typical of the position of writing program administrators in departments of English. Should composition programs separate from departments of English or try to continue communicating within a situation in which they are treated with condescension? For the moment, I'll choose the latter, adopt Miller's belief that the "political goes by way of the ethical," and read the language in which Miller characterizes composition in an effort to demonstrate why I still see difficulties.

Composition and Disciplinarity

I begin by comparing Miller's treatment of composition studies to his account of other academic enterprises. Feminism, for example, cannot be reduced: "You can't say feminism holds such and such" because it is "a very diverse movement." Feminist theory has had an effect on the makeup of doctoral exams ("even when the candidate is male"). Feminism even expands out of the academy into the 1992 presidential campaign, and as Fish avers, "You measure the value of a theory by the way it becomes effective outside the academy." And new historicism calls upon us to read "non-literary" texts "just as carefully and with just as much intelligence and imagination as you would read Shakespeare." Cultural criticism expands into African American studies. Both cultural criticism and deconstruction have "an understanding that the way you make changes is not by abstract political pronouncements but by the active work of reading or teaching something."

Feminism is described as breaking institutional boundaries such that "everybody's work is transformed." Social criticism intervenes in the institution "by changing what's actually taught in the classroom" and "by the active work of reading or teaching something." Cultural criticism sees that "we have to transform rather than repudiate" theory. Western theory is "transformed" by translation into Chinese. Miller himself has "transformed" Burke. Deconstruction has been "transformed" in Edward Said's *Beginnings*. "American studies ... is in the midst of a radical transformation" into ethnic multiculturalism. And composition "will be part of that" ethnic multiculturalism because "ESL is a large part of the challenge in teaching English composition at a place like Irvine," although "it's not that people who have English as a first language can't be very bad writers—they often are."

Whereas "transformation" is the figure for literary studies, the language of containment and remediation describes writing and its teaching. This account of composition studies is so condescending and reductive (and widespread) that many compositionists want to leave their institutional "homes" and strike out on their own. But Miller does not think that's a good idea. In "The Function of Rhetorical Study at the Present Time," he writes, "The worst catastrophe that could befall the study of English literature would be to *allow* the programs in expository writing to become separate empires in the universities and colleges, wholly cut off from the departments of English and American literature" (203; emphasis added). In this interview, he describes a discussion at Irvine about "whether composition ought *to be taken away* from the English Department and *given* to some dean, made a cross-school program" (emphasis added). One can't help noticing that in these sentences composition programs become objects to be given and taken away, allowed to go and come. Then, he asserts that "composition ought to stay in English departments, not to help composition but to help English departments. It's good for them to have the composition people."

Miller's response to Olson's obvious question (Why should we stay where we are treated with contempt?) is simply astounding: Composition programs might be "weaker from the point of view of having clout with the administration, getting money.... [Composition] does gain something from having the strong budgetary support of an English department." Composition programs in state universities, staffed by part-time faculty who have no benefits, merit pay, or hope of tenure, do not seem to me to have gained very much from the budgetary support of English departments. These programs do make money, however, and English departments have gained much (release time, research leave, low teaching loads for persons who do not teach writing) from *that* strong economic support. This exchange is more persuasive as a discussion of symbolic capital: the English department lends the prestige of the humanities to composition's service function. On the whole, though, I find actual capital more useful: I wholeheartedly support his recommendation of "a stated separate budget for composition within the English Department to secure the support for composition."

To perceive composition studies as having both a research and a service function (analogous with literary studies) would probably require changing the name and the institutional identity of the English department. Composition studies can be seen as central to the conceptual project of departments of semiotics or departments of rhetoric or departments of cultural studies, but not to traditional departments of English. Any of these names, and any of the corresponding shifts in the hierarchical structures of value, would be good for compositionists. But when Olson asks whether Miller believes that the future of literary criticism and the English department itself lies in departments of rhetoric, Miller's reply preserves the traditional notion of English departments with the traditional privileged position for literary studies. Such departments, he says, have obligations to teach literary history, and that "could only with difficulty be put under the rubric of rhetoric." Are we to infer that he believes that literary histories are in some sense *not* rhetoricized? Pressed, Miller is "prepared to say that that's *part* of rhetoric, but it's obviously stretching it a little bit." But if, like Kenneth Burke, Miller believes that "literature ought to matter to individual human life or to society," then surely departments of English should look at how the writing of literary history has excluded the "works by women and so-called minorities" who now appear on the Ph.D. exams at Irvine (even when the candidate is male), and compositionists with their exciting "methodological and theoretical" tools should "be there." And although Miller grants the "obligation to teach an understanding of ethnic communities within the larger community," he thinks that "to call this rhetoric might unnecessarily limit it." But then, a curious turn: texts, Miller says, are best taught by *reading*—"that's where rhetoric, a rhetorical approach, is necessary... [and] there's a kind of link... a natural alliance... between the young people who do literary theory ... and the people who do composition theory ... something a good department would want to advance."

Here is what I see happening. Three terms—*rhetoric, reading*, and *composition*—are in play. *Reading* is the privileged term; *composition* is reduced and contained. *Rhetoric* is presented by Olson as a bridge term, one that entails the other two, forming a synthesis in which writing and reading, understood deconstructively, could operate together "responsibly" to produce the reformed institution Miller calls for in which "teaching and writing about literature and culture [are seen] as being an active intervention." But Miller opposes adopting the term *rhetoric* to name the reformed, reconceived English department, and he brings in the stretching and limiting opposition to say how. But the stretching and limiting of "rhetoric" becomes an aporia in which I get (first) lost and then (of course) very interested. If rhetoric is "the investigation of figures of speech, rather than the art of persuasion, though the notion of persuasion is still present," how would it be "limiting" to ask how women, "so-called minorities," and canonical figures find, in any situation (literary and non-literary), the available means of persuasion? And how would it be "stretching" rhetoric to investigate how these texts are included, excluded, and otherwise appropriated into literary (or any) histories? The "natural alliance" between literary theory and composition theory has as its project to investigate how language makes selves (or subject positions), knowledge, and value. The advantage (to composition studies) of the renamed department is that the renaming would, in the context of the generational change Miller describes in this interview, tend to efface the tropes of containment that have governed us and our work for so long. It would also provide an institutional venue for addressing questions of what Miller calls the "ideality of the literary object" by investigating the generic boundaries of the literary as well as opportunities to look at the rhetorical construction of knowledge.

It's hard to see why Miller opposes the naming, and the more he explains, the more confusing he gets. Olson asks how, having deconstructed the writing/reading opposition and thereby permitted us all to see how "reading is itself a kind of writing, or writing is a trope for the act of reading," Miller would prevent composition from being resubsumed under "English as reading." He responds by urging us to "persuade the rest of the English department that it's their responsibility to teach reading." "Composition people," he says, "have got to depend to some degree on the people in the English department and other language departments to do some, if not most, of the teaching of reading," even in the sense that includes writing. But then (is he changing his mind?): "Insofar as that's a *rhetorical* skill, it goes along with Stanley [Fish's] suggestion that they ought to be called departments of rhetoric." Even within what Miller calls "rhetorical reading," he seems still to preserve the hierarchy in which literary studies is privileged over composition.

This privilege is legible in Miller's surprising response to the question about whether he considers himself a writer. His demurral suggests that he reserves the name "writer" for authors of literary texts. There seems to be a quadripartite division in Miller's use of the term. First, there are Writers: artists, like George Eliot, William Carlos Williams, and Wallace Stevens, in whose company he does not count himself. Then, in an MLA President's column reprinted in *Theory Now and Then*, Miller distinguishes a "primary writer" like Blanchot from "the more humble metier of 'secondary writing' as you or I might be obligated to practice it" (301). After Writers like George Eliot, primary writers like Blanchot and secondary writers like Hillis Miller and the rest of us, we have (presumably) students in freshman comp and ESL classes.

How might one understand this quadripartite class system in the context of institutionalized English departments? A further gloss is perhaps available in *Versions of Pygmalion*, wherein Miller approvingly quotes Henry James' belief "that writing, say writing *The Golden Bowl*, is a thing done that does other things in its turn," and he wonders, "In what sense is reading novels, poems or philosophical texts, teaching them, or writing about them a thing done that does other things in its turn?" (15). His answer seems to be that such privileged Writing promotes ethical reading, an obligatory activity that "means a suspension of other responsibilities and contractual obligations, to my family, my institution, to my students and colleagues, whose 'secondary' texts I have a perpetually mounting obligation to assess" (19). And ethical reading can promote teaching. Teaching is "the public expression or allegory . . . of the act of reading." And "you teach in the way you've learned that you ought to." This notion of teaching as the replication of cultural value through institutional authority inevitably relegates professional attention to the production of texts as a "secondary" activity performed on secondary texts by secondary people.

The notion that teaching composition is "making people able to write" sustains these institutions of authority. But then, late in the interview, Miller makes a surprising turn: "The key to teaching writing probably is to convince students that . . . they're in some kind of situation that they've got to write their way out of." This "ethical" account of teaching writing strikes me as quite wonderful (even though Miller draws all his examples from literary texts) and quite at odds with his positions elsewhere in the interview.

A Question of Ethics
Many thinkers and teachers who choose to call themselves compositionists share Miller's belief that "quite a lot is at stake in the choice of what you study in a course, in what you write about, and in how you do it." And it is for that reason that so many of us are looking critically at the rhetorical construction of the disciplines and giving careful critical attention to teaching the ways in which those constructions reduce and exclude people. Attention to the work

of rhetoricians like Chaim Perelman and Stephen Toulmin has prompted compositionists to call into question the very conception of disciplinarity as a traditional system of procedures and techniques for testing answers to paradigmatic questions. Researchers in composition borrow procedures from several disciplines, but they do not always use them in traditionally sanctioned ways. Rather, like Kenneth Burke, they "go off in all directions" seeking post-disciplinary solutions to concrete problems. Miller would, I suspect, find those "composition persons" useful allies in his argument with the philosophers who accuse him of crossing disciplinary boundaries to study and "transform" Kant's *Critique*. Instead, although it seems to be okay for him to read philosophy deconstructively, he worries about "younger," postmodern thinkers who lack formal disciplinary training in the fields they study. He implies that he finds it irresponsible of them not to train themselves in the disciplines at issue.

It seems to me that Miller most often applies the adjective *responsible* to courses of action that preserve the status quo. Those whom the institution has treated well tend to think of it as responsible and want to preserve it. But those who do not perceive themselves as having been treated well by the institution tend to see its behavior as irresponsible and to seek alternatives. I honor Hillis Miller's contributions toward making our institution more responsible than it is, but he must know that for *ethical* reasons, many "composition people" may decide—soon—no longer to "be there."

University of Toledo
Toledo, Ohio

Works Cited

Harkin, Patricia. "For Its Own Sake: Humanizing Composition Studies." *Works and Days* 8 (1986): 79-91.

Miller, J. Hillis. "The Function of Rhetorical Study at the Present Time." *Theory Now and Then.* Durham: Duke UP, 1991. 201-16.

——. *Theory Now and Then.* Durham: Duke UP, 1991.

——. *Versions of Pygmalion.* Cambridge and London: Harvard UP, 1990.

Learning About Learning About Deconstruction: An Epi(tryingtobe)gone

Jasper Neel

Hillis Miller has been a friend to composition studies for fifteen years. He has repeatedly and successfully used his great influence to make research in the teaching of writing legitimate. And I take great pride in saying that Hillis Miller has been a good friend to me. In 1980 when I was teaching at Francis Marion College, a small liberal arts college in South Carolina, I received an NEH research fellowship. In the proposal that won me the fellowship, I admitted that I knew little about "Theory," but I explained my hunch that "Theory" might offer a way to bridge the broadening chasm between literature and composition, an accomplishment that seemed important to me (and apparently to NEH) at the time. I decided to spend my leave in New Haven, for New Haven in 1980 was where "Theory" was being written and spoken. One could stand on the sidewalk outside Naples Pizza—the noontime gathering spot for the "Yale School"—and read the pun that someone had inscribed in the wet concrete, "Derrida *etais ici.*" *Deconstruction and Criticism* was hot off the press, and English departments were abuzz with a sense of life that we baby boomers (at least this baby boomer) had not seen before.

Linda Peterson, who was still an untenured assistant professor at Yale, arranged quarters for me in Branford College, where I settled down for a four-month stay. I approached Geoffrey Hartman and Hillis Miller by explaining that I wanted to know more about pedagogy. Miller and Hartman, of course, were wise enough to know that "Theory" would remain sterile if it did not affect pedagogy: "Theory is of no use," as Miller puts it in his interview with *JAC*, "unless it's used for something," even if "using it means changing it." In my first meetings with Hartman and Miller, I explained that I wanted to try to write a book linking theory in general and deconstruction in particular to the field of composition studies. I was astonished (I remain astonished even today) that two such eminent scholars—they literally had the academic world at their door in those days—would take the time to help an obscure assistant professor from an obscure college work in a field that seemed quite remote from Yale. Neither of them knew me very well, and neither had any obligation to me whatsoever, yet both were exceedingly kind. They invited me to their seminars, took me to lunch, introduced me to Harold Bloom and Paul de Man, and generally opened the doors of Yale intellectual life to me. Miller even invited me to his home. By the end of my stay, Miller and I had begun meeting occasionally at my apartment in Branford for a run up Prospect Hill to the Divinity School; on one occasion we went for a run through the countryside near his farmhouse.

Without the letters of recommendation from Hartman and Miller that grew out of my four-month stay in New Haven, I would never have been able to move from Francis Marion to Northern Illinois (a university with a Ph.D. program in rhet/comp); without the education I received at Yale, I would never have been able to write *Plato, Derrida, and Writing*; without that book I would not have gotten tenure at Northern Illinois and certainly never would have ended up at Vanderbilt. Thus, my personal debt to Hillis Miller is profound. He (and his colleague Geoffrey Hartman) opened the way that has become my career (a career that, though certainly modest by the standards of Hillis Miller, nevertheless astonishes me). Indeed, all of us in composition studies owe Hillis Miller a debt because he has used his influence and his many national positions (including his presidency of the MLA) to make our work legitimate.

I remember the months at Yale fondly. Hanging around with the "Yale School" and seeming to be "in the know" was exhilarating. More particularly, however, I remember two conversations with Miller that occurred near the end of my stay. Those conversations (which I am sure Miller does not remember) have become a metonomy both for my own relationship with deconstruction and for my concern about the effect deconstruction has on composition studies. Before each conversation, I spent several days working through my understanding of the term *deconstruction*. Once I had my thoughts "straight," I inflicted myself on Miller long enough to articulate those thoughts. Each time, Miller replied thoughtfully and patiently that my notions were insightful and interesting, but not quite correct; and he went on to point out weaknesses, oversimplifications, and gaps in my reading. A few days before leaving New Haven to return to South Carolina, where I would resume teaching basic writing to poorly prepared students at my brand new (established in 1975) commuter college, I was preparing myself for a third and final try at articulating my notions of deconstruction. In doing so, I finally realized both what Miller was trying to teach me *and* what he was trying not to teach me.

On the one hand, Miller was trying to teach me that deconstruction—insofar as it labels something as diverse as the reading strategies of Bloom, de Man, Derrida, Hartman, and Miller—is not a term or name that can bring order and hence peace to one's intellectual life. Nor is it a methodology that will organize and inform daily pedagogy. In short, my logocentric, highly authoritarian strategy for "defining" deconstruction was itself a misunderstanding *of* deconstruction. My desire to "name" and "understand" deconstruction demonstrated my own intellectual shortcomings.

On the other hand, Miller was trying to conceal from me my role as the mark in a shell game. As one of the reigning gurus of deconstruction, Miller could not allow a bandwagon rider to define the term, for once such an epigone succeeded in defining deconstruction, the definer him- or herself could begin making decisions about the value of deconstruction. In other words, once "deconstruction" became a normalized, domesticated "activity" speakable by one of its epigones, deconstruction would be indistinguishable from "existentialism," "structuralism," or any other twentieth-century term that, having been tamed, has ossified.

A Doubled Need

This double situation—on the one hand learning about deconstruction while on the other learning about learning about deconstruction—led then and leads now to a nightmarish conundrum. How does a group—any group, no matter what its size—decide to privilege a few important voices while silencing all of the other voices? Of course, this is not a new conundrum; even in fourth-century Athens, the most radical democracy the world has yet known, only one percent of the people on the Pnyx actually spoke with influence and authority. To be who he was in 1980, Hillis Miller needed me (well, not me personally but someone to play the role "learner"). In an opposed way, I needed Hillis Miller then and continue to need him now so that I can play the role "student" or, for purposes of this text, "respondent." Unfortunately, this doubled need for teacher and pupil foregrounds metonymically the field in which I work. Composition studies seems to need Hillis Miller (or Richard Rorty, or Stanley Fish, or Mary Field Belenky, or whomever) in order to have something to say to itself. While composition studies most emphatically does not need "leading intellectuals" to have work to do—the students come by the millions each fall—composition studies does seem to need "leading intellectuals" to have something to say about what it does.

As the *JAC* interviews make plain, some voices deserve to be heard above all the others, and none of the voices that deserve to be heard lives in the body of a rhet/comp person. Few would dispute that Miller's is one of the voices that deserve to be heard, just as few would dispute Miller's claim that Derrida, Heidegger, Husserl, and Hegel are other voices that deserve to be heard. "Some people," as Miller puts it, "are better readers than others." The best readers, like Miller or Derrida, always ask us to allow them a certain authorial space. "Try to notice," Miller asks, "whether I might conceivably not be speaking for myself but doing what any literary critic has to do: trying to speak for the author that I'm discussing or even for some imagined position which I'm then going to differ from." *"Caveat lector,"* as Hartman puts it, because the texts of the "boadeconstructors" are always situated (Bloom, et al. ix). And the situation of their texts, Miller explains in his interview, prevents any sort of straightforward reading:

People will say that Derrida talks about "the free play of language in the void" or something, and you go back and find he's really talking about Lévi-Strauss in that passage and the formulation is only made possible by the reading of the particular author. I think it's often forgotten in what you might call pedagogical accounts of Derrida, accounts used in teaching him, that almost all his work is the reading of some text or other. That's certainly true of my own work.

With its space secure and its "meaning" complicated far beyond any sort of summary, a privileged voice such as Miller's can then be free to make the standard demands: responsibility, tradition, truth, democracy.

Miller warns against the irresponsibility of undertaking cultural studies without knowing the necessary original languages or the "protocols of social science research"; he requires that anyone undertaking a study of any intellectual phenomenon (deconstruction in particular) study its history back through several centuries; he insists on such notions as "truth and falsehood" and "good and bad readings"; and he insists that both he and Derrida want "to use deconstructive thinking as a way to imagine the possible movement toward a better form of democracy." Thus, he assumes the role of spokesperson for and defender of academic responsibility, historical integrity, truth, goodness, and democracy. And in a typically American way, he assumes this role with an air of humility, refusing to call himself a writer and claiming to be no more than a teacher: "My writing is an adjunct to teaching. Though it's something I do seriously, I think *writer* is too big a word for what I do."

I suspect that most people who have known Miller would grant him all these titles. Though he is an aggressive, tenacious opponent, even his bitterest professional antagonists would be likely to grant that he is humble and that he does stand for responsibility, integrity, truth, goodness, and democracy. In light of all this—in light of responsibility, integrity, truth, goodness, democracy, and humility, especially when those traits are joined with my personal and everyone's professional obligations to Miller—how am I to "respond"?

By pointing out the danger.

A Danger to Composition

The danger, as I have already argued in responding to Derrida's *JAC* interview two years ago, is both real and significant. Were the notions Miller and Derrida articulate to prevail, composition studies would become philosophical literary criticism. As he made clear in his 1990 interview, Derrida is "on the side of philosophy"; he stands foursquare against sophistry and a free-standing rhetoric. Rhetoric "as a separate discipline," he fears, "may become a sort of empty instrument whose usefulness or effectiveness would be independent of logic, or even reference or truth." "Contrary to what some people think I think," Derrida continues, "I would be on the side of philosophy, logic, truth, reference, etc." While warning about the danger of oversimplifying, Derrida nevertheless says, "If the sophists are what Plato thinks they are, I'm not in favor of the sophists" (16-17). In language almost identical to Derrida's, Miller carefully separates both himself and deconstruction from sophistry—whether the sophistry of Protagoras and Gorgias, or that quite different sophistry of *Protagoras* and *Gorgias*. "I would be more willing," Miller picks up Derrida's language, "to say that *Plato* is the founder of deconstruction than to say the sophists were." Though Miller, like Derrida, warns that we know very little about the sophists, he draws a clear distinction between deconstruction and sophistry, arguing that the texts of Protagoras and Gorgias bear "no relation to what deconstructionists say." Miller hedges this by directing us to "go back and read Plato"; if we do, Miller assures us, we will see that Plato is "not what [we've] been led to expect."

Well, I *have* gone back and read Plato. I even learned Greek, in part because I know what Miller thinks of scholars who cannot read a text in its original language. And I found *exactly* what I expected. Through his Socrates, Plato creates the voice with which Jacques Derrida and Hillis Miller speak. And the metaphysics of that voice privileges thinking over speaking, speaking over writing, philosophy over rhetoric, and truth over sophistry. If composition studies decides to speak with Plato's voice, composition research will embark on an unending journey toward truth, a journey that no mortal can ever complete; as a result, composition studies will be indistinguishable from philosophy or literary criticism. Indeed, the discursive practices and analytic strategies used in composition studies will grow directly out of Platonic hermeneutics, leaving composition studies forever trapped in the role Aristotle gives it, the role of *paraphues*, a doubly dependent, mixed metaphor type of offshoot—an inquiry unable to sustain itself without the root and branch systems of literary criticism and philosophy (*Rhetoric* 1356^{a}20-35). Thus, when Miller calls for composition to remain in English departments on "principled reasons," he is being absolutely honest. He does not seek the money that follows the teaching of writing; rather, he seeks the utterly Platonic intellectual enterprise in which communication lags behind and serves thinking, thereby allowing thinking to remain prior to and independent of its vehiculation, thereby giving truth a never-quite-realized but entirely safe residence. With such truth safely privileged, teachers can discharge their "responsibilities" by "displaying" what they "know."

Call an intellectual a sophist, in other words, and—even if the intellectual is a "boadeconstructor" like Hillis Miller or Jacques Derrida—you will have a fight on your hands. "Sophist" is the one thing an honest, truthful, clear-thinking, responsible intellectual cannot be.

Philosophy, however, is not the only danger Miller's reclamation of composition entails, for he has a very particular notion of rhetoric, a notion that he has consistently made clear at least since 1979. Miller defines rhetoric as the study of figures of speech. This definition, it seems to me, generates two possible responses. One response would be to point out that in the strictest, most classical terms, Miller makes rhetoric into a subset of itself. At least since Aristotle, rhetoric has consisted of five canons (invention, arrangement, style, memory, and delivery) and three appeals (ethos, pathos, and logos). If Miller had his way, this classical rhetoric (the sort of rhetoric that Burke, Corbett, Horner, Lunsford, Perelman, Toulmin and numerous others have tried to articulate recently) would be reduced to one part of one part. Invention, arrangement, memory, delivery, ethos, pathos, logos, and most of style would be gone. The study of metaphor (which is only one part of style) would be left. I do not know one single rhetorician or composition studies person who would consider such a reduction wise. Asking rhetoric to undergo such radical surgery would be like asking literary criticism to pay attention only to lyric poetry, leaving to others everything from novels, plays, and films to nonfiction prose and longer poetry. A second response to Miller's reduction of rhetoric to a subset of itself would be to point out that Miller changes rhetoric into a particular kind of philological hermeneutics. While one can easily imagine a rhetoric with this focus, all of us who learned to teach writing by teaching New Criticism in the 1970s know how sterile and ineffective this focus would make our pedagogy.

A Question of Pedagogy

So, how might I reconcile my genuine feelings of debt and my unquestioned high regard for Hillis Miller as a friend and advocate with my reservations about his notions of what composition ought to do? Unseemly as it will be, I will say that Miller simply does not understand (and of course I recognize the statistical probability that I am doing nothing more than trying to reverse roles with him so that I can prevent his occupying any location from which he might speak). I will offer two examples.

The first example has to do with pedagogy. By 1986 Miller had already weighed in against "libertarian pedagogy." Then, as now, Miller saw teaching as an interchange between the teacher and a text. Students are not "partners" in the interchange; rather, they are "witnesses or overhearers." Miller fears a pedagogy in which teachers engage directly in an interchange with their students, a pedagogy "in which the students all say what they want and the teacher just facilitates this." Such pedagogy "frees" the teacher from the teacher's major responsibility, Miller argues, and obviates the sort of display that Miller equates with good teaching.

What Miller does not seem to understand is that the only meaningful texts in the composition class already belong to the students. One cannot teach composition by "displaying" one's "interaction with the text at hand" because no "text at hand" exists as an object of study whose power and beauty allow for a professional explication. While one can imagine a composition classroom in which a teacher "displays" the teacher's "activity of reading" as the teacher "interacts" with a representative student paper, I doubt that anyone would take such pedagogy seriously. What Miller has in mind, indeed what Miller cannot see beyond, is the demonstrative explication of a canonized text. That, for him, *is* teaching. Anything other than that falls into the category of irresponsible professional behavior. Incredibly, Miller claims that libertarian pedagogy was already at work in the Yale English department thirty years ago. In those days, William Wimsatt and his colleagues merely assigned topics and sat back to listen as the students did the teaching. Is it possible that Miller cannot see the difference between graduate seminars at Yale in the early sixties and Jane Tompkins' classes at Duke today? No one at Yale, least of all the students, thought the students were free to express themselves or make up their own educations. Students at Yale in 1960 were doing everything in their power to imitate Wimsatt; that Wimsatt did little directly to show them what he wanted did not free them. Quite the contrary, it showed just how rigid his desires were. Those desires were so rigid, so clear, and so unassailable that no one needed to "demonstrate" them. I suspect that the only difference between Miller's pedagogy and Wimsatt's is that Miller demonstrates what he wants while Wimsatt left the students to figure it out for themselves.

The second example of the danger Miller offers comes at the end of his interview. After a long and interesting paragraph about the ethical dimension of writing, Miller ends by saying "I don't know that saying this ... will help at all in *teaching* writing." The reason his speculation probably won't help with *teaching* writing is that Miller is and always has been a literary critic. And, like it or not, literary criticism has less to do with teaching writing than do philosophy, linguistics, and anthropology and no more to do with teaching writing than do economics, management, or even civil engineering.

So, would it be rude to thank Hillis Miller (profusely and with genuine gratitude) for his help while completely ignoring his advice? I hope so. While an experienced, committed composition teacher can surely learn a great deal about how to do scholarship by looking at the way Miller does it, such a composition teacher must listen to Miller at all times with the acute awareness that the explication of canonized texts is probably the most indirect and least probable way of teaching writing. While one can surely teach writing through such demonstrative explication, one is much more likely to generate a pedagogy that excludes all those who cannot, like the Yale graduate students of the sixties, figure out all by themselves what the teacher wants.

Vanderbilt University
Nashville, Tennessee

Works Cited

Aristotle. *The "Art" of Rhetoric*. Trans. John Henry Freese. Cambridge: Harvard UP (Loeb), 1991.

Bloom, Harold, et al. *Deconstruction and Criticism*. New York: Seabury, 1979.

Derrida, Jacques. "Jacques Derrida on Rhetoric and Composition: A Conversation." *Journal of Advanced Composition* 10 (1990): 1-21.

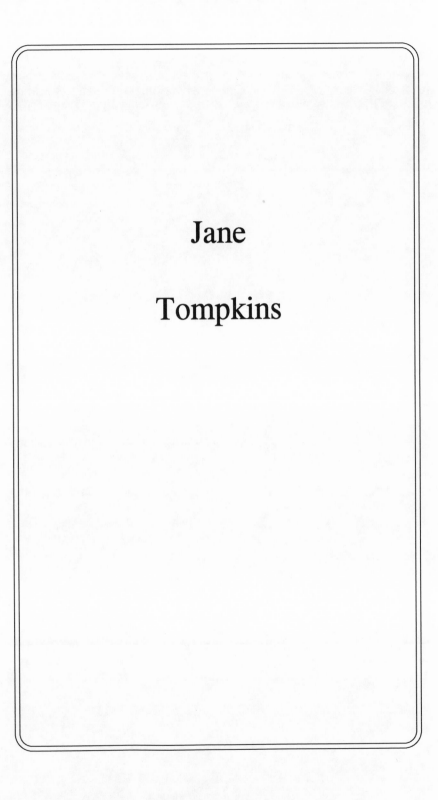

Jane

Tompkins

Jane Tompkins and the Politics of Writing, Scholarship, and Pedagogy

GARY A. OLSON

Jane Tompkins is intensely "aware of the extent to which *writing* for people in our profession is a kind of ego activity," and she likens this egoism to the kind of "performance model" of *teaching* she so roundly decries in her well-known "Pedagogy of the Distressed." In contrast, Tompkins sees writing as "a mode of self-refinement and self-development which is an end in itself." That is, she has "come to understand writing as a way that people like us have of taking care of ourselves." Not only is writing "almost like a grooming activity, or something that you do in the mode of self-care, like getting a massage or working out," but it's also a form of "self-discovery." Consequently, Tompkins is very serious about writing, both her own scholarly writing and the teaching of composition.

To assist in her own writing, Tompkins relies heavily on an Elbow-style writing group composed of two or three of her colleagues who provide "continual 'real world' feedback." In the interview recorded below, Tompkins says, "This writing group has been an essential aid in pushing me forward in the directions I need to go as a writer, and it has been a continual source of support in the process of composition." This is why she recommends writing groups "as a way not just to write but to exist in the academy." Similarly, Tompkins is enthusiastic about the field of rhetoric and composition and finds "enormously valuable" the "theoretical and practical writing about teaching rhetoric and composition that has been turned out in the last ten or fifteen years." In fact, she believes that "the most interesting thinking and ideas in higher education about classroom teaching come from the field of rhetoric and composition."

The fact that Tompkins has thought extensively about pedagogy over the last several years is reflected in this interview. She discusses legitimizing "personal response, private experience, as a source of knowledge," "coercing" students into taking responsibility for their own learning, and constructing "radical" or alternative kinds of classroom arrangements. Despite the apparent success of her experiments with radical pedagogy, Tompkins plans to move back toward a somewhat more traditional pedagogy so as to avoid the intensity, the "precariousness," the "conflict and supercharged stuff" that characterized her recent alternative classes: "What I'm going to strive for next fall is to create a situation in which there will be a greater degree of safety for the students and for me... because I think the safety itself is freeing in a way that this constant vertigo . . . is not." Nevertheless, she remains optimistic that "teaching reform is in the air and here to stay."

Tompkins discusses several other issues pertinent to composition, English studies, and academic life in general. Retreating from her previous rejection of reader-response criticism, she claims to have "come back around to believing in reader response as a great pedagogical approach to literary study" because she is "so interested in students now." Reader response is an important "way to put students at the center of the study of literature." And Tompkins characterizes right wing attempts to halt the expansion of the canon as "largely ineffectual" because the "demographics are against it": "I don't see people pulling back from assigning fiction by ethnic, black, or women writers on account of what Dinesh D'Souza and Lynne Cheney say." In addition, she elaborates on the "very painful and almost crippling" divide between "the scholarly and the personal" perpetuated by the patriarchal academy, and she says that women need to "heal" themselves and to "heal that division." She blames her anger at "the male critical establishment" and her "sense of injured merit, deprivation and resentment" for causing her to buy into the atmosphere of "extreme status-consciousness and the desire to scramble up the ladder that is so palpable at professional conferences." But before such destructive competitiveness will cease, argues Tompkins, "The culture of the institution is what needs to change."

Agreeing with Noam Chomsky that the move away from patriarchy is "an evolutionary development," Tompkins argues that "we're attaining a much more flexible, sophisticated, and subtle understanding of gender and sex." This increased understanding is due both to the woman's movement *and*, she is careful to point out, to the men's movement. Says Tompkins, "I tend to think that the men's movement is a natural evolutionary outgrowth of the women's movement, that if the women's movement is going to succeed at all it is absolutely necessary for there to be a change in the way men conceive of themselves along the lines now being laid out in the men's movement...."

Jane Tompkins' strong commitment to writing, to teaching, to students and their personal development makes her an important ally to those of us in rhetoric and composition. She has struggled with many of the same questions about composition, pedagogy, teacher authority, collaborative writing groups, and survival on the margins of the academy. Tompkins says that she feels "indebted" to compositionists, "especially for their pedagogical experimentation and insight." Perhaps her own experimentation and insight will be of use to us in our continued search for more effective pedagogies.

Q. Clearly, you pay a good deal of attention to your writing. Especially in your most recent work, you've been attempting to subvert traditional ways of writing scholarship. In contrast to the typical sterile, voiceless academic prose, your scholarly writing is warm, inviting, and intensely personal. Do you think of yourself as a writer?

A. Yes I do, but only very recently have I thought of myself that way. It's a great pleasure to think that I *can* think of myself as a writer because, like most people who go into literature, I suppose I admired writers excessively and looked up to them. Although I didn't realize while I was in graduate school and for the first twenty years of teaching that I really aspired to be a writer more than a critic, now that I've made this crossover, I'm absolutely delighted. Let me say, though, that I think it's a false dichotomy: a scholar/critic versus a writer. It's a dichotomy we've been sold in some way by the tradition we work in, and it's not useful to us anymore. One sign that it's no longer useful is the quantity of autobiographical writing that is appearing—not just from women, but from men as well. And men respond to this kind of writing just as much as women do. (Well, maybe not as many men do, but many men respond very positively to it, and some are practicing it.) So, now that I think of myself as a writer, I want to encourage everybody who goes to graduate school and engages in the kind of writing that we do in graduate school to think of themselves that way, too, because I think it can only enhance the reach and quality of the work that gets done.

Q. Would you describe your writing process? Do you use a word processor? Are you a continual reviser?

A. Well, once I used to write longhand, and then I used a typewriter, and then (actually fairly early on) I switched to the computer. I was a very slow writer, extremely slow, and I felt that the technology of the computer would allow me to revise better. I was a compulsive reviser, though much less so now than say twelve years ago. I got a computer in 1981, and I got it precisely because I revised so much and therefore had to be constantly retyping. I was looking for something that would relieve me of that. What I found was what everyone told me I would find: that the benefit is not simply in the ease with which you can revise, but rather in what it does to your process of composition. That is, the initial writing itself is freed up by the things the computer makes easy. Whether it's just because of the difference in the writing technology or because (probably more likely) I've had a considerable degree of success (my writing has met with a lot of positive response), I write much more easily now, and sometimes I don't have to revise much at all. So, the *kind* of writer I am has changed with the change in my status and in my self-confidence. My book *West of Everything* was put forward by Oxford for a Pulitzer Prize in the category of nonfiction. I found this out a few weeks ago, and damned if I haven't been able to stop myself from writing since then. I think it's one of maybe hundreds of nominations, but anyway Oxford picked it for *its* submission. I guess what I'm saying is that your writing process, in my experience, is very much a function of your psychological, technological, and other circumstances.

I'm just beginning to change my notion of the role writing has in my life now, and I can't predict exactly how it's going to turn out in the end, but in a sense it's parallel to the change that's taken place in my teaching. Just as I've tried to step back from what I call the "performance model" of *teaching*, where your ego is very much at stake, to a different mode where presumably your ego is not so much on the line (although, in fact, it still is), I've become more aware of the extent to which *writing* for people in our profession is a kind of ego activity. I'm not in the least degree free from that myself, but the recognition that that's the case makes me question somewhat the role that writing has played for me. It may be that I will write less in the future and try to change the arena of my activities from writing to what you might call *action*—that is, doing things. I've been smitten with Natalie Goldberg's books, *Writing Down the Bones* and *Wild Mind*, and in so far as I understand it, writing for her is what she calls "a practice" akin to the practice of meditation. (She's a Zen Buddhist and her whole understanding of what writing is comes out of her Zen background.) In that way of thinking, writing becomes a mode of self-refinement and self-development which is an end in itself, and so the product or performance dimensions of it become secondary or perhaps not important at all. I think all of us in our profession use writing in that way whether we know it or not.

I don't know whether Goldberg talks about this since I haven't read everything in those books, but I've recently come to understand writing as a way that people like us have of taking care of ourselves. When we can't get to our writing, we feel deprived and we feel hungry for it, not just because we're afraid we won't get our articles written so that we won't get our job or our promotion (although certainly those fears apply), but because there's a need that we have to perform this activity *for ourselves*. It's almost like a grooming activity, or something that you do in the mode of self-care, like getting a massage or working out. It's a form of attention that seems to be directed outward toward an object outside of yourself, but somehow the effect strangely is to have attended to yourself in some way. That's the way I'm coming to understand it. To that degree, I don't know that I'll be able to give up writing very easily.

I also see writing as a form of self-development and self-discovery, as a way you can come to know yourself and learn about yourself, or just as a mode of learning pure and simple. In that regard, my sort of proof text is a line from Robert Pirsig's *Zen and the Art of Motorcycle Maintenance*: "The motorcycle you're working on is the motorcycle of yourself." When Pirsig talks in an extended passage in that novel about something he calls "gumptionology," which is the science of what it takes to fix a motorcycle, I read that as being about writing and have always so read it. That approach to writing—that is, you think you're working on the motorcycle and you're really working on yourself—is one that I've recently come to.

Q. Many scholars insist on having colleagues read their work before submitting it for publication. It seems that one advantage you may have being in Duke's English department is the careful reading of any number of prominent scholars. Do you share drafts of your work with your colleagues?

A. I have a writing group that has been in existence for five years now, and those are my "main men," so to speak (they're all women), the people to whom I show my work and from whom I get the feedback that helps me write. This writing group has been an essential aid in pushing me forward in the directions I need to go as a writer, and it has been a continual source of support in the process of composition—a process that otherwise is extremely lonely.

Q. So, you get together to read and respond to each other's drafts?

A. Our format has changed over the years: we expanded from three to four, and that meant some changes; then, because the group was bigger, it wasn't working out so well and we changed again. We meet every two or three weeks at the house of one or another of us. Right now we're in a mode in which we don't read anything in advance; we just bring our work to group. Only two people are on in any given day so that there's enough time to be given to each person's work. Right now we're supposed to keep the meeting to two hours—one person gets an hour and then the other person gets an hour—but it's usually prefaced by a half an hour of conversation in which we try to catch up with one another, find out what's going on in each other's lives, talk department gossip, or say whatever we need to get off our chests. In the very beginning of the group, which I formed as a result of reading Peter Elbow's *Writing with Power*, we had some protocols about the kinds of feedback that were or weren't appropriate to give, and now and then we review this. Basically, people ask for the kind of feedback they want to have on a given day, and they can also ask specific questions that they want us to answer. For all the members, the group has been a mainstay and a wonderful help, but this isn't to say that the group hasn't had a lot of problems and that we don't have to stop from time to time and talk about what's been going on among us and what our gripes are and what we'd really like to be getting out of it. We're about to do that again when we all get back from vacation.

Q. So there's continual attention paid to the social dynamics of the group as well as to the writing that's brought into the session.

A. That's only slightly overstated. That is, we have slowly learned that it is necessary to pay attention to those dynamics, that they won't just take care of themselves, that things build up under the surface and we have to talk them out and deal with them one way or another. I think we're getting to the point where we can anticipate them a little better. I strongly recommend writing groups as a way not just to write but to exist in the academy. It gives you a kind of base of support that is both personal and institutional, as well as continual "real world" feedback for what you're doing. Also, the earlier you can show something to somebody, the better off you are as far as I'm concerned. We show each other the absolute raw stuff as it comes out, and that's the best way to do it.

Q. As someone who has obviously done a considerable amount of thinking about teaching and writing, what are your thoughts about the future of rhetoric and composition as a discipline?

A. I'm afraid I don't have too many thoughts per se about that, since I have not been trained in the field of rhetoric and composition. I've taught composition for about fifteen years, but I did it in a "seat of the pants" way. I received no training in it and just did it the best I could. My views are of a person who isn't particularly well informed. I'm very glad that the field of rhetoric and composition has come into its own, which I think it has in the last five or ten years, that it's now recognized as a legitimate territory of knowledge. I think that it's enormously valuable to have the kinds of theoretical and practical writing about teaching rhetoric and composition that has been turned out in the last ten or fifteen years as a resource for people who do that day to day. And in my fairly recent experience in getting to know what's going on in pedagogy across the country, I have found that the most interesting thinking and ideas in higher education about classroom teaching come from the field of rhetoric and composition. In my mind, there's no doubt about that. I feel indebted to people who have been working in that field, especially for their pedagogical experimentation and insight.

Q. In criticizing your own education you write, "It took massive doses of repressive cynicism and academic cool administered continuously throughout graduate school to dampen my ardor for big subjects, moral commitment, and quasi-religious enthusiasm about literature. But I learned to hide my feelings about what I read, especially from myself, and to transmute the energy into work that was acceptable." How do we construct a pedagogy in which "feelings" and emotions play a major role? And, then, how do we justify it to critics?

A. It may sound surprising, but I've never really thought about it in those terms. I did teach the course several years ago when I was beginning the experimentation on emotion that I write about in "Pedagogy of the Distressed." It was a feminist theory course on the subject of emotion. I have never taught a more traumatic course in my entire life. I've tried some pretty radical things since then, but nothing was as traumatic as that course. It was a double whammy in the sense that it was a women's studies course. From what I understand in talking to my colleagues in women's studies, often women's studies courses operate as a kind of escape valve for people's emotions which are unable to be expressed in other places in the university, and so they all get dumped into this one available outlet. So there was that going on; plus there was the open invitation I issued at the beginning of the semester for people to express their feelings; plus there was a certain chemistry in that particular group of people that produced a lot of conflict and supercharged stuff. All of those things added up to a pretty traumatic experience, although it was one from which I benefited enormously—and so, I think, did many other members of the class. While I'm not eager to rush out to greet such an experience again, I have to admit that it was not one that I want to put down because it was difficult.

How do you construct a pedagogy that allows for emotions? So far, I don't have any methods at all; in fact, I don't even announce it as a goal in my courses. But I do think it's important. I guess the way I attempt to incorporate emotions is to have personal experience count for a lot; personal response to literature (or whatever the subject matter) is to be central to any consideration of it. As soon as you have legitimized personal response, private experience, as a source of knowledge about a text, it seems to me you've also legitimized feeling or emotions, since at least for me the two are almost identical, although I'm sure they're not for everyone. I guess my answer, then, is not to remain within the established orbit of possible sources of knowledge about a given text but always to open that up to the experience of the individuals who happen to be in the room.

Q. And presumably such a pedagogy, given what you've written in "Pedagogy of the Distressed," would be much more student-centered and one in which you allow students the opportunity to take intellectual risks.

A. It's not so much the opportunity to take intellectual risks as it is that students are in effect being coerced into taking responsibility for their own learning. I prefer the word *responsibility*; they're forced by me because I step back and won't do it myself. The last experimental course I taught on the undergraduate level, which was last fall, was the most radical one that I've done because I did not provide the students with a syllabus. I did provide them with initial readings. We read a book and a couple of essays and discussed them in the first couple of weeks, but after that I just turned the course over to the students and said, "It's yours. We can read what you want; we can do what you want." This, too, was a somewhat traumatic course, though not like the emotions course was. There was a lot of fear involved for me. Every single day for about seven weeks (and that's a long time) my heart was in my throat when I walked into that class because I did not know what was going to happen, whether it was going to be a good or bad day, whether the experiment was working or not. It wasn't clear to me for the first seven weeks of the course whether it was working. Now, with *that* degree of precariousness (and the students felt it as well) come certain constraints. What I'm going to strive for next fall is to create a situation in which there will be a greater degree of safety for the students and for me, which I suppose means within certain limits a greater degree of predictability because I think the safety itself is freeing in a way that this constant vertigo, which was very exciting and wonderful in its way, is not.

Q. You say something like that in "Facing Yourself," that school should be a "safe" place like home: "Slowly, I've come to think school should be a different kind of place from what it's been, at least from the way it was for me. More like the way home was supposed to be. A safe place, somewhere where you belong, where you can grow and express yourself freely, and where people matter more than information and ideas."

A. Yes—if home *were* safe. That's the irony of this. In thinking about school, I tended to use home as the contrast, but in working on the book I'm now working on—which is about pedagogy, a section of which is devoted to my own early experiences in school—what I finally had to do in order to explain what was going on for me at school was to take myself home to see what was happening there. And lo and behold, I was terrified when I was at home, too. In many respects, home was a lot safer than school, but there were ways in which it wasn't safe or a good place for me either. So that's a construct I had been using that I now see has holes in it.

Q. In "Pedagogy of the Distressed" you criticize what you call the "performance model" of education that dominates our classrooms. In reaction to this traditional method of teaching, you advocate a type of liberatory learning based in part on Paulo Freire's radical pedagogy. You write, "I went from teaching as performance to teaching as a maternal or coaching activity because I wanted to remove myself from center stage and get out of the students' way, to pay more attention to them and less to myself." Does this mean that you view liberatory learning as a "feminist" or at least "female" pedagogy?

A. No, not in any essentialist way. I think that women may be more comfortable doing it or may gravitate toward it more readily than men, but I don't want to cordon it off and label it feminist or female because I don't want men to have any sense that it's off limits for them. The chapter called "Connected Teaching" in *Women's Ways of Knowing* has been extremely important for me and very validating; in fact, that whole book has been validating, and I feel very indebted to the work that those four women did. In many ways, the kind of teaching I do is, you might say, historically feminist, or by circumstances feminist. And it's probably because I *am* a woman that I'm doing it, but I don't see it at all as the province of women. In fact, I've found that many men are very interested in it, are already doing it in certain ways, have thought a lot about it, have written about it.

Q. You also discuss in "Pedagogy of the Distressed" the "antipedagogical indoctrination" that is so much a part of graduate education and the "fear of pedagogy" that predominates in the academy. Given the increasing attention scholars and educators are paying to student-centered approaches, do you believe this attitude is changing?

A. There certainly is a movement in higher education now that you might call a student-centered pedagogy movement (that's so ill phrased). I've been going to the meetings of a group called the Association of General and Liberal Studies; these are people interested in "general education." General education refers to the broad-based background in the liberal arts that students have traditionally gotten in their first two years of college or university. The people who attend this meeting are interested in various forms of liberatory pedagogy, especially teaching that goes under the name of "collaborative learning," "cooperative learning," the "decentered classroom," and various "non-authoritarian modes of learning." I find it extremely inspiring and invigorating to associate with these people, none of whom are at the top-ranked universities in this country and many of whom are administrators. Whether it constitutes an across-the-board movement is hard to say, but Harvard, Stanford, and such places now have elaborate centers for teaching and learning, and it's gotten to be the trend these days for upscale universities to institute teaching/learning centers and to have a variety of instruments that their faculty can use to upgrade and in various ways improve or fiddle around with their teaching. What this will amount to in reality, in actual change in classroom practice, I do not know. At the AGLS meeting I attended two years ago, the dean of a small college in Colorado talked about the fact that at her school she had sponsored innumerable activities directed toward changing classroom styles to less hierarchical modes, but when she walked the halls of the classroom buildings and looked into the classrooms, in room after room the students were sitting in their seats and the teacher was standing up in front of the class lecturing or writing on the blackboard. The physics of it hadn't changed. Although I could be wrong about this, I suspect that in most cases the physics of it still hasn't changed; the phenomenology is still pretty much the same. But having said that, teaching reform is in the air and here to stay; its course is yet to be run. It will be interesting to see what happens. I'm optimistic.

Q. In developing your own forms of student-centered pedagogy, you were influenced heavily by Freire. Some critics have claimed that Freire's writings and pedagogy are sexist and male oriented (though Freire does make an attempt in *JAC* to refute such charges by declaring his "camaraderie" with women and the women's movement). Do you see Freire's model as sexist? Do you believe there is a need to develop a distinctly female-oriented radical pedagogy?

A. Well, Freire can be criticized for a number of things in addition to sexism. For example, he uses high theoretical Marxist jargon, which is exclusionary; and he doesn't really admit the existence of his own revolutionary agenda, which is the whole motivation for everything he's doing. So, *there* are two "biggies" right there; plus, it is true that his language is sexist. But still and all, his notion that in order for people to be empowered education needs to be a practice of freedom is an incredibly powerful insight and has been enormously useful to me and to thousands of people. I'm very thankful to Freire and therefore loathe to criticize him for whatever his limitations might be. The answer to the second question, whether we need a radical pedagogy for women, has to depend on the circumstances in which you teach. As soon as I started to think and write about teaching, I became aware that teaching is always in a situation; it's always taking place in a certain time and place, with these people and not those people, under these conditions and so forth. Your pedagogy has to be accommodated or adapted to where you are. So I would say that a specifically feminist pedagogy would by all means be called for. For example, there's a project in North Carolina called "Motherread" which is helping pregnant mothers who are in high school become literate. It seems to me that if you don't have a feminist pedagogy for *that* you're really out to lunch. So I would say, yes, depending on the circumstances there may be a need for a specifically feminist approach.

Q. It strikes me that you frequently do what few scholars have the courage to do: to continually expose yourself in print, to make yourself vulnerable, to reveal your most private thoughts and fears. Could you elaborate on the role scholarship plays in your life and the reasons you incorporate such personal matters into your work? Do you consider this a feminist approach?

A. I have so mixed up the scholarly and the personal that I'm hardly willing to recognize the distinction anymore. I've gotten to the point where I can say that scholarship has no role in my life, and my life has no role in my scholarship. I really don't even want to carve the pie up in those pieces; it's not useful to me to do that. That's kind of an agenda, of course, as well—an agenda, again, that's specific to a time and place. It's something I've gotten caught up in in reaction to a certain history, and if I were differently situated, I might want to keep a rigid separation between my private life and my work because of some other chronology. But right now, for me and for a lot of women, the divide, the separation, has been very painful and almost crippling, and so now we're trying to heal ourselves, heal that division so that we don't feel that in our professional lives we have to somehow twist ourselves out of shape. Is it feminist? It's *de facto* feminist. That is, it's primarily women (at least in the last few years in this country) in our discipline who have done this sort of thing. But I think that the basic impulse is one that men can participate in and appreciate too. Although (because of the way women were socialized in this culture) it was more natural and inevitable that women would do this first and in greater numbers, there's nothing essentially female about it.

Q. In *New Literary History* you argue that we need to "speak personally in a professional context," especially in critical articles, because "to adhere to the conventions is to uphold a male standard of rationality that militates against women being recognized as culturally legitimate sources of knowledge." Given how academic power structures work, however, isn't such personal-oriented scholarship only possible for people such as yourself who have gained substantial stature in the field?

A. I've had people ask me that question a lot. In order for it to be legitimate for anybody, *somebody* has to do it. It's *safe* for me to do it because I do have a certain level of stature and so I'm *able* to. I hope to be making it safe and legitimate for other people to do it as well. When I'm asked that question, it always seems that there's a certain resentment or hostility behind it which I find it difficult to take responsibility for. Would people rather that I didn't do it? That's what's always behind this question.

Q. Noam Chomsky commented in *JAC* that "for cultural reasons, the move away from patriarchy is a step upwards, not just a change. It's a step toward understanding our true nature." Do you agree that the "move away from patriarchy" is occurring and, also, that such a move is "evolutionary"?

A. Yes, there is a movement away from patriarchy; that's pretty clear. Is it evolutionary? The term *evolution* is one that has a lot of baggage connected with it; there are different kinds of evolution that people talk about. He means it in a Darwinian way? I think it's *better* for us now to move away from patriarchal structures because of the kind of world we now live in. The historical circumstances that obtain for people in the sorts of societies that people like you and I inhabit seem to me to require some of the skills and attitudes toward life that have been, at least in the recent past, identified more with women than with men. I think that maybe, yes, quite in a Darwinian (that is to say a survivalistic) sense, it *is* an evolutionary development.

Q. Recently in *JAC*, Stanley Fish commented that "feminists who rely in their arguments on a distinction between male and female epistemology are wrong" because "there could not be such a distinction between ways of knowing." Do you agree?

A. I don't really think much about epistemology anymore. My thinking is not at that level. The question is what's behind a question like that? What are the real-world consequences of it? How does it play out in terms of what you do in the classroom or how you teach people to write or what sorts of models you give them? I think it's true that because women are socialized differently from infancy they find themselves much more comfortable in certain kinds of learning situations than in others. If you want to call that a difference in epistemology, I don't really care, but I think that in a *practical* sense it's true. I've experienced it myself; I've seen it. Belenky and her coauthors have pretty well proved that experientially women function somewhat differently from men (or *many* women function differently from *many* men) in certain kinds of learning situations. There's a huge amount of crossover, and you can't generalize, and some men are more like women in that respect, and vice versa; but yes, I think that there are differences in optimal learning environments for some men and some women.

Q. In "Saving Our Lives" you describe a women's studies meeting during which there was "a largely hostile discussion of the new men's movement." You report that you were "amazed at the glibness, almost blitheness, with which women were willing to dismiss men's pain in tacit favor of their own oppression." You then talk about "the terrible price men have had to pay for having a certain model of masculinity put before them." Certainly, it seems healthy to point out that both men and women are socialized into prescribed gender roles and suffer their own kinds of pain, but how do you answer the feminist response that at this point in time it is essential that women privilege and come to terms with their own pain, since this is exactly what has been suppressed for so long?

A. What I have to say about men's pain and the need to recognize it is not meant to preclude or in any way come before women's recognition of their own considerable distress and suffering, so the two are not mutually exclusive in any sense. I think the question arises from a feeling that social agendas may revert to former priorities if too much attention is paid to the men's movement. That's my sense of where these criticisms are coming from. I have a fairly optimistic reading of the men's movement. I tend to think that the men's movement is a natural evolutionary outgrowth of the women's movement, that if the women's movement is going to succeed at all it is absolutely necessary for there to be a change in the way men conceive of themselves along lines now being laid out in the men's movement, and that the welfare of women in large part is dependent upon the success of that development because we don't live in separate worlds; we're all part of the same social fabric. So, I don't think it's a correct analysis of the situation to say that if people pay attention to the men's movement the clock will be turned back thirty years. I could be wrong; it could be that the retrograde elements of the men's movement will become more and more prominent and will succeed in a more permanent than temporary backlash, but that's not my sense of the way it's going. I believe we're attaining a much more flexible, sophisticated, and subtle understanding of gender and sex than we had twenty-five or thirty years ago, and that's all to the good.

Q. Twelve years ago, you argued in *Reader-Response Criticism* that while reader-response critics defined their work as a radical departure from the values and principles of New Criticism, a close analysis demonstrates that they had not revolutionized critical theory "but merely transposed formalist principles into a new key." In retrospect, what do you believe is the contribution of reader-response criticism?

A. I'm coming back around actually. In a sense, I left reader-response criticism behind in 1980 when I published that book—I was going on to other things—but I've come back around to believing in reader response as a great pedagogical approach to literary study because I'm so interested in students now. What's happened is that the focus of my attention in the classroom has moved away from the subject matter to the students, and *they're* really what I see when I walk into the room. Reader-response criticism is a way to put students at the center of the study of literature, so I think its "contribution" is similar to that of feminist criticism, in that it legitimized a certain kind of personal response to literature (or whatever the subject matter might be) and so had a kind of integrative effect or performed a unifying function in terms of making a connection between peoples' lives and what went on inside classrooms in colleges and universities.

Q. Some years ago you wrote, "What is most striking about reader-response criticism and its close relative, deconstructive criticism, is their failure to break out of the mold into which critical writing was cast by the formalist identification of criticism with explication." Do you still believe that deconstructive criticism has failed to escape this formalist mold?

A. I wouldn't go along with that statement anymore. At least in some of its manifestations, deconstructive criticism has broken out of that mode. The example I'm thinking of, though, might not be accepted by anybody as deconstructive criticism: Hélène Cixous' *The Laugh of the Medusa*. I take that to be written in a deconstructive mode, or in a mode of discourse that was enabled by the writings of people like Derrida and Lacan. In effect, Derrida's writing freed language up in so dramatic a way from the conventions that had governed writing about literature that the eruptive and uncontrollable energy of the prose, and also of deconstruction's sense of language itself as sort of ceaselessly reproducing itself with a difference, made for kinds of writing that went beyond explication and crossed the line over into writing in the Barthesian sense, which is self-creation so to speak.

Q. Some critics have argued that deconstruction has outlived its usefulness.

A. I don't think that the insights of poststructuralism have yet been fully absorbed, even in the literary academy much less the culture at large. I think it's still alive and has a lot of work to do of the kind it has been doing for the last twenty-five or thirty years. Of course, history marches on. First you put down your right foot; then you put down your left foot. Has the right foot outlived its usefulness? Sure things are going to change, and deconstruction in its original form will no longer be able to cut any ice at a certain point, but it isn't for all of that something we should condescend to.

Q. In *West of Everything* you demonstrate that the western is an "answer" to the domestic novel, "the antithesis of the cult of domesticity that dominated American Victorian culture." In such novels, "the viewpoint women represent is introduced *in order* to be swept aside, crushed or dramatically invalidated," and women are in fact used to "legitimize the violence men practice in order to protect them." Why have you devoted so much of your professional energy to a genre that expresses such male violence and misogyny?

A. People have asked me that question before. They've asked, "What's a nice girl like you doing working on westerns." It's not an easy question to answer. First, it seemed a logical next step after having studied the major popular fictional forms of the nineteenth century, which are the women's novels. I think the major popular fictional form of the twentieth century has been these men's things in various forms of adventure stories—stories about gangsters, detectives, spies, science fiction heroes, and so forth—of which the western is kind of the key one. There is sort of a natural historical move from the one to the other. Another reason is that I think that the book for me was an attempt to come to terms with my own attitudes toward men. What happened in the end was that I recognized the extent to which I had, so to speak, become a man or had introjected the cultural imperatives that control male conduct in our society and that I'd done so in order to succeed or function in the academy. So what the book was in a way—not as I was doing it, but in retrospect—was an attempt on my part to recognize what I had done to myself or what I had become, an attempt to understand that and also to sympathize with it. That's why when I write about the western it's both with love and hate: I don't have a single attitude toward it.

Q. In *Sensational Designs* and much of your other work on American fiction, you attempt to open the canon, to "move the study of American literature away from the small group of master texts that have dominated critical discussion for the last thirty years." Do you believe recent attempts to open the canon are headed for success despite vocal attacks by the right wing?

A. It already has succeeded. The canon is radically different from what it was twenty years ago, and people everywhere are teaching all kinds of texts that wouldn't have been thought of previously. I think it's a *fait accompli*. The pressure from the right wing has been largely ineffectual, it seems to me—though not completely, as witnessed by what happened at the University of Texas. I don't see people pulling back from assigning fiction by ethnic, black, or women writers on account of what Dinesh D'Souza and Lynne Cheney say. To the extent that such pressure influences opinion and, therefore, has an effect on where funding goes and those sorts of things, I do think it is something to think about, but I think the demographics are against it. The racial and ethnic composition of the student body in colleges and universities is fact number one; the racial, ethnic, and gender composition of the professoriate is fact number two. These demographic trends are not reversing themselves; they're moving further in the same direction. The canon or the curriculum has followed demography, and it probably will continue to do so.

Q. You have frequently criticized the values and workings of the academic world. For example, in "Report from a Conference" you characterize our typical professional conferences as being pervaded by a "high-performance, dog-eat-dog atmosphere" in which "the who's in who's out game is being played with such ferocity that when you get on an elevator, you can cut the status consciousness with a knife." And in "Fighting Words: Unlearning to Write the Critical Essay," you claim that academics often engage in out-and-out violence: "ritual execution," "bloodlust," and intellectual "assassination." What is it about the academic environment that fosters this behavior? What realistic changes can we make?

A. Well, speaking for myself, I was most moved to behave in this way—which I certainly have done and haven't completely ceased doing—by a sense of injured merit, deprivation and resentment, a feeling that I had not received my just desserts. That made me angry and made me want to lash out at the establishment, which in my case took the form of attacking the male critical establishment that had controlled the canon and our approaches to it. So, generally speaking, I think it's out of a sense of personal injury of some kind that people engage in vicious polemical fights with one another, and it's also related to the extreme status-consciousness and desire to scramble up the ladder that is so palpable at professional conventions. Solving this problem would virtually mean bringing about some kind of utopian society because the university doesn't operate in a vacuum; it's an extension of a very competitive, success-, status-, and money-oriented world. In a sense, we're no different from the business world in that respect, though the currency is somewhat different. One way that I'm working on right now to alter this somewhat has to do with the culture of the university as an institution and the kinds of values that individual universities foster or discourage by the ways in which they conduct their own internal business. It seems to me that the departments that I've visited that have been some of the happiest places to work have not been at all privileged monetarily and have had virtually no professional visibility; nevertheless, a lot of the people in these departments got along with one another very well, respected themselves professionally and personally, and had a sense of reward and fulfillment in their daily work. How can that be? It seems to me from the cases I've observed that it was because the institution itself was attending to its own needs, to the things that would make its personnel feel good about themselves. There was a lot of attention given to the way faculty members would interact with one another on a daily basis, and the administration had a good sense of what departments needed and what kinds of encouragement they deserved to have. I'm back to metaphors of housekeeping and domesticity and sort of maternal attention to the maintenance and procedural aspects of life, but I do feel that universities, in particular, because their eyes are supposed to be firmly focused on the distant frontiers of truth, neglect the kind of social, psychological, and even in certain cases physical upkeep that makes the capacity to go searching for truth possible in the first place. What I'm saying is that more of a spirit of collectivity, a commitment not simply to finding the latest truth in your subfield but to the people you work with in your department and to the institution as an alma mater for the students who are coming through—a much more local focus for people's energies, drives and ambitions than a focus on becoming nationally known for this or that discovery or contribution—might help to defuse and make less tempting or desirable that kind of combat and grasping after visibility that seems to characterize the profession so much of late. The culture of the institution is what needs to change.

Q. In one of your typical moments of stunning honesty you write, "I learned what epistemology I know from my husband. I think of it as more his game than mine. It's a game I enjoy playing but which I no longer need or want to play. I want to declare my independence of it, of him. (Part of what is going on here has to do with a need I have to make sure I'm not being absorbed in someone else's personality.) What I am breaking away from is both my conformity to the conventions of a male professional practice and my intellectual dependence on my husband." Do you believe that marriage has changed the critical acceptance of your work?

A. That's hard for me to answer because some people don't know I'm married to Stanley Fish, so they aren't influenced by that. Some people do, and it's very difficult for me to know how that fact has influenced their reception of my work since it's not the kind of thing that people tell me. Certainly, in professional/social situations the fact that I'm married to Stanley influences people's behavior toward me all the time, and how they behave toward me depends often on which side of the fence they're on. If they're more interested in the kind of work *he* does, they'll often pay more attention to him; or if they're traditionally oriented toward the man as the more important member of a couple, they'll pay more attention to him; or if they want his favor, and he's an extremely powerful person in the profession, they'll pay more attention to him because they want to be in good with him. Those things are obvious and happen all the time, though less so now than they did in the past when we first got together. So, if the reception of my work in the world is a mirror of the way in which people react toward us as a couple in social situations, extrapolating from that, then I would say it probably has influenced them quite a bit. But how that gets processed in each case would depend very much on the circumstances of the person who is reading it.

Q. Do you believe that this danger of being absorbed into your spouse's personality is unique to your situation, or is it a more general problem that all academic women face, or is it even more general and a problem that all academics, men and women, face when they're both in the academy together?

A. I no longer feel that way; that's not an issue for me. At the time that I wrote it, the very fact that I *could* write it meant that it was just about to become no longer an issue for me. I finally had to say it, and it felt really good to say it. Having said it, I never had to worry about it again. In fact, I don't worry about it at all. How people feel about themselves is one thing; how other people see them is another. Whereas I got rid of that some six years ago, I'm sure most people still see me, if they see me at all, totally in Stanley's shadow. Those are two somewhat different things, how I feel and how I'm seen. As far as academic couples in general are concerned, sure it's a problem because this is a new phenomenon. We're not used to having men and women in couples have separate professional identities. Culturally, we're just now developing the sensorium or the cognitive apparatus for apprehending that, and I think that it's coming. It exists now in some quarters, and as the phenomenon becomes increasingly more common, people will be able more and more to see members of a professional couple as separate and not see one person as somehow influenced by the profile of another. I feel that sort of thing is in the process of being elaborated and is evolving right now.

Q. Are there any misunderstandings or criticisms of your work that you would like to take issue with or elaborate on right now?

A. In reviews of *West of Everything*, a couple of reviewers have taken exception to the two animal rights chapters in the book, the horses chapter and the cattle chapter. In fact, one review said, "You know the book is taking a turn for the worse when she asks the question, 'Why doesn't Roy Rogers eat Trigger?'" In other words, the sort of pro-animal rights stand I take in the chapters on horses and especially cattle is seen by a lot of people as a kind of kooky, flaky, idiosyncratic (I don't know what their vocabulary would be) aspect of my work, but generally people like the book and so are willing to bracket it and say, "Oh well, she has that quirk." But they still see it as a quirk. I don't see my position on that issue as in some way a special case that has to be forgiven, or as isolated from the rest of what I'm writing about in the book. In fact, I discuss it in the book as very much an extension of my understanding of the models of human pain, suffering, and self-mortification that characterize the western. So a sensitivity to and an awareness of pain and suffering within one's self becomes extended to an awareness of it in other people and indeed in other beings, and animals are simply there next to us or are in our lives as possible objects for that kind of attention. Also (and this doesn't really come through in the book), for me an awareness of what our relation to animals is is inseparable from a kind of environmental consciousness that I and so many people now have, especially more and more children. I think of this new attitude toward the welfare or rights of animals as being part and parcel of an increased consciousness about what our relationship to the physical environment (which we're interdependent with and which is alive just as we are) needs to be.

Encounters with Jane Tompkins

Susan C. Jarratt

I confess that I have mixed feelings about Jane Tompkins. I'm glad she discovered pedagogy, writing, and the West. But, curiously, I find myself already in those places she discovered, a native in habitats stumbled upon by an anthropologist. How does the native feel when the anthropologist decides to study his or her culture? Flattered, exposed, welcoming, objectified. My response to the interview traces its themes back to my encounters with Tompkins on three different occasions.

Encounter One: Teaching the Teachers
When Jane Tompkins delivered her "Pedagogy of the Distressed" talk at Miami University, I was indeed distressed; in fact, I was really angry. Here was Tompkins, a person with a major reputation in literary criticism and theory who had seemingly just discovered the concept of pedagogy, coming to lecture a group of people many of whom had spent their professional lives working on pedagogy. She announced that she had read Paulo Freire a few months before and was very excited about her discovery. Freire had already been studied in our field for years. The publication of her essay as a lead article in *College English* only made me angrier. When a graduate student comes across a new find and makes a major change in his or her thinking, writing, or teaching, it doesn't often make for a major publication. But when a first-rank, mainstream literary scholar discovers teaching, this is big news.

But I'm no longer angry about Tompkins' lecture or her essay. As letters reacting to her essay were published in *CE* and as she responded, I began to rethink her status in the profession of literary studies and her experience as a woman in the academy. The account of her life as the member of a two-career academic couple carrying the heavier domestic and teaching load—in short, as a wife—made me more sympathetic. I also had second thoughts about the ways Tompkins' disciplinary history in literary studies and in elite universities kept her at a distance from composition as a discipline. These changes, however, didn't affect my puzzlement about her lack of study in our field before she made her pronouncements. One of the letters of response to her article, after praising her, gently informed Tompkins of the twenty-five-year existence of NCTE. This was a lack Tompkins might have remedied in the years following her entry into the domain of composition, but, unfortunately, the anthropological stance persists in the *JAC* interview.

Tompkins' claim to a fifteen-year history as a writing instructor does not lead her to identify herself with "people who do that day to day"; she's still an outsider by choice. Though Tompkins feels "indebted" to people working in the field and acknowledges good work about writing pedagogy, she doesn't yet have many thoughts about the discipline, claiming that her pedagogy involves "no methods at all." While having read Elbow on writing groups influences her own writing practice, Tompkins doesn't speak about applying Elbow's ideas in her own classroom. Not being trained in the discipline is a handicap impressively overcome by many first-generation rhetoric and composition scholars, including Lisa Ede and Elizabeth Flynn. Compositionists would have expected Tompkins, more than the other major scholars in philosophy, linguistics, and literary theory featured in these interviews, to have done some homework in the field, especially given the fact that she's writing a book about pedagogy. Though I'm no longer angry, I'm disappointed at her continuing distance from composition studies. In this interview, her response to the field remains primarily at the level of feelings rather than intellectual or scholarly engagement.

If she were reading in the field, Tompkins would find her current ideas about Freirean-style pedagogy moving in the same direction as others who attempted at one time a direct imitation of Freire's democratization methods but now see the need for adaptation. We are now listening to what Freire has said about differences in contexts, observing that the needs and positions of U.S. students—their literacies—are different from those of Freire's students. The next stage in critical pedagogy will attend to a double agenda: encouraging students to take responsibility, as Tompkins suggests, for their education, along with recognizing the need for knowledge exchange—knowledge about how language works dialogically, and about material and social conditions for the production of discourse in various cultural contexts. Critical pedagogues like Henry Giroux, Ira Shor, and Kathleen Weiler have moved in this direction, but there is a great need for feminists and others associated with social movements in the U.S. to articulate responses to this challenge. I found myself speculating about how the new book on pedagogy might weigh in on this issue. We might take a clue from Tompkins' idea about performance.

Tompkins describes traditional teaching as performance, with the teacher exercising authority and delivering information. In moving away from that mode, Tompkins implies she is no longer a performer, only herself. This understanding of performance differs from some current feminist readings of subjectivity in general, and gender in particular, as performances (for example, see Bizzell and Butler). The idea is that everyone is performing a self, a gender, all the time, and that institutional positions such as teacher and student are always performances as well, with a range of possible choices about how to carry out those performances. On this analysis, Tompkins chooses not her real self over a performing self, but rather changes the kind of performance to one that allows for more emotion in the classroom.

Opening the classroom to emotion and personal experience is a tactic endorsed by teachers from a number of positions: certain feminisms, cultural studies, critical pedagogy, and expressivist composition. But this tactic serves different ends in these different contexts. In service of what political project can we see Tompkins' "liberatory" teaching, then? When she speaks of getting students to take responsibility, Tompkins sounds somewhat like advocates of critical pedagogy. But her characterizations of students and of the act of writing suggest different alignments. Tompkins focuses on the experiences of "the individuals who happen to be in the room"—single collections of life-experience presumably undifferentiated by social factors such as class, race, gender. Further, Tompkins' way of talking about writing as self-discovery casts her as the subject of expressivist pedagogy: a writer on an internal journey. In the comparison of writing with therapy, she sounds much like Elbow, advocating writing as "self-development, self-discovery." Though I don't share this view of composition theory, I respect those who advance strong and serious arguments for it. But Tompkins' further comments in this vein, references to writing as grooming, like "getting a massage or working out," seem to trivialize the focus on the individual, making writing sound like a yuppie pastime.

Much ink has been shed in the arguments about expressive versus social constructionist theories of writing. As with many important debates, much rides on the definitions of its terms. Not only does Tompkins seem unaware of those debates in composition theory, she seems to be several stages behind that dialogue in her treatment of the writing subject so unproblematically as a given, "natural" self. I feel quite certain that Tompkins is very aware of current theories of subjectivity but is purposely avoiding them—to be accessible, to try to cut through an alienating theoretical language, to reposition herself and her writing in the academy. Tompkins' career trajectory leads her away from theory in general; she wants now to uncomplicate and merge personal and academic, home and school. While I respect a personal decision made at some professional risk in an exposed public arena, in my view, Tompkins' stance is not the most productive one for composition studies now. The most exciting advances in arguments about composition and literary studies are coming out of current work in feminist theory and cultural studies, places where "experience" and "self" are both valued and analyzed. Especially given the current work exposing the negative feminization of composition, turning for answers to key questions in composition theory toward an unmediated experience of the personal, strongly associated with the feminine, is a bad idea.

Encounter Two: Feminism, or How Political Is the Personal?
When I picked up the issue of *New Literary History* centered on feminist epistemology, it was with an uneasy feeling. Already knowing I had major intellectual objections to the key essay, I placed myself in the positions of the

feminists who were asked to respond. How would I have handled such a task? How would I have negotiated my conflicting desires to argue, critique, even displace the feminist author's views with my own and to preserve solidarity among feminists, a marginal group in academic knowledge-production? Tompkins' response to the situation struck me as perfect. She acknowledged the difficulty, responded to the author as an academic woman in a male-dominated field, while at the same time encasing a critique of the essay within her response. Her creative approach to the task exemplifies critique in the strong sense: respectful, engaged, and committed.

I often include her essay, "Me and My Shadow," on reading lists for graduate seminars, and it surprised me the first time female graduate students reacted with anger and resentment to it. They said, "Tompkins has the leisure, the freedom to respond in such a relaxed way because of her status. If one of us tried to write such a piece, it would never be published." Tompkins addresses the complaint in the *JAC* interview effectively. Should she not move into a personal mode because it is possible for her to do so and not for others? No.

The more interesting question is how she deploys the personal, the autobiographical: what kind of personal self she creates or performs. As in her remarks about the function of writing, Tompkins keeps alive the idea of a self uncovered, discovered. In the questions about deconstructive writing and the reference to Cixous, there was an opportunity to refigure the relation of writing to "self," but instead "self" gets collapsed back into "self-creation" without any exploration of text or performance in deconstruction.

One self Tompkins was neither confessing nor professing in this interview was the feminist. Throughout the interview Tompkins resists identifying her practice with feminism, which she seems to equate with "female." The text is full of qualifications of the term: her teaching is "historically feminist, or by circumstances feminist"; the current relationship between the personal and the academic is for Tompkins "*de facto* feminist." In many moments, the evocation of feminism suggests to Tompkins the exclusion of men; to be "feminist" is to be "cordoned off." Again, this response can be placed in her own personal history. Her relation to the academy features competition and "personal injury," to which she responded by attacking the "male critical establishment." As Tompkins recreates that history and its present for herself, she implicitly associates feminism with that attack, but she then implies that softening it, moving away from it as she is now, requires moving away from feminism.

The most telling moment of this limited definition of feminism comes in her response to the question about a need for a specifically "female-oriented radical pedagogy." Tompkins speculates that a "specifically feminist pedagogy" would be needed in specific circumstances. The example she gives is a literacy program for pregnant women in North Carolina. Only "other" women need feminism? The implication here is that feminism is a benevolent, philanthropic enterprise aimed at a group of "women" in reduced circumstances. This is a reform, not a transformative feminism: a matronizing (rather than patronizing) gesture which fails to acknowledge the larger structures of gender power, the possibility that patriarchy affects women and men in every class and in every classroom.

This interview creates an odd picture of feminism, the political movement and intellectual operation within which Tompkins' life and work make sense. At times it seemed that Tompkins defines feminism as many of my undergraduates do: an aggressive, woman-promoting, male-deriding, in-your-face movement that has nothing to do with them, that wishes only to exclude men. Certainly, there are feminists and feminisms that fit that description. But so many of the ideas and plans Tompkins presents in the interview and in her work—the critique of Westerns as misogynist, the need to reconnect the personal and academic, the need for understanding students and teachers as whole people with emotional and material existences as well as intellectual—all these projects have deeply feminist connections. That Tompkins is silent on those and offers in place only an interest in the responsibility or pain of the individual throws her comments by default into a liberal theory of democracy in which people are individuals with separate emotions and lives and with responsibilities within a social contract system. This stance is disappointing and not consistent with the Freirean source. Despite Tompkins' attempt to distance herself from the epistemology of her husband, she speaks more to an audience of potentially hostile men than to feminists or even other women.

At moments, Tompkins aligns the genders in a more productive way. Her remarks about a men's movement suggest a relational change and note potential problems with this particular men's movement. I also appreciated her response to the question of Freire and sexism. It's too easy to ignore Freire's intellectual history and context, to pick up on the exclusive language and dismiss the conceptual and liberatory power of his work.

Encounter Three: Beautiful Blue Eyes
Jane Tompkins came to Miami University again, this time to talk about Buffalo Bill. As a native Texan, I once again felt "discovered." She suggested that her visit to a museum in Wyoming constituted an unmediated encounter with "the West"; it was an attempt to cut through the layers of aggrandizement and reaction by confronting Bill face to face. Ergo the eyes, noted in the Lawrence Ferlinghetti poem she distributed with the lecture. I thought about buffalo eyes—those wild and totally guileless marbles of fear. Because you only see them in movies as the camera gets close when they're about to get killed. I also thought about all the pairs of cunning blue eyes I've seen under the brims of cowboy hats in kicker bars. Picture Harlin in *Thelma and Louise*. There's no innocently cutting through that Western, male ethos, descended directly from B.B. Cody. I think about the boy in my brother's high

school class who had a beautiful eye (color unknown) kicked out by a cowboy boot in a totally typical little brawl one night. I didn't need to go to a museum to encounter "the West."

But then Tompkins knows all this. That's why my reactions are mixed. I was puzzled by the questions on *West of Everything*. What better to do with Westerns than put our best critical energies into exploring their violence and misogyny? I also wondered about the question on animal rights. Why not talk about Indians instead of animals, especially in 1992? The "Indians" chapter has been anthologized for writing classes and written about by at least one compositionist (Schilb). Tompkins anticipated the sharp focus on Native Americans this year, examining the way knowledge is created.

Through writing this response I discovered that Jane Tompkins likes to discover things and that I don't like to feel "discovered." Writing this response wasn't much like massage. It felt more like scraping a pumice stone over rough and calloused skin—callouses that protect, skin that gets red and painful.

Miami University
Oxford, Ohio

Works Cited

Bizzell, Patricia. *"The Praise of Folly*, The Woman Rhetor, and Post-Modern Skepticism."
Rhetoric Society Quarterly 22.1 (Winter 1992): 7-17.

Butler, Judith. *Gender Trouble. Feminism and the Subversion of Identity*. New York: Routledge, 1990.

Schilb, John. "The Role of Ethos: Ethics, Rhetoric, and Politics in Contemporary Feminist Theory." *Pre/Text* 11 (1990): 211-34.

Lit/Comp: A Response
to Jane Tompkins

Elizabeth A. Flynn

I can't resist beginning my response to the Tompkins interview with a reflection on the significance of the times our paths have crossed. The interview itself and Jane's open and warm demeanor seem to welcome this approach.

Personal Encounters
My first encounter was in the form of an appreciative letter from her after a mutual friend, Frank Hubbard, had sent her a copy of a paper I had delivered, "Women as Reader-Response Critics," at the Midwest Modern Language Association Convention in 1982. In the paper I argued that the approaches to reader response of Tompkins, Susan Suleiman, and Louise Rosenblatt were gendered in interesting and important ways. Jane clearly liked the piece. I then sent her a draft of "Gender and Reading," an essay she was less comfortable with since it seemed to assume that there was a single correct reading of the three short stories under consideration and to judge student responses in accordance with how well they conformed to this single interpretation. Thanks to comments by Jane and others, the revised version of "Gender and Reading" is considerably less rigid in its insistence on the one true meaning of a text. Jane's reaction to the essay suggested to me at the time that her theoretical stance was (and no doubt still is) considerably closer to a poststructuralist perspective than is mine.

There was much more at stake in my next encounter, for she was the referee that Johns Hopkins University Press selected to review *Gender and Reading*. She was enthusiastic about the manuscript but not about the introduction to the book and a few of the contributions, including a very early draft of mine. I substituted "Gender and Reading" for the premature piece, Patsy Schweickart and I decided to drop two or three others, and we revised the introduction.

In the summer of 1985, between the acceptance of *Gender and Reading* and its publication, I had the good fortune of having lunch with Jane at the School of Criticism and Theory. I was in Evanston for the weekend so a friend who was attending the School, Ellen Messer-Davidow, made the arrangements. *Sensational Designs* had just been published, and Jane talked about her writing group, about the difficulties she had had writing the book, about her vulnerabilities as a writer, and about the discomfort she had felt in the job interview for the position at Duke (for she had not yet joined the faculty there). I remember thinking at the time that a collection of essays about the writing processes of women like Tompkins would be wonderful.

Our paths crossed once again during the winter of 1991 when she and Andrea Lunsford participated in a session on feminist pedagogy that I had organized for the MLA Division on the Teaching of Literature. Coordinating the session necessitated several phone calls early in 1991 which became long and intense because they occurred while I was engaged in one of my many struggles with my university's bureaucracy. I felt quite comfortable sharing the details of my situation, and the support Jane provided was much-needed. Having read the Tompkins interview, I now realize why Jane was so helpful. She feels that departments need to provide "maternal" attention to its members, providing them the encouragement they deserve and nurturing a spirit of collectivity, a "commitment not simply to finding the latest truth in your subfield but to the people you work with in your department and to the institution as an alma mater for the students who are coming through." She sees that "a much more local focus for people's energies, drives and ambitions than a focus on becoming nationally known for this or that discovery or contribution—might help to defuse and make less tempting or desirable that kind of combat and grasping after visibility that seems to characterize the profession so much of late. The culture of the institution is what needs to change."

The MLA session itself, which coincided with the publication of Jane's second book, *West of Everything*, was very well attended, and a number of people told me afterward that it was the best session of the conference. I had asked Jane and Andrea to speak for only fifteen minutes and then to allow the members of the audience to respond to their presentations. Andrea spoke of obstacles placed in the way of pedagogies that encourage collaboration at her own university and elsewhere. Jane spoke of a course she was then teaching at Duke that aimed to break free of the boundaries of the traditional classroom. Students conversed about what was happening in their lives as much if not more than what was happening in the texts they were reading, made field trips to places such as the local Toys R Us store, and were invited to dinner at Tompkins' house where they received gifts from her.

The excitement of the pedagogical approaches described and validated in combination, perhaps, with the unusual structure of the session produced a lively conversation and a temporary but powerful feeling of shared community. By the end, participants were exchanging addresses and calling for a continuation of the session at the next year's MLA. (Judith Fetterley and I conducted a workshop on feminist pedagogy at the 1992 MLA.)

Opportunities for Dialogue

Forums such as the MLA session and the Tompkins interview provide excellent opportunities for dialogue between literature specialists and composition specialists and for a recognition that the two communities have different but complementary areas of expertise that can be mutually beneficial. They will never satisfactorily engage each other, though, until they are seen as equal, and we are far from achieving this goal. As Susan Miller points out in *Textual Carnivals*, composition has been regarded as a practical, "how-to" field without intellectual rigor. Its domain is the realm of immature student writing in contrast to literature's domain of quasi-religious textual ideals. According to Miller, compositionists respond to their institutional status in ways that closely parallel responses by other groups marginalized by class, race, or gender.

Tompkins' appreciative stance toward the field of composition studies represents to me a hope that the lit/comp binary, with its inevitable privileging of literature over composition (or theory/practice over teaching) can be deconstructed. Tompkins, after all, is a professor in one of the premiere literature departments in the country and is married to one of the foremost literary theorists in the nation. If *she* has discovered that compositionists are far ahead of literature specialists in the area of pedagogy, and if *she* recognizes the value of pedagogical work, then there is a possibility that others trained in literature will as well.

The Tompkins interview reminds me of the *JAC* interview with Mary Belenky, in that both scholars revealed an interest in and respect for the field of composition studies. It is not surprising that Tompkins speaks appreciatively of the chapter "Connected Teaching" in *Women's Ways of Knowing*. I learned in preparing for the 1991 MLA session that Jane has been becoming increasingly interested in pedagogy recently, is writing a book on the subject, and is discovering that exciting pedagogical exploration and experimentation is going on within composition studies. As she says in the interview, "The most interesting thinking and ideas in higher education about classroom teaching come from the field of rhetoric and composition." I learned, too, that she has been conducting pedagogy workshops with compositionists such as Bill Coles of the University of Pittsburgh. She was delighted to be paired with Lunsford, a well-known compositionist, at the MLA session.

The interview suggests, though, that the gap between faculty whose primary allegiance has been to literary studies and faculty whose primary allegiance has been to composition studies is often considerable. The former tend to see themselves as writers, as producers of scholarly essays that are well-crafted, intellectually sophisticated, and well-researched. The field of literary studies privileges scholarship over teaching. Students of literature are trained to write books and articles on literary topics, be they theoretical or critical. They learn to produce sophisticated prose and sustained arguments. The writing in journals such as *PMLA* is unquestionably mature, authoritative. Jane's development as a powerful writer, although recent, is characteristic of people with her background, training, and situation: a Yale Ph.D. in literature and a position in one of the strongest literature departments in the country.

Compositionists, in contrast, are generally not from ivy league universities and are generally more committed to pedagogical innovation than to the production of scholarly writing. It is only recently, after all, that compositionists have begun to produce book-length studies, and, until recently, much of the writing that has been done in composition studies has more closely resembled reportorial writing done in the social sciences than the stylized essays produced within literary studies. For the most part, compositionists are far ahead of literature specialists in the area of pedagogy but have not had the opportunities to develop as writers that literature specialists have had because they have been burdened by heavy teaching loads and labor-intensive administrative responsibilities.

Pedagogy and Disciplinary Expectations
Although Jane recognizes the need for innovative approaches to the teaching of literature and appreciates the work of compositionists, she is clearly considerably more comfortable in the role of writer than she is in the role of teacher. She is an accomplished writer, an excellent stylist, and a careful researcher. Her work has been well received. As she mentions in the interview, *West of Everything* was selected by Oxford University Press for nomination for the Pulitzer Prize. Although it is only recently that she has begun to think of herself as a writer (there were long stretches in her career, apparently, when she did not write), she is obviously entirely comfortable with the role and extremely productive and prolific. She describes writing in positive terms. She says, "It's a great pleasure to think that I *can* think of myself as a writer." She is "absolutely delighted" that she has made the crossover from critic to writer. Writing for her is "a mode of self-refinement and self-development which is an end in itself." Writing is a kind of grooming activity, a way that people have of taking care of themselves. She participates enthusiastically in a writing group. She speaks of having gained self-confidence as a result of writing and finds that one's writing process is very much a function of one's psychological, technological, and other circumstances.

Jane sees parallels between the changes that have taken place in her writing and in her teaching. Just as she has moved from writing as a kind of ego activity to writing as a form of self expression, she has moved from a belief in the "performance model" of teaching to a student-centered classroom. Clearly, though, she feels considerable discomfort in her role as innovative teacher. She speaks of the "precariousness" of her recent experiments with alternatives to traditional pedagogical approaches. As a result of her innovations, her classroom has ceased to be a "safe" place for her. She admits that when it comes to pedagogical matters, her views are those of a person "who isn't particularly well informed." She speaks of a feminist theory course that became a "pretty traumatic experience." For her, making changes in her traditional pedagogical methods is "difficult." She describes an experimental undergraduate course as another traumatic course. She says, "There was a lot of fear involved for me. Every single day for about seven weeks (and that's a long time) my heart was in my throat when I walked into that class because I did not know what was going to happen, whether it was going to be a good or bad day, whether the experiment was working or not." The class produced a "constant vertigo."

Perhaps sensing that Tompkins is vulnerable when it comes to discussing pedagogy, many compositionists and feminists have been critical of her work in this area. A compositionist friend who attended the MLA session said she found Tompkins' discussion of what she was doing in her classroom to be embarrassingly undertheorized. A feminist friend had a similar response and observed that only at an elitist institution could faculty risk spending a class session at Toys R Us. I was a panelist at a conference several years ago in which a compositionist spent thirty minutes critiquing Tompkins' work in a rather unfriendly way. I had dinner with some colleagues recently at the annual meeting of the National Council of Teachers of English who expressed the sentiment that in attending to pedagogical matters, Tompkins is colonizing territory that should remain the province of compositionists. They felt, too, that her gestures of appreciation for work in composition ring false because they do not seem to coincide with participation in the composition community by attending composition conferences or reading the work of compositionists. The reaction is a kind of reversal of the usual situation in which the literature specialist is disdainful of the theoretical naivete or immature scholarship of the composition specialist. Tompkins' entry into the conversation about how best to create student-centered classrooms has clearly angered a number of compositionists.

My own reaction has been somewhat different. I welcome Jane's entry into the conversation and appreciate her candor in admitting that her experiments have been distressing as well as her recognition that in this area compositionists are considerably more knowledgeable than she is. I see the gestures she is making toward the composition community as sincere and valuable ones that should be emulated by her colleagues in literature-dominated departments of English. She is taking an important first step that may encourage others to follow.

At the same time, I see Tompkins' recent discovery of student-centered pedagogies to be a sad commentary on the inattention paid to pedagogical concerns by the literature community. I remember my first reaction to "Pedagogy of the Distressed" very vividly. The essay brought home to me the extent to which the reader-response movement within the field of literary studies has enabled theoretical and critical work but not pedagogical work.

I realized that despite the fact that Tompkins had edited *Reader-Response Criticism* and had been at the center of the response movement for a time, her work in the area had had little or no impact on her teaching. I realized, too, that this was probably the case for many other reader-response theorists and practitioners in literary studies and that individuals such as Louise Rosenblatt and David Bleich who were primarily interested in teaching were in some ways anomalous. Rosenblatt's field is primarily education rather than literary studies, and David Bleich has become a compositionist. Only recently has Tompkins discovered that reader-response criticism provides a way to "put students at the center of the study of literature." She now sees it as making a similar contribution to feminist criticism in that it legitimizes a certain kind of personal response to literature and so has "a kind of integrative effect or performed a unifying function in terms of making a connection between peoples' lives and what went on inside classrooms in colleges and universities."

The fields of literary studies and composition studies have developed in very different ways in the past few decades. Literary studies has become a field that values interdisciplinarity and that has considerable theoretical sophistication. It has expanded its concerns from explications of individual literary texts, defined narrowly to include traditional literary genres, to considerations of the nature of textuality itself and to an exploration of relationships between texts and culture defined broadly. What it has not done, though, is to focus attention on what it means to teach literature and how this might best be done given that student populations are increasingly diverse. Tompkins' interview and her work on pedagogy suggest that this may be changing. Literature specialists may be discovering that as their work turns in the direction of cultural studies, and as they become increasingly aware of the importance of the reader in the literary transaction, they cannot ignore the political implications of their pedagogical practices. If attention to pedagogical concerns becomes widespread within literary studies, then there is a possibility that the differences between the fields of literary studies and composition studies will be reduced, as will the differences in the relative status each is accorded within English studies. I see Jane Tompkins not as a colonizer but as a potential equalizer. As she is well aware, we have knowledge and know-how that can help mitigate her distress.

Michigan Technological University
Houghton, Michigan

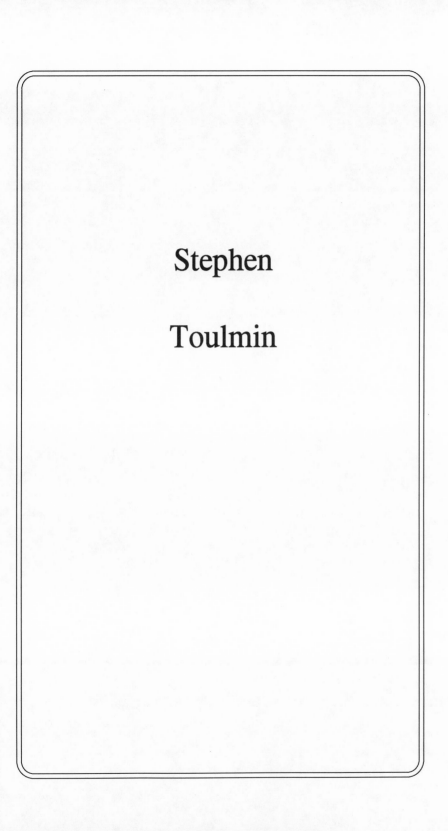

Stephen

Toulmin

Literary Theory, Philosophy of Science, and Persuasive Discourse: Thoughts from a Neo-premodernist

GARY A. OLSON

British logician Stephen Toulmin suggests that his many books could be "regarded as sketches toward a *'novissimum organum,'*" in that they are all "in different ways concerned with rationality, reasonableness, the operations of the human reason, and so on." For decades he has waged a relentless attack on rationalism, associating it with "a kind of worship of algorithms, a worship of formal arguments, and an insistence on getting the 'right answer.'" He argues that we need to reconceptualize rationality as non-systematic, but he views this project to be in sharp contrast to that of Jean-François Lyotard and the deconstructionists, which he interprets as an attempt to replace rationality with absurdity. For Toulmin, a postmodern rationality would be situational and contextual, much more akin to "reasonableness" than to "rationality" as strictly defined. This is why he applauds the recent tendency among philosophers to engage in applied, contextual philosophy, such as the philosophy of law, the philosophy of science, or the philosophy of art: "I think philosophers often do their best work when they turn their skills to helping to hoe other people's vineyards ... clearing away the underbrush that stands in the way of understanding." It's also why his own recent work entails spending time each week in the University of Chicago Hospital, "working alongside doctors whose business is to think about and discuss and arrive at conclusions about the moral problems that arise in the context of the clinical practice of medicine."

Thus, like Stanley Fish, Richard Rorty, and many others, Toulmin sees "no legitimate role for theory" and advises that we "be prepared to kiss rationalism goodbye and walk off in the opposite direction with joy in our hearts." These views are entirely understandable given the fact that Toulmin's mentor at Cambridge and his principal intellectual influence was Wittgenstein, from whom he inherited "a kind of classical skepticism." As a committed pragmatist, then, Toulmin's life's work has concerned "the recovery of the tradition of practical philosophy that was submerged after the intellectual triumph of theory in the seventeenth century." Clearly, to Toulmin, "pragmatism is not just another philosophical theory on a parallel with the others." Yet, he is wary of the "many people who have claimed to break with Descartes in the last few years," seeing many of them (including Lyotard) as "really rejecting Descartes for Cartesian reasons."

In the interview recorded below, Toulmin discusses these and several other issues relevant to scholars in rhetoric and composition. Noting the importance of clear writing and ample revision—especially in philosophy, "where obscurity is regarded as a mark of profundity"—he offers Toulmin's Law of Composition: *"The effort the writer does not put into writing, the reader has to put into reading."* He criticizes Chaim Perelman's "new rhetoric" for failing to open "up the broader perspectives within which the new rhetoric functions as richly as I would like to see done." In fact, much in the spirit of many of us in rhetoric and composition, he argues for a substantially broad conception of rhetoric: "What we call 'rhetoric' has to be understood as including dialectic, topics, all those bits of the discussion about argumentation that are not analytic." In addition, he takes issue with strict social constructionist theory and with Chomskyan nativism, approving only of "weak" versions of both: "I would need a lot of convincing in a very specific case before I was prepared to concede a particular grammatical structure was hard-wired in"; nevertheless, it seems "to go without saying that in many important respects the human capacity for language not only is an inherited capacity, but it has certain physiological preconditions, not least neurophysiological preconditions." In addition, Toulmin comments on feminism and the woman's movement, crediting the latter with making him "in important respects emancipated," and saying, "I really felt through much of my life this business of living in an oppressively structured society."

Of course, most compositionists know of Toulmin through his work on persuasion, detailed in his *The Uses of Argument*. Toulmin states that he didn't think he was "writing a book on the theory of rhetoric, or really even on the theory of argumentation," nor was he even certain that he was "writing a book with a model in it." Nor, for that matter, is he convinced today that "the Toulmin model could be used equally well for argumentation in all fields or of all kinds." This last position is in keeping with his general stance against theory: "No algorithm is self-applying." Thus, "every text has to be understood in relation to a situation." For decades scholars have observed that Toulmin based his model of argumentation on a jurisprudential model, but he takes this opportunity to correct this common misunderstanding, claiming that he added the comparison with jurisprudence as an afterthought. He also points out that he's dissatisfied with the book's discussion of "backing," commenting that were he to write the book today he would substantially strengthen the treatment of backing.

Given Toulmin's attempt to dismantle rationalism and his concern with establishing a useful postmodern philosophical tradition, his project shares numerous similarities with that of the poststructuralists. Yet, he seems to have no patience for the French deconstructionists. Acknowledging that he cannot make "the investment of time needed in order to penetrate their terminology" because he is "too old," he nonetheless believes that deconstruction is "game playing so far as I'm concerned." It's no wonder that he prefers Montaigne to "nearly everybody I've read who's consciously postmodernist." Consequently, Toulmin would rather be known as a "neo-premodernist" than as a postmodernist; he believes "the thing to do after rejecting Cartesianism is not to go on through the wreckage of the temple but to go back into the town where this heretical temple was built and rediscover the life that was lived by people for many centuries before the rationalist dream seized hold of people's minds." Perhaps the work of this eminent neo-premodernist will be of use to many of us in rhetoric and composition as we continue to construct a discipline responsive to the intellectual challenges of a postmodern age.

Q. You've written an impressive number of successful books, articles, and lectures over the last several decades. Do you think of yourself as a writer?

A. Yes, I suppose I think of myself as a writer. I get more direct and intense satisfaction out of writing something to my own satisfaction than I do out of, for instance, teaching; and if the choice is between being a writer or being a teacher, I'm a writer. I'm not sure that just being a writer is an honorable way of spending a whole life, but that's another matter.

Q. We in rhetoric and composition are interested in how successful writers compose. Would you describe your writing process? For example, do you outline before drafting? Do you revise substantially? Do you use a computer?

A. Well, I've been writing for more than forty years, and the process has changed (some people never leave the quill pen behind). I wrote out my first ethics book with pen and ink. What I tend to do most often now (though not with the most difficult material) is to talk a draft into a tape recorder, have that transcribed onto a Macintosh disk, and then do the really hard work, which is the editing, on the word processor. To me, this is the most satisfactory, up-to-date technique given what's available. I underline, though, that the really hard work is the editing. When I wrote things with ink or when I had a typist who typed things out, I was inhibited because it embarrassed me very much to send the same thing back for retyping seven or eight times just because I wanted to rephrase things or to move a clause from one place to another. So, I find the word processor a great invention from the moral as well as the technological point of view: I don't have the sense that I'm exploiting the secretarial help in the way I did. Let me say, too, that by and large I never begin to write anything until I have the whole thing worked out. I don't embark on a writing project to see how it looks. I typically, even in my books, even in the *Cosmopolis* book, have a pretty accurate idea about what will go into every stage.

Q. So, you give a great deal of thought to the subject before actually dictating a text.

A. It's not that I think about it; it's much more like architecture. I have to have a sense of the architectonic of it, a sense of where I'm headed and how it's all fitting together. Obviously, some of that goes down on paper or in the computer in the form of headings and a sort of blocking out of rough chapter sections and so on, but the actual writing process, which may be the dictating process, really begins only at the point at which I know what the entire opus is supposed to be. I said a moment ago that editing is the most important factor. Having lived all these years with the texts of philosophers, let me say that there are few things more irritating in reading a philosopher (well, it's partly irritation, partly the joy of discovery) than when you read a text for the seventh time and suddenly realize what it is the writer is trying to say. Especially if it is a very good point that you've previously come to recognize for *yourself*, it's a little irritating that it hadn't been made clear that this is what the person was saying. I have this trouble particularly with a man I immensely admire: John Dewey. I have a sense sometimes that he just kept writing and periodically tore off the lengths and sent it to the printer. I'm quite sure that Dewey didn't do what I do, and I almost mean this dead literally (though a lot of it actually goes on in my head subvocally rather than vocally): I go through all my material repeatedly to see how it will *sound* to a reader and how the rhythms of the prose will come out and contribute to the reader's understanding. The effect of this is that a lot of people say to me, "Oh Stephen, you're so lucky to be able to write so clearly." To which I state Toulmin's Law of Composition: *The effort the writer does not put into writing, the reader has to put into reading.* The only trouble is that since I put immense effort into the editorial stage so as to make sure not only that I have said what I wanted to say but that it comes off as having a kind of natural rhythm, I rather resent being told that this came easily.

Q. Quite a few compositionists will be pleased with your emphasis on the revising and editing processes.

A. It's especially important in philosophy, where obscurity is regarded as a mark of profundity. As a result of deliberately avoiding being obscure, philosophers have at any rate made *some* effort to write with non-Germanic clarity, and thank God on the whole this has been part of a longstanding tradition among philosophers of English origin from John Locke and David Hume on.

Q. Who would you say has had the most influence on you intellectually?

A. Well, let's take a whole string of people. If we're talking about who influenced me philosophically, well obviously Wittgenstein. I went to his classes in Cambridge in the last couple of years of his time there; I wrote the Wittgenstein/Vienna book with Allan Janik; and certainly Wittgenstein's whole approach to philosophy was tremendously influential on me. In certain respects, attending Wittgenstein's lectures gave me the courage of previous convictions; that is, I was already strongly inclined to move in the direction that he encouraged us to move in: toward a kind of classical skepticism. I've written an essay in which I draw attention to the parallels between Wittgenstein and Sextus Empiricus, with Montaigne as a kind of intermediate figure. It's not that I think for a moment that Wittgenstein had read these people, but I think that where he ends up in regard to all matters of technical philosophy is in a classical Pyrrhonist position of saying that the thing to do with philosophical questions is not to answer them but to avoid answering them and to step back and ask, "How on earth did we get into this trap?"

Wittgenstein was a major influence partly because, like him, I began in physics; my first degree was in math and physics. I earned my living during the Second World War working on radar, and I discovered that my reasons for being interested in physics were not the same as those of my successful colleagues in the discipline. When I was given a piece of apparatus to work with, I tended to break it. It was clear that I was not going to make a living as an experimenter. Besides, most theory had by that time become too brazenly mathematical. (Sometimes when I'm talking to scientists, I say that I've spent the years since 1942, fifty years now, trying to figure out what it was I'd been taught at Cambridge.) So, I started in the exact sciences, then moved to the philosophy of science, then to the history of science, then to the broader sociology and politics of science, and finally to the whole place of the exact sciences in the overall march of intellectual history. I see it as a sort of constant building; it's kind of the reverse of Peer Gynt: whereas Gynt starts outside the onion and starts taking it to pieces, I see myself as having started in the empty center and built the onion around it layer by layer. So that's the point about my being a physicist. Wittgenstein had, of course, been terribly interested in physics to begin with and to the end of his life acknowledged Heinrich Hertz as one of the major writers from whom he had got ideas and in whom he found something of his own philosophical attitudes. He had wanted to work with Ludwig Boltzmann, but Boltzmann committed suicide just before Wittgenstein was due to go there. (It was a time of suicides, as you know; Durkheim writes about it.) However, you were asking about influences, and the next point is that although I found Wittgenstein's general philosophical method very congenial, I didn't find his approach to ethics anything like as congenial.

Q. That was your first book.

A. Well, yes. I don't think that at that stage I understood at all clearly what Wittgenstein's attitude toward ethics was. He didn't really talk about it very much, certainly not in his regular lectures. What I found particularly unsatisfactory was his failure to pay any attention to the long-term intellectual significance of history. Like so many people who have claimed to break with Descartes in the last few years, Wittgenstein was just a tiny bit inclined to attack Descartes with Cartesian weapons. (As you know, I think Lyotard and such people are really rejecting Descartes for Cartesian reasons.) And Wittgenstein follows Descartes; he says in one of the early notebooks, "What is history to me? Mine is the first and only world." That is, there is a strong element of narcissism that comes out in a form of a philosophical solipsism, and *that* he does not really get the better of philosophically until around 1930. However, that meant that at a certain stage it was quite apparent to me that you couldn't really get the account of the operations of the human reason that I was interested in without looking at how concepts change; that was how I got onto the human understanding project, but this was after having again read, and been encouraged by reading, Collingwood. Collingwood is a strong influence at a certain stage. Actually (and perhaps I'll write an essay about this sometime), for those who are interested, the entirety of my work could in fact, from a certain point of view, be regarded as sketches toward a *"novissimum organum"*; that is, all my books are in different ways concerned with rationality, reasonableness, the operations of the human reason, and so on. In fact, I've often put a little teaser at the end of works, not with any intention of teasing people, almost as a kind of reminder to myself about what it is I ought to be thinking about next. There's a little postscript at the end of *The Uses of Argument* in which I say, "Strictly speaking, all this examination of argumentation and concepts and the rest should be conducted with an eye to the historically changing character of argument forms and basic concepts," and I mention Collingwood there as being a philosopher for whom that's a starting point rather than something to be disregarded.

Q. *The Uses of Argument* has received an enormous amount of attention. Are you surprised by the overwhelming critical reception of that book and of the so-called Toulmin method of argumentation?

A. It was not initially overwhelming, particularly in England. I was still living in England when I wrote that book. If ever a book imitated Hume's *Treatise* by falling stillborn from the press but, like Hume's *Treatise*, turning out to have a longer life than the obstetrician predicted for it, it was *The Uses of Argument*. I published it in England, and Peter Strawson wrote a dismissive review in *The Listener*, the BBC's intellectual weekly; that was the end of the matter so far as my colleagues in England were concerned. The few who bothered to read it said, "Oh, it's an antilogic book" (pragmatism wasn't in vogue yet in England). So, I was surprised that it kept selling so well, and then I discovered that it was being used up and down the Mississippi Valley. Recently, I spent two days at a boot camp in Kalamazoo with members of the Speech Communication Association who have a subgroup that deals with what they call "communication ethics." I'm deeply aware of the book's reception; I feel I have to do something to pay back what these people have done for me. However, when I wrote *The Uses of Argument*, I certainly didn't think I was writing a book on the theory of rhetoric, or really even on the theory of argumentation. I wasn't clear that I was writing a book with a model in it. I had two agendas in writing the book. The deeper agenda arose out of a perception about the argument in epistemology—particularly empiricist epistemology, from Locke to Kant, and again from Mach and Russell on through to the Cambridge people like G.E. Moore and the younger people. This argument was largely generated as a result of confusion between substantive arguments and formal arguments and sprang from a demand that substantive arguments meet formal criteria of a sort that seemed to me (and to Aristotle) inappropriate. So, I wrote the book seeking to demonstrate that these epistemological problems would dissolve if only you looked more seriously at what substantive argumentation was about. Now, that's the deeper agenda. The more superficial agenda was that, after all, I had already by that time written first the *Reason in Ethics* book and then the little *Philosophy of Science* book, and it seemed natural to give a more general account of the kinds of considerations I'd been concerned with in these two special cases. On the face of it, *The Uses of Argument* was intended to show people explicitly on a more general level the points that had been exercising me when I wrote first about ethics and then about science in the earlier books.

Q. Many compositionists use your method as a kind of heuristic for helping students develop argumentative essays. Do you approve of this pedagogical application of your work?

A. I'd approve of anything people find fruitful, so long as they don't use my ideas dogmatically. I was having a chat with the people at the SCA communication ethics meeting, and they were a little unhappy when I said that it wasn't plain to me that the Toulmin model could be used equally well for argumentation in all fields or of all kinds. I wanted to say, "I have a lot of mottoes of the form, 'No algorithm is self-applying,' or 'No theory is self-validating.'" So, you have to find out as you go along in what areas this model works best and in what areas one has to use it with qualifications.

Q. Some scholars in composition and others in speech use your method as a tool of discourse analysis, as a critical tool for examining persuasive essays and speeches. Are you also pleased with this application of your work?

A. If you give people a crutch, they can walk into a marsh, or they can walk down the center of the road. If I help people get to the right conclusion more quickly, I'm pleased. I'm quite uncritical in general about this, though I might well be critical in particular cases.

Q. Many scholars in numerous disciplines are preoccupied with the nature of persuasion. Clifford Geertz, for example, has spent decades pondering exactly what makes a text in anthropology persuasive. (He said recently in *JAC* that it has more to do with an author's ethos than with presenting a body of facts.) What would you say is at the heart of persuasion? What above everything makes a text persuasive?

A. I have to start with a prefatory remark. We find ourselves in a situation in which the word *context* is used to mean two quite different things: on the one hand, the larger text of which a particular text is a part, the other bits of text which are around it; on the other hand, the situation, the situation into which a text is put. I have to be rather careful because in writing *Cosmopolis*, at a certain stage about halfway through it, I realized that all the things I'd said about "decontextualization" and "recontextualization" were really "desituation" and "resituation." I suppose it might have been a good idea if I'd gone through it with my word processor's search and replace; however, my editor convinced me that people wouldn't be grateful with being stuck with neologisms and that if there is this ambiguity in words like *decontextualize*, we're stuck with it for the time being. With that said, I believe every text has to be understood in relation to a situation. In this I agree with Habermas that all knowledge is related to a human interest of one kind or another. This human interest may be that of molecular biologists, in which case what makes a text persuasive has something to do with the role of that text in whatever conceptual clarification and refinement is occurring in a particular corner of molecular biology. And that's not a simple matter; it isn't a matter of finding out that two and two make four. The whole of philosophy of science is concerned with deciding what's at issue when a new paper is regarded as having made a deep and important contribution to molecular biology, for instance. Obviously, the less well-defined the situation within which a text is made public and the shared goals of the author and the audience toward which the publication of the text is intended to make a contribution, the harder it is to say what makes something persuasive. When Mr. Churchill gave speeches in the House of Commons in the early 1940s, they were, as I recall, wonderfully persuasive, but in a different kind of way from the texts in molecular biology. We can reread those speeches now and admire the craftsmanship involved in their composition and the flawless actor's way in which throw-away phrases and such things were inserted, but when we reread them now there's nothing to say they're persuasive because the occasion for persuasion has passed. We can see what *might* have made them persuasive, but that's a piece of historical reconstruction now.

Q. So there's nothing inherent in a speech or a text that ensures persuasion; it's always contingent upon a specific context or situation.

A. All language functions in situations. I'm still enough of a Wittgensteinian to believe that there has to be a *Lebensform* [life-form] in order for there to be a *Sprachspiel* [language game]. Unless there are human beings engaged in shared activities, there is no scope for language to be put to use in a way that will convey anything.

Q. It's been almost four decades since you published *The Uses of Argument*. Have you thought of any ways to refine your model, or would you like to alter or retract any part of it?

A. Oh, sure. If I were writing it again today, especially knowing what kind of audience would actually want to make use of it, I would say a great deal more in particular about the variety of different things that go by the name of "backing." It's too much of a kind of carpetbag concept in the book. When Rieke, Janik, and I did the *Introduction to Reasoning* book much later, we did something to make the discussion of backing a bit more sophisticated, particularly in the final chapters where we talk about argumentation in different spheres. Philosophically speaking, the discussion of backing is the part that's least satisfactory in the original book and needs a lot of brushing up.

Q. Many scholars in communication talk about the "Toulmin revolution" in argumentation, characterizing your work as *descriptive* (as opposed to older *prescriptive* models) and as in the forefront of the "process view of human communication." However, others, such as Charles Willard, attack your descriptive diagrams for creating "conceptional confusion" and for unjustly simplifying the phenomena they seek to describe. What is your response to criticism that your descriptive diagrams are reductive and fail to account for the true complexity of persuasive communication?

A. Well, they can't be said to fail to do something they were not intended to do. I know Charlie; he and I always have a nice argument. He's a bull terrier: he likes to go into a situation and find a rag that he can chew hard on. I'm one of his pet rags. But I like him; he's a nice fellow, and he's serious. He's got points he wants to make, and he's certainly entitled to make those points. To the extent that the Toulmin model has developed a life of its own, he's welcome to tear it apart. It doesn't affect my ego.

Q. It's been said that you based your model of argumentation on the workings of jurisprudence in order to move away from the traditional model of logic based on mathematics and a form of reasoning that seemed too abstract to be relevant to real-world situations. Similarly, the "critical thinking" movement that swept the nation in the 1970s and 80s was an attempt to situate logical reasoning in realistic scenarios, to contextualize logic and argument. What is your opinion of the critical thinking movement? Do you see your work on argumentation as a part of that movement?

A. There's an assumption in the first part that's false. For the record, I didn't base *The Uses of Argument* on a jurisprudential model. I wrote the book almost entirely, and then at the very end it occurred to me that as a way to add a bit of clarity to the exposition, the comparison with jurisprudence would do no harm. I brought that in right at the end; it wasn't in my mind or part of my plan when I was first working up the content of the book.

Q. That's interesting, because numerous commentators have made quite a point about your basing your model on jurisprudence.

A. I know; people just assume things without bothering to inquire. You're the first to raise this with me, and, therefore, I take the opportunity to correct this widespread misapprehension. For what it's worth, I believe I was right to think that it was illuminating to use the jurisprudential model and the "court of reason." In some ways, I regret that things did not happen the way they're reputed to have happened.

Q. So, do you see your work in trying to situate logic this way as related to the critical thinking movement?

A. I was never part of the critical thinking movement. I only have a kind of newspaper reader's gossipy acquaintance with the movement and therefore don't know much about it. I never attempted any involvement in it.

Q. Your work on argumentation is often cited along with Chaim Perelman's (his coauthor, Olbrechts-Tyteca, seems to get lost in the shuffle) as the two works that have changed the face of argumentation. What is your assessment of Perelman's "new rhetoric"?

A. Let me step back and say something larger, first. I said earlier that I had great admiration for John Dewey. Some people commenting on my general philosophical approach have noted how surprising it was for a pragmatist to be born in England. As you've probably gathered, it does seem to me that pragmatism is not just another philosophical theory on a parallel with the others. I think the long-run thrust of pragmatism is concerned with what I call the "recovery of practical philosophy," the recovery of the tradition of practical philosophy that was submerged after the intellectual triumph of theory in the seventeenth century. So, although the birth of pragmatism was painful—in that William James, for instance, generated pragmatism from within an extraordinary epistemological framework that was deeply pre-Wittgensteinian—by the time you get to Dewey, Dewey already had remarkably well-formed all the main sense of what practical philosophy should be and also a deep understanding of what was wrong with the tradition from Descartes on. (His *Quest for Certainty* book is still worth reading.) What I find interesting is that Richard Rorty claims to be an admirer of Dewey, and yet he seems to miss an awful lot of the points that Dewey is sound on. In particular (and this is curious in somebody who knows the whole Wittgensteinian move), Rorty still has a highly individualistic attitude toward all philosophical issues and even toward language: anybody's welcome to invent their own language, so to say, and if you want to talk a different language that's your privilege. But Dewey is quite clear that language functions within collective enterprises, and we get involved in all these different things in which we share language with our fellow baseball players, or our fellow Democratic party members, or our fellow ornithologists, or our fellow criminal defense lawyers. And we share not only the language but the *Lebensform* which provides the situations within which different language games can operate. Thus, it seems to me that looking back down the road, historians of philosophy will see this revival of practical philosophy, of which pragmatism is a phase, as a major change in the history of philosophy. Now, it's not surprising if parallel sorts of things happen in different places. It's difficult to be a pragmatist in a country whose philosophical life is dominated by Leuven, one of the most conservative Catholic philosophy schools in Europe. Was Perelman Jewish? I suppose so. (Just a few weeks ago I was at a conference in Lisbon organized by Michel Meyer, who is Perelman's leading surviving student and who runs the successor program at the Free University of Brussels.) His new rhetoric is fine, though it's narrower than I would like it to be. Neither Perelman nor Meyer really opens up the broader perspectives within which the new rhetoric functions as richly as I would like to see done.

Q. You've said, "Since the mid-1960s, rhetoric has begun to regain its respectability as a topic of literary and linguistic analysis, and it now shares with 'narrative' an attention for which they both waited a long time." What role do you see rhetoric playing in a postmodern age?

A. I think "rhetoric" is kind of a code word. When I refer to my own work as sketches for another organon, what goes with this is a sense that what needs reviving is not just rhetoric but all the bits of the organon that are not analytic. And I think theoretical philosophy as it has existed since the seventeenth century has generally attempted to confine the discussion of argumentation and the validity of arguments to the zone occupied by the *Prior* and *Posterior Analytics* of Aristotle. Why? For the very good reason that it appeared that one could keep those under sufficient control to say (roughly speaking) that there was only one valid answer to any given question, and only one valid form. Whether the argument was valid or not is a question that can be established and to which the answer can be given without peradventure, whereas once you get into ethics, politics, poetics, rhetoric, and the other things that Aristotle also regards as worth including in his entire series of linked projects, the thing becomes inescapably hermeneutic. So for me, what we call "rhetoric" has to be understood as including dialectic, topics, all those bits of the discussion about argumentation that are not analytic. Whether it's prudent to go on calling these things "rhetoric" when there are still many people for whom the word *rhetoric* has all kinds of bad overtones, is another question.

Q. Siegfried Schmidt has argued in *New Literary History* that "if literary science is to . . . liberate itself from the (self-adopted) ghetto of the 'humanities,' it must evolve into a consciously and *critically argumentative* science." He then proceeds to outline such a "science" based almost entirely on your method of argumentation. What is your opinion, first, of this kind of use of your work and, second, of attempts in general to create a science of literary criticism?

A. I would regard it as a catastrophe. Where does Mr. Siegfried Schmidt come from?

Q. I assume he's from Germany, since he was at the University of Bielefeld when his article was translated from the German by Peter Heath.

A. In that case, we're deceived by the translator because I'll bet he used the word *Wissenschaft*. The word *Wissenschaft* does not mean the same as the word *science*; it means "discipline." Obviously, if the question reads, "If literary criticism is to become a serious *discipline*, it has to do this, that, and the other," that's different from saying in English that it has to be a "science." Also, I don't like this "self-adopted ghetto of the humanities." I don't know who or what he is referring to. I'm not going to say anything of the shallow relativistic kind, but it's the general "situation" problem again. The point is that when you find yourself getting involved with arguments that come out of a situation in another country, you have to do a bit of checking to determine what was at stake in the debate from which this thing was taken. For example, Habermas comes here to Northwestern most years, and we have a jolly two or three days when he's here. He gives a couple of lectures, usually on Kant's ethics as being the ultimate font of universalization and impartiality and the rest. He and I have a kind of joking relationship: he gets up and denounces the neo-Aristotelians, by whom he means some people in Germany who call themselves neo-Aristotelians; then I get up like St. Sebastian, take the arrows full in my chest, and say, "I'm happy to be a neo-Aristotelian." So we chew that one a bit. Sometimes I ask my colleague Tom McCarthy, "What's really biting Jürgen; why does he have so much investment in his pragmatics being universal?" Tom explains how different it was growing up in Germany after the Second World War from growing up in England just before and during the Second World War. We really do come out of situations in which what reasonably mattered to us was very different. For me it's of crucial importance that Descartes died two years after the end of the Thirty Years War, while Leibniz was born two years before the end of the Thirty Years War. They lived in totally different situations, and what an intelligent young man would have regarded as of supreme intellectual importance in the 1630s was quite different from what an intelligent young man would have regarded as of supreme intellectual importance in Germany in the 1680s. This is the "situation" factor.

Of course, being a classical skeptic helps one in this respect; it enables one to make this point. If I thought there were definitely right answers to overly general philosophical questions, then I wouldn't be allowed to say this; this would be what they call the "genetic fallacy" and things of this kind. But since, like Wittgenstein, I think that to try to answer philosophical questions definitively on that level of generality is a piece of self-deception, then the question is, "What was at stake for people that they felt it indispensable to find some self-validating proposition like *cogito ergo sum* or some principle of judgment that would compel the attention of scholars of all kinds, like the 'principle of sufficient reason'?" I used to find Leibniz totally opaque until I realized that he was the first ecumenist. He spent thirty years trying to organize a congress to which theologians of every orientation would come and arrive at agreement about which of the basic doctrines of Christianity stood to reason—conformed to the principle of sufficient reason—and which were sufficiently idiosyncratic that everybody could see that different people would have different opinions about them but that it wouldn't matter.

Q. What, then, do you see as the role of literary theory, especially if it is not going to be looking for universals?

A. Now you approach a very delicate area for me. I find the role of theory in literary studies exceedingly limited. Basically, I don't believe that this is an area in which there should be a concern with theory. In my experience, a preoccupation with theory in this area does more harm than good.

Q. For the same reasons that we talk about theory being limited in a general sense, or is there a specific reason?

A. I think it's worth specifying the reasons. The first step you take in developing a theory is to abstract: you find some examples that seem to exemplify with particular clarity some patterns that you would like to use as general patterns about which to develop a method of theoretical analysis, and you choose initially to ignore both all other situations which don't exemplify the patterns so clearly and also all other features even in those situations which are not directly relevant to the pattern from which you are abstracting. You end up with an analysis that is abstract. This is what in practice abstraction is. Now, that's okay if at the end of the day you understand that you have to argue your way back to real life before what you say has any direct application to the particular regard with which you're concerned. You can't just say, "Texts that don't fit the criteria of my theory are bogus." The question arises, "What light if any does your theoretical analysis throw on these other texts that are somewhat different from the ones from which you arrived at your initial abstraction?" Most of the authors whose literary productions I find commanding my attention, irresistible, and seizing my imagination, are attempting to show us something about our lives in all their complexity in a way that would be falsified quite misleadingly if one were simply to use them to abstract some bits and throw the rest away. Consider Tolstoy. I reread *Anna* every second year. There is this sense that you can quarrel with the old man; you can dislike his attitudes in certain respects; you can be unclear what his attitudes are from reading to reading. Every time I reread *Anna*, I have a slightly different sense of what the author's attitude toward his heroine was. It's a very rich and complex book, both for authorial reasons and, of course, because of the way he stuffs detail into the picture.

Q. Do you have a literary critic in mind who would provide the kind of illumination you're talking about while avoiding limiting abstraction?

A. Saul Bellow, when he writes criticism, is quite good. I remember being heartened when Bellow gave his Nobel lecture. (I've heard him give some very bad lectures, but that was one of his better ones.) I share his sense that any literary theory which entails, for example, that Tolstoy is not a great novelist is self-refuting—or self-discrediting, rather. I wouldn't want to say self-refuting; that would be giving it too much credit. That's my feeling, and, to that extent, Mr. Siegfried Schmidt seems to me to be a bit of a barbarian if he really regards the humanities as a ghetto. I'm enormously grateful for having been a physicist; on the other hand, all the very best physicists I know are also deeply interested in those aspects of life which the humanities are there to record.

Q. What about the use of the French deconstructionists in literary criticism? Do you have any opinion about that?

A. Honestly, about ten years ago I had to decide whether to make an investment: the investment of time needed in order to penetrate their terminology. I decided I was already too old for that to be a prudent investment. My sense is that they take us about as far as the *Tractatus*, that there's a great deal of humane wisdom even in the *Philosophical Investigations*, and it's game playing so far as I'm concerned. It's very unfair of me to say so without having made this investment, but it's based on a partial judgment that is not totally uninformed.

Q. You take Thomas Kuhn to task for his theory of how knowledge in science is created, saying that "the contrast between normal and revolutionary change has acquired something of the same spurious absoluteness as the medieval contrast between rest and motion." Do you disagree generally with the thesis that knowledge is a social construct?

A. I never know what that phrase means. Saying that knowledge is a social construct need only be to say the same thing I've already said—namely, that for me all questions about knowledge have to be situated. If being a social construct only means situated, well yes. But I'll tell you, I don't like the word *social*. It's too narrow. It pushes one in the direction of sociology and politics in cases where more may be at stake than sociology and politics. Just to mention another influence on me, I spent a fair amount of the most impressionable years of my growing up at King's College Cambridge, and one of the people who was there in the later part of my time at Cambridge was E.M. Forster. He was very old and was retired. He was like a door mouse: he was so tiny and retiring, you could feel his whiskers twitching. He was like a character out of Beatrix Potter. He had an enormous sensitivity for priorities. He wrote the famous essay "Two Cheers for Democracy," in which he says he's full of admiration for democracy and is quite prepared to believe that it is the best sketch for a form of government one could have; nevertheless, he reserves three cheers for, how does he put it, his "beloved republic." Forster was, I suppose, the chief literary figure who understood G.E. Moore's *Principia Ethica* in its kind of practical moral interpretation. And in his *Essays in Biography*, John Maynard Keynes explains what Moore meant to the Bloomsbury people and how they took his rather abstract arguments and turned them into a kind of gospel, so that the chapter on the Ideal, the last chapter in Moore's *Principia Ethica*, became a kind of moral handbook so far as they were concerned. Moore, who belonged to a generation very much concerned not to reject utilitarianism so much as to criticize the preoccupation of its parents and grandparents with the sewers and public works, so to say, called parts of his theory "ideal utilitarianism"; but that was because for him the goals of action should not only be concerned with eliminating disease and hunger and other important issues, but it should also be concerned with the pleasures of friendship and the appreciation of beauty in art and nature and so on. So Forster was very much a Moorian in that way, and, in particular, he could not bring himself to believe that we were right to esteem society above our friends. I've never thought of it this way before, but one can say that there are certain parallels between Forster and Tolstoy in this respect. I have argued that Tolstoy did not believe that moral relationships were possible except with other people who lived within walking or at most horse-riding distance from you. Tolstoy's conception of the moral universe is of those people with whom you have occasion to interact on a day-to-day basis.

If I may, let me just expand on this a bit because it's a very nice point in some ways, especially if you're interested in the late nineteenth-century novel. There was a very intelligent conservative politician called Edward Boyle who died ridiculously young. I remember having an amusing conversation with him in which he was explaining how there were certain nineteenth-century novelists—the one he chose to talk about was Thomas Hardy—who could only have written after the invention of the railway and before the invention of the automobile. Chekhov is similar: everybody in Chekhov is always dreaming of going to Moscow in the same way that everybody in Hardy is dreaming of going to London. This comes out in *Anna* as well. One of the central things in *Anna* is that Anna finds herself in a series of situations that become progressively intolerable to her; she can't cope. Because the moral demands made on her are for one reason or another too intense, too unbearable, what happens again and again is that she goes down to the railway station and gets on a train to go *somewhere*. *Where* the train is going is the last matter of importance. Right at the end, of course, she is doing it again, only this time a train journey is not enough. This is why, in someways, the invention of the private car made it much harder to distinguish between the people with whom we are actively engaged in a moral way from day to day, and other people. At any rate, all of this is because I said I wasn't happy with the word *social*. The point is that it's clear that *social* includes the *micro social*: "me and my friends." Do you see what I'm saying?

Q. Yes, but I think those people who consider themselves "social construc- tionists" are beginning with both Kuhn and Rorty and are saying that knowledge, and therefore reality, is *only* a social construct; it's not external to human discourse.

A. This is quite different. I don't mind them saying it's a social construct; it's the moment they start saying it's *only* a social construct that the trouble starts, because they then immediately bring in some object of contrast which had previously only been implied, and if you really get them to specify what they mean by that which they're contrasting, it turns out to be a load of old rope. Put it this way: theories in physics are constructed socially as external; the externality of their reference is part of the account. This isn't to say that theories in physics are as they stand metaphysical or open to attack as foundationalist. This is a point that Karl Popper grinds on and on about. This is what he has in mind when he talks about the "third world," which I think is an unhappy way of putting it. To say knowledge is a social construct and not external is open to precisely the same difficulties as Kant's references to the *Ding an sich* [the thing in itself]. Kant keeps saying, "You can't say anything at all about the *Ding an sich*." But what's he just done? You see, that's the problem. If Kant had really understood about the *Ding an sich* with, so to say, full Wittgensteinian seriousness, he would have avoided saying that; he would have found some way of gesturing in the direction of that which we can't say anything about. I think it need do no harm to say that all theories are social constructs if all you mean is that concepts are human products and that you have no theory without concepts.

Q. In a recent book about feminist epistemology and the construction of knowledge, philosopher Lorraine Code argues that the sex of the knower is "epistemologically significant" and that it is time to move beyond mainstream epistemology, which, she argues, is Cartesian and is modeled after physics. What are your thoughts about this work?

A. I think the defects of the Cartesian tradition come up most strikingly in the shortcomings of psychology. Certainly, psychology is growing out of this, but it's clear right through the middle of the century. I never understood why academic psychologists wanted their subject to be like physics. It is much more natural to think of it as like biology. Think of some of the early masterpieces of psychology, such as Hermann von Helmholtz's *Physiologi- cal Optics*, which is concerned with sense perception. It's essentially a treatise on sensory psychology, and it's done within a strictly biological framework. I think it's important to understand that mental functions and even higher mental functions are refinements and extensions of organic functions; so unless you understand all the different languages of biology (and there are at least four independent languages within biology, not least the evolutionary one), you really don't have a proper launching off ground to develop either psychology or epistemology. So I agree with Code, though I should point out that it wasn't even the model of physics; it was the model that Descartes held out as being what physics *ought* to be. Physics itself has changed a lot.

Q. You say that "sexual emotion appeared the gravest threat to the hierarchical Nation-State" and that traditionalists could preserve the class basis of society only by "expelling sex from the realm of respectability." One of the final blows to modernism and its defense of nation-states was the new attitude toward sex, emotions, gender discrimination, and the role of women. Do you credit this monumental change of attitude at least in part to the women's movement?

A. Sure, the women's movement is a very important expression of it, though I hate to take on single causes in a situation of this kind. I personally feel immense gratitude for the women's movement. I think it's made an awful difference to my life.

Q. In what way?

A. On every level. I happen to enjoy cooking. In our household, my wife is an attorney, so I have more time to cook than she has, though she tends to cook on weekends. That's a silly example. The fact is that I really felt through much of my life this business of living in an oppressively structured society. I really felt it very much on my pulse. I was not able to articulate it to myself; I only knew that in my relations with people from other classes, other races, and the other principal gender, I always had the sense that these relationships were distorted by irrelevant external social demands. This has always been a source of pain for me. I could go on about this, but I won't. This is becoming a sort of testimony at this point, but I'm sure some people will resonate to it. I think some of the things that happened in the late sixties and early seventies left *me* in important respects emancipated, because I have a sense that nothing is any longer seeking to have me treat women or blacks or working class people, or aristos for that matter, with attitudes that are based on anything other than what I take the people to be. For example, I go to and fro between America and England. (I don't go back to England more often than I can help, but I have so many family members there that I really have to visit.) Within two minutes of landing at Heathrow, I realize that people are reacting to me on the basis of what they perceive me as being, not on the basis of what they find me to be. They don't wait to find out what kind of person I am. They react to how I am dressed, most particularly to what my voice sounds like. To that extent, it's still a country in which interpersonal relations have a strong stereotypical component which is based on such perceptions, and I could never stand that; it's just a knife in my guts.

Q. So beyond the personal impact on your life, you do see the women's movement as being successful in general then.

A. I know there is a fair number of women, especially in the intellectual world, who feel that not much has been gained. If one's doing economic statistics and so on, I understand that. My wife's in family law, and given how the shoe pinches in family breakups and so on, it's obvious that women very often still get a raw deal. On the other hand, in terms of the general quality of social relations, I think there has been a major transformation. I don't know how widespread it is in terms of going from country to country. For instance, I think France is still basically a male chauvinist culture. When you're in France, turn on the early morning television and watch French MTV. It's terrible. I blush to look at those things—the women always in kind of slave positions as it were.

Q. American MTV is not much better.

A. Yes, but there's a kind of tongue-in-cheek quality about it. In France, it's clear they don't understand the images they themselves are generating.

Q. You've expressed "grave objections" to the strong nativist position of Chomsky and others that "the human language capacity is specific and unitary," and you seem to support instead a weaker version of the nativist thesis. Would you clarify your thoughts about innate language capacity, especially given the fact that nativism in general seems to be in such disrepute?

A. Is it? I didn't know that. Things change so quickly. Chomsky's own opinions change so quickly. It seems to me to go without saying that in many important respects the human capacity for language not only is an inherited capacity, but it has certain physiological preconditions, not least neurophysiological preconditions. One subject that I've from time to time read about is clinical neurology, particularly aphasiology, the study of the aphasias, the apraxias, the agnosias—all the different cognitive disabilities that are associated with different kinds of brain injury. It's obvious (and you only need a minimal acquaintance with that literature, which is not very hard to get because the fundamental phenomena are so striking) that in certain respects we must be born with a tendency to develop brains having a particular kind of complexity, in order, as they say with computers, to "support the software." The question is just how much is hardwired in (forgive the jargon). In regard to basic grammatical structures, for me the presumption is that they *aren't* hard-wired in. I would need a lot of convincing in a very specific case before I was prepared to concede a particular grammatical structure was hard-wired in. I remember when Chomsky gave his John Locke Lectures in Oxford. I went to all of them. Chomsky was very dismissive whenever anybody brought up evolutionary questions, and his attitude was that "anybody who asks about the evolutionary precursors of language doesn't understand what language is." I quote him; those are his words. It seems to me that if there were a species in which the linguistic structures were hard-wired in on the level of detail that Chomsky supposes, this would be a recipe for a species that is too stereotypic to survive. I think the arguments which are used to suggest that transformational grammar is hard-wired in could also be used and have been used by people to argue that Newtonian mechanics is hard-wired in, or Euclidian geometry, and so on. For instance, there is a well-known essay by Konrad Lorenz in which he claims that geese perceive the world in a non-Euclidian way, whereas human beings perceive the world in a Euclidian way. He's inclined to the view that the brains of geese must be correspondingly different from the brains of human beings. Now, I'm skeptical about that. I think the fact is that there are very interesting arguments to be gone into about why Kant was able to make such play with the uniqueness of Euclidian geometry; however, I would be prepared in the last resort to argue that the uniqueness of Euclidian geometry is rooted in pragmatic considerations, not in anything native about it that one can indeed show how it is that categories of everyday colloquial talk about spatial relations takes forms of which the Euclidian account represents a kind of legitimate idealization. There are plenty of people who don't talk that way because they don't live those lives. If you live in a jungle surrounded by mountains and you don't have enough flat land to survey and measure, and then if somebody asks you how far away a certain village is, you'll tend to answer, "Two cigarettes." You'll turn the spatial question into a temporal question. You take the question, "How far away is that village?" to mean "How long does it take to get there?" which of course is the practical question if you're living in the kind of country where cars and airplanes and so on are not available.

Let me add one more point related to nativism. Some years ago I was at McMaster University at Hamilton in Ontario, and I met a very interesting philosopher called Albert Shalom, a Jewish Québecois who had just published a book about Collingwood. We started talking about Wittgenstein, and he said cheerfully, "But of course, Wittgenstein is a cultural relativist." My eyebrows went up and I asked him to expand on this. He explained, "But of course, agreement in concepts is possible only where there are shared forms of life; different cultures have different forms of life; ergo, all concepts are culturally relative." Three months later, I met David Hamlyn (who edited *Mind*) at London University, and I reported this conversation with Shalom. He laughed airily and said, "But of course that's wrong; of course, Wittgenstein is a nativist." Again my eyebrows went up, and I asked him why he said this. He replied, "Obviously, we understand each other perfectly well across cultural boundaries; therefore, all the basic forms of life must in some way or another be hard-wired in." He didn't use that phrase, for this was some years ago, but he meant they must have some kind of physiological basis. Now, what I want to say about this is that it's clear to me that Wittgenstein deliberately avoided taking a position on this subject for reasons that seem to me to be partly arbitrary but generally sufficient. They're arbitrary in that what he's doing is seeking to draw a line between philosophical and scientific issues, and what he is refusing to do is to admit this question of nativism or relativism into his philosophical discussion. On the other hand, it seems to me that there is a perfectly good point to be made, which is that you can't generalize about it; there may well be *some* concepts, *some* modes of perception, *some* cognitive categories that turn out to be, at any rate with certain qualifications, cultural universals.

There is a very interesting woman at Berkeley, Eleanor Rosch, who has done a lot of work on cognitive categories, beginning with questions about how it is that color language has some pervasive similarities across many cultural boundaries. She was led to the conclusion that, indeed, we are so equipped in terms of our color vision that some colors, so to say, demand to be recognized (or, as she puts it, are "salient in perception"), whereas there are others that we find it harder to recognize and name. She has extended this work in many ways. But all of this is something we have to find out as we go along. The idea that we could produce arguments for demonstrating that the entirety of transformational grammar must somehow or other be physiologically available to people seems to me to be just a wild overgeneralization. Of course, it's quite compatible, as you've said, with a weaker kind of nativism. My nativism is one in which any claim that some aspect of language use has an inherited physiological basis has to be established afresh by real evidence, such as medical evidence—for instance, from research into people who have had particular kinds of brain injuries. Such work is very interesting. For example, there was a wonderful man called Alexander Romanovich Luria, who was a student of Vygotsky. He did some extraordinary work during the Second World War while in a hospital looking after people who'd been wounded in the head, and what he discovered is that people who grow up in ideographic cultures and people who grow up in alphabetic cultures display differences in syndromes of aphasia with the same brain injury. In alphabetic cultures, there's a direct relationship between language as it is spoken and heard and language as it is written and read. Indeed, there's a fair amount of evidence that when the likes of us, growing up in an alphabetic culture, learn to read and write, we do so in a way that establishes neurological pathways that are in certain respects parasitical on the pathways that have already been established in learning to talk and to understand spoken language, whereas if you're Chinese and you grow up with ideograms, this sort of phonological relationship isn't available to you. So to that extent, learning to write in Chinese is much more like learning to paint than it is like learning to write in alphabetic language: you paint a picture of the idea; you don't produce a written record of the word.

Q. So the notion of how you handle concepts is different.

A. To the extent that handling concepts is what goes on in the public domain, it could very well be the same; but to the extent that some of these operations become internalized, yes, they'd be different in different cultures.

Q. A large portion of *Cosmopolis* concerns deestablishing received views about when the modern age began. Why is this so important?

A. It's important because the most striking change that took place in the culture of Europe and that deserves to be marked as the transition from one age to another is that which followed the general availability of printed books, as a result of which you get a lay culture alongside and eventually displacing the ecclesiastical culture. If there's any single feature characteristic of what we call the Middle Ages, it is the dominance of the ecclesiastical culture and the associated creation of a transnational community of scholars, chancellors and clerics of different kinds whose task was both to define and transmit the received culture; they were the bearers of culture, and they decided what belonged in it. Of course, there were wandering scholars and other eccentric folk whose goings on we're beginning to appreciate better, thanks to such people as Helen Waddell and Carlo Ginzburg; but still, the received culture as it exists almost down to 1500 is the culture as defined and transmitted within this community of scholars who were also clerics. Of course, there was Chaucer, and of course there were exceptions (especially in Italy, where the Renaissance began early), but still I see this as the vital transition. Things that happened in the seventeenth century, with the emergence of the exact sciences and Cartesianism and all the rest, would have been impossible if not for events occurring at the very end of the fifteenth century but primarily in the sixteenth century. After all, it's not for nothing that Erasmus, Rabelais, Cervantes, Montaigne, and Shakespeare all lived in a situation in which there was a minimal amount of exact sciences to pay any attention to. Their conception of what there was to write and talk about was formed in this situation. This is why we call them humanists; their preoccupations were those of the humanities, and they were the people who recovered and made more widely available the bits of classical antiquity that had never been properly attended to in the High Middle Ages: Plutarch, Sophocles, Ovid, and the rest.

That's only the beginning of an answer; the reason why this is important is that, as I argue at the end of the book, it's only by placing our inheritance from the exact sciences within the context of our inheritance from the humanities that we give ourselves an agenda which has a future. Think of the 1992 Rio Conference. The idea of more heads of government meeting in the same place at the same time than ever before in history—the idea that Rachel Carson did *this*? This is an extraordinary exemplification of what scientific thinking becomes when it finds the salient points at which you can touch political nerves. I'm not saying that I overrate the Rio Conference, only that it's phenomenal that it happened. The issues that the conference was intended to address have some very deep, difficult, and important intellectual questions associated with them. It's impossible to say those questions are only scientific ones or only humanistic ones, because they are precisely the kinds of questions that arise within this new overlap of the exact sciences and the humanities.

Q. You say in *Cosmopolis*, "The opening gambit of modern philosophy becomes, not the decontextualized rationalism of Descartes' *Discourse* and *Meditations*, but Montaigne's restatement of classical skepticism in the *Apology*. . . . He believed that there is no general truth about which certainty is possible, and concluded that we can claim certainty about nothing." Yet, these values are often cited as "postmodern." In fact, some composition scholars point directly to Montaigne and his "open-ended inquiry" and his "resistance to closure" as desirable facets of a postmodern pedagogy. What are your thoughts about this seeming contradiction?

A. At the meeting with the speech communication people, one comment seemed to me to be both extremely intelligent and amusing. Somebody was wondering what to call the attitude I'd been presenting in my lecture for them and came up with this wonderful phrase: "neo-premodern." I confess that in some ways I'm more a neo-premodernist than I am a postmodernist. I think the thing to do after rejecting Cartesianism is not to go on through the wreckage of the temple but to go back into the town where this heretical temple was built and rediscover the life that was lived by people for many centuries before the rationalist dream seized hold of people's minds. I'd never thought of calling myself a neo-premodern, but there is a sense in which this does capture some of my preoccupations. I didn't know that others were actually seeking to develop a pedagogy based on postmodern ideas. I'd be interested to see what this cashed in for and how it was worked out in detail.

Q. So you don't find a problem with people using Montaigne as a precursor to postmodern ideas?

A. I think Montaigne is much better than nearly everybody I've read who's consciously postmodernist, so I think the idea of their reading Montaigne and learning from him is desirable. They may end up writing in a less grandiosely theoretical and more illuminatingly concrete style. Montaigne may help to cure them of their habits of abstraction. By the way, since we're speaking of Montaigne and since you mentioned Geertz earlier, let me point out that one of the important points I argue in *Cosmopolis* is that there was no reason in the world that we shouldn't have had a perfectly well-formed program for cultural anthropology by the end of the seventeenth century, given the impetus Montaigne potentially provided. But because of this shift of attention to rationalism and the goal of unique theories, the kinds of questions that cultural anthropologists were to ask during the twentieth century came to appear not intellectually serious. So I think the creation of cultural anthropology was deferred for two-hundred years as a result of the intellectual influence of the rationalists, and that seems to me to have been a pity. That's an exaggeration but an exaggeration in the right direction. One could make the point that Diderot and others in the intervening period had a feel for these issues; on the other hand, persuading the academic world to take cultural anthropology seriously was like pulling hen's teeth—it was a problematic business.

Q. You argue in *Human Understanding* that if we are ever going to be able to increase our understanding of human understanding we must halt the increasing tendency to compartmentalize academic areas and disciplines, "For the very boundaries between academic disciplines are themselves a consequence of the current divisions of intellectual authority, and the justice of those divisions is itself one of the chief questions to be faced afresh." And in *Cosmopolis* you say, "The intellectual tasks for a science in which all the branches are accepted as equally serious call for more subdisciplinary, transdisciplinary, and multidisciplinary reasoning." How can we stop the trend toward increasing compartmentalization and instead encourage the kind of intellectual border crossing that you espouse?

A. On a certain level, I'm less pessimistic than perhaps I was earlier. If you take a historical view, what you find is that transdisciplinary inquiries are always being started up, and it's sort of a natural sequence that after awhile what had previously appeared to be transdisciplinary comes to appear to be centrally disciplinary. I can't tell you how transdisciplinary and eccentric molecular biology was when it was first thought up; it was the ultimate transdisciplinary activity. Now it's almost stuffy; it's really one of the central pillars. I honestly think the situation is better now than it was thirty years ago; I think people are more aware of the danger of compartmentalization, and I think that federal funding agencies such as the National Science Foundation and the MacArthur Foundation are more on the lookout for new interbreedings between established academic disciplines. I see these groups as facilitators; there's a better recognition that it's no good feeding all the financial support into the long-established disciplines because you'll end up getting stereotyped stuff again and you'll miss the winners.

Q. You have written, "When Wittgenstein and Rorty argue that philosophy is at 'the end of the road,' they are overdramatizing the situation. The present state of the subject marks the return from a theory-centered conception, dominated by a concern for *stability* and *rigor*, to a renewed acceptance of practice, which requires us to *adapt* action to the special demands of particular occasions. . . . The task is not to build new, more comprehensive systems of theory with universal and timeless relevance, but to limit the scope of even the best-framed theories and fight the intellectual reductionism that became entrenched during the ascendancy of rationalism." This is reminiscent of Geertz's "local knowledge" and Fish's campaign "against theory." Do you believe there will be *any* role for theory in the postmodern age other than the limited scope you refer to?

A. I don't know what people mean by "theory" in this situation. To talk Rortian for the moment, there's a contrast between theory with a capital *T* and theories with small *t*'s. As I said, I was a physicist and lived among scientists, and so I have a general feel for the way all of *that* language goes. Their theories tend to have small *t*'s, and it's plain that there will always be lots of them. This is "theory" in the sense of playing hunches and thinking of possible explanations of things not necessarily confined to science. You know, detectives involved in criminal investigations have their theories about who did it, and Miss Marple is full of theories with small *t*'s. When people ask about the future role of theory and they're talking about theory with a big *T*, I'm inclined to shake hands with Rorty and say there is probably no legitimate role for theory with a big *T*; we should be prepared to kiss rationalism goodbye and walk off in the opposite direction with joy in our hearts. However, all those theories with little *t*'s (and some of them may aim prematurely to achieve slightly more grandiose things than are there to be achieved) will be part of what goes on in the intellectual world in the future as in the past. It seems to me that when we look back historically and discuss matters of an ideological tendency, we tend to see the things that happened in previous centuries too much in terms shaped by the categories we inherited from rationalist philosophy. The early decades of the social and behavioral sciences were terribly damaged by the tendency to think that what the inductive logician said about science was the same as science, so people busily tried to put psychology into a form that would be acceptable to the inductive logicians. But if you'd really been a physicist and knew about the life of the exact sciences as it goes on at places like Rockefeller University, then you knew that what the inductive logician said was really beside the point.

There's a very interesting group of people now doing what they call the ethnography of science; there are many of them, but Sharon Traweek comes to mind. (I've always had the feeling there should be a subject of this kind.) What I'm leading to is a wonderful essay by the late Peter Medawar called "Is the Scientific Paper Fraudulent?" He points out that a scientific paper tends to be presented in such a way that it looks as though it were a historical narrative, but that's absolutely irrelevant to what it's there to do. There's no guarantee whatever that the way things are presented in the paper was historically the order in which they were done in the actual lab or in the research inquiry which is being reported on. The purpose of the scientific paper is to make a point, to provide substantive foundation for some new twist in the science in question.

Q. It's persuasive, argumentative.

A. Yes, it's intended to be persuasive, argumentative. But that means there are all kinds of limitations on the view of science you get if all you have to go on is the printed texts. I always enjoyed sitting in the bar at Rockefeller University at the end of the afternoon and listening to scientists talk to each other because what they talked about among themselves when they weren't writing papers was much more revealing about what was bugging them, why they were having difficulties, what they hadn't yet figured out, what kind of sense they were going to make of their results; it's all quite a different story. So an intellectual history based on the categories of rationalism is like an account of science that only looks at printed texts. You must dig down and find out what the people are really up to and why certain things are perceived as difficulties and others are glossed over; that's part of reinserting the activity of science within the humane world.

Q. You write that the thesis of *Human Understanding* is that "in science and philosophy alike, an exclusive preoccupation with logical systematicity has been destructive of both historical understanding and rational criticism." You go on to say that people "demonstrate their rationality, not by ordering their concepts and beliefs in tidy formal structures, but by their preparedness to respond to novel situations with open minds." Then, in *Cosmopolis*, you argue that in the postmodern age we don't need to replace "rationality" with "absurdity," as you say Lyotard and the deconstructionists believe; rather, we need to reconceptualize rationality as non-systemic. How would you characterize this new postmodern rationality? How would it work?

A. First, within this new situation we should be much less tempted to contrast "rationality" with "reasonableness." One of the mysteries of the whole rationalist era was the way in which reasonableness was pushed aside as not being intellectually serious; only rationality counted. I think this was associated with a kind of worship of algorithms, a worship of formal arguments, and an insistence on getting the "right answer," with the assumption that there *is* a "right answer." Let me give you an example. I have tended, over the last few years, to spend about one half-day a week in the University of Chicago Hospital working alongside doctors whose business is to think about and discuss and arrive at conclusions about the moral problems that arise in the context of the clinical practice of medicine. Now, there's no way you're going to answer *those* questions by some kind of formal algorithm. I'm not saying that mathematics is entirely irrelevant, but in the last resort the question of how the decision to turn off the life-support system is going to be arrived at is one that (I certainly wouldn't want to say this is an "irrational" or even a "nonrational" question) has to be dealt with with an immense awareness of all that is at stake: what the possibilities are, what the presumed wishes of the unconscious patient are, what the attitudes of the family are, and a lot of other factors. I'd be inclined to say that this is a nice exemplar of the demands of rationality, the demands of reason within the new situation where theory has a highly circumscribed status. I talked earlier about the Rio Conference and the questions that arise in ecology. There is a point in *Cosmopolis* (and also in my "Recovery of Practical Philosophy" lecture) at which I say that the crucial questions now have to do with environmental issues, medical ethics, psychiatric issues, and things of that kind. If there is a mind-body problem left, one could only throw some light on it by philosophers sitting down with and among and listening to working psychiatrists—clinical psychiatrists, not just psychiatrists theorizing but psychiatrists who are actually figuring out how they can help patients and what is feasible and what can be done.

There is a more general point I should make. At the speech communication conference, I talked with a woman who'd been trained at Berkeley's Department of Rhetoric. She commented, "Everything we do these days, all the dissertations written in the Berkeley rhetoric department, are always about the rhetoric of this, the rhetoric of that, the rhetoric of the other. They never talk about rhetoric as a subject that could be discussed in isolation from all the other enterprises within which language is used in ways that students of rhetoric are interested in." It seems to me that philosophy is in the same position. Ronald Dworkin writes about current problems in law from a philosophical point of view, and his long complex essays come out in *The New York Review*. Philosophy of science is done increasingly by people who understand the problems of science from *inside* science. My friend and colleague David Hull writes about evolutionary biology as a result of being continually engaged in the study of evolutionary biology and discussions with biologists; so philosophers are engaged in helping to clarify the way ahead for evolutionary biology as much as people like Dworkin are engaged in, for instance, finding ways of stymieing the promotion of Judge Bork. Arthur Danto's essays in *The Nation* on contemporary art are both very philosophical but also very much concerned with the actual substance of what's going on in the New York art scene. Hence, you've got philosophy of law, philosophy of science, philosophy of art. I think philosophers often do their best work when they turn their skills to helping to hoe other people's vineyards, which of course is John Locke's old crack about being an underlaborer clearing away the underbrush that stands in the way of understanding.

Q. So a new kind of rationality would be contextualized within specific areas.

A. Yes. The trouble is that the word *rationality* is like the word *rhetoric*. It's got too much of a historical burden now; it's too much concerned with the development of algorithms and the use of formal procedures. As I've said, we need to break down the distinction between rationality and reasonableness. It would be much less misleading to say that we have to make sure that we make the decision whether and when to turn off the life-support system in a "reasonable" manner than to say that we have to have a "rational" procedure for making that decision.

Q. It's akin to the big and little *t*'s of theory; now we have a big and little *r*.

A. Yes, that's actually a very interesting thing to say because the critical theory literature oscillates between using the word *rational* with, as it were, a small *r* and then referring to "rationality" in a way that I think immediately suggests a capital *R* in Rorty's sense. The arguments built around the concept of rationality tend to be themselves Cartesian, even if they are turned against the inheritance of Descartes. They are Cartesian in that you can only understand what is being said by understanding it as referring to some sort of foundationalist mode of talking about the products of the human reason, and that's not there for us anymore.

Q. You've put forth numerous controversial propositions in several disciplinary areas, including logic, philosophy of science, and rhetoric. Such work has led to a considerable amount of criticism. Are there any criticisms or misunderstandings of your work that you would like to address at this time?

A. I have shamelessly failed to pay attention to criticism of my work. I have a colleague at the University of Pittsburgh, Adolf Grunbaum, who is so hurt by criticism that if you write even a friendly three-page note in some journal he'll come back with a twenty-one page correction of your misunderstandings of his position. He was once sleepless for a long time because *Philosophy of Science Quarterly* had devoted a whole issue to his ideas, and there in print were all of these papers by people who he thought were his friends and who thought of themselves as his friends, but the papers were so full of misunderstandings that he didn't see how he would ever succeed in correcting them. It's unfair of me to cite Adolf; he's a nice fellow but feels he can't let anything pass. I'm absolutely the opposite: I quite shamelessly let everything pass because I'm much more interested in writing the next book. To return to the very first thing we were talking about, I know well that I put as much work as I possibly could into making what I said plain and intelligible. And I do find that a surprisingly large number of people turn out to have read my work and understood perfectly well what I was saying. On the whole, the people who are captious are those who have their own axe to grind. They use what they take my views to be, not always in as friendly a spirit as Charlie Willard, as a whipping post of some kind or another. It's all a question of priorities. By the time the criticisms of any one book come out, I've moved into another area, and I feel disinclined to go back and root around in a field I've left.

"The Good Man Speaking Well," or Business as Usual

ARABELLA LYON

I remember first reading Stephen Toulmin on aims and commensurability. Responding to Kuhn's vision of competing paradigms, he wrote,

> When two scientific positions share similar intellectual aims and fall within the scope of the same discipline, the historical transition between them can always be discussed in "rational" terms, even though their respective supporters have no theoretical concepts in common. (*Understanding* 126)

On first read, Toulmin's adage—disciplined discourses are "always" commensurable if common aims can be found—seems more than simply useful; it explains the success of many amazing scientific and non-scientific communications. It helps me understand why I can order coffee in Paris though I do not speak French and why I can teach multiethnic classes of basic writers by emphasizing our common goal of academic success. In addition to providing an explanation for communicative accomplishments, his adage suggests a strategy for revising unsuccessful communication; that is, if at first you don't succeed, find common aims. But in my initial encounter, what I found *most* appealing was that Toulmin provided a one-line rebuttal, a bulwark, to all the chaos and danger of incommensurable discourses theorized by postmodernists. If people find common aims, then they can reason together, deliberate together, and agree on action. Toulmin, ever "the good man speaking well," provides a stable approach to traditional democracy and education in a changing society.

My naive hope for the enterprises of deliberation and reasoned commonality has long since vanished. Toulmin, however, continues to believe we can come together and reason our way to common action, and his many projects, though philosophical, are all concerned with situated, micro-social, persuasive knowledge, and therefore continue to be used in the research and teaching of rhetoric and composition. Without a doubt, Toulmin's contributions to our field are magnificent, and yet I come away from his interview deeply, sleeplessly troubled.

Rhetoric and Pluralism
In her recent *JAC* response to Clifford Geertz, Lisa Ede notes that Geertz's pluralism is both attractive and suspect, and this theme, though she pursues

others, is worthy of more analysis, especially in the context of Toulmin's interview. The Toulmin interview, because it enacts both the attractive and suspect aspects of pluralism, dramatizes pluralism's appeal as well as the problems that it presents to a community. And I would argue that his enactment of pluralism may well be key to understanding the politics of our own field. After all, rhetoric and composition, even in its dual name, engages the problematic of pluralism.

Pluralism, the attempt to place everything in the field of persuasion, is always an ambivalent term, a term pulled between tolerance and dominance, multiplicity and commonality, marriage and seduction. Feminists, most concerned with its dangers, have best analyzed the implications of its allures and perils. For instance, Annette Kolodny characterizes feminist pluralism attractively as "the acknowledgement that we do not and need not adhere to identical ideologies" in order to "continue talking to, arguing with, and learning from one another" (Gardiner et al. 667). But Ellen Rooney's suspicious characterization may be more revealing. She finds that pluralism is often a centrist effort to contain both radical relativism and beliefs based on monistic theories or radical subjectivism; to control these disruptive positions, pluralism conceives the grounds of meaning as based in a persuadable audience and constructs every interpreter "as an effect of the desire to persuade" (22, 1). Since many pluralistic activities limit what is heard by whom, Rooney sees some pluralisms as "*nothing but* the desire to adjudicate other theories and thus other practices from above" (32). By Rooney's account, pluralists seek to arbitrate ideas, ideologies, and actions at a level above the committed and uncommitted. So while Kolodny theorizes an ideal practice of feminism, Rooney analyzes its practice in literary theory and finds it suspect.

With either understanding of pluralism, Kolodny's or Rooney's, we can see that it is implicated in theories of rhetoric based on persuasion, conversation, dialogue, dialectic, and reason. Toulmin professes this familiar kind of rhetoric, and his interview reveals precisely the ambivalence between the appealing theorization and suspect practice of pluralism.

Toulmin is, in fact, a pluralist (perhaps a required attribute of the "good man"). He welcomes diverse applications of his work, provided they are not "dogmatic." He encourages transdisciplinary inquiry, dismisses insistence on the "right answer," and values persuasion, whether in scientific texts or at the Rio conference. And if the interview itself is insufficient evidence for his pluralism, in *Cosmopolis*, he writes,

> There may be no rational way to convert to our point of view people who honestly hold other positions, but we cannot short circuit such disagreements. Instead, we should live with them, as further evidence of the diversity of human life. Later on, these differences may be resolved by further shared experience, which allows different schools to converge. In advance of this experience, we must accept this diversity of views in a spirit of toleration. (30)

Here, Toulmin expresses both a tolerance of difference and the expectant hope of convergence. Unlike Kolodny's, Toulmin's *purpose* is neither the preservation of nor respect for difference, but rather convergence. His pluralism desires to construct others as a persuadable audience, *not* as subjects with different but valid ideologies.

The desire for convergence—not in itself terrifying, and certainly inherent in any persuasive activity—optimistically requires bilateral movement: both audience and rhetor reconsider their position and that of the other and somehow come to share each other's experience. Predictably, it is hard to find a clear instance of this. Ideally, in our field, rhetoricians would read experimental studies, and experimentalists would quote the sophists; but, as we know, practice deviates from the ideal: after graduate school, this rarely happens at levels sufficient to transform individual or disciplinary practice. Toulmin hopes for ideal practice, a dialectic between audience and speaker, but his practice deviates, too *(Uses* 19). Toulmin's desire to adjudicate from above, from *his* reasoned space, as well as his fear of monistic theories and relativism are enacted repeatedly throughout the interview—most noticeably in his *dismissal* of various intellectual perspectives, his *domestication* of feminism, and his *refusal* to read critics.

Toulmin clearly dismisses monism and relativism, positions which Rooney characterizes as unacceptable to pluralists. The move to dismissal is most explicit in his discussion of alternative interpretations of Wittgenstein. He raised his eyebrows at Albert Shalom's assertion that Wittgenstein was a cultural relativist and again when David Hamlyn asserts that Wittgenstein was a nativist. Rather than draw the conclusion that interpretations of Wittgenstein are wildly divergent, he instead says, "It's clear to me. that Wittgenstein deliberately avoided taking a position," and rejects the interpretations of other scholars. His dismissal of Chomsky and postmodernists repeats the pattern, but the structuralist Chomsky's monistic view warrants hearings and discussions prior to "grave objections," while Jean-François Lyotard simply is dismissed as absurd, and deconstruction as not "a prudent investment." Despite his promise not to "short circuit" disagreements, Toulmin, at times, refuses the activities that create informed disagreement and deliberation. When the assumptions, questions, debates, and vocabulary differ significantly from his, when faced with a "historical transition" in his discipline, the good man fails to seek the new "'rational' terms" of discussion; he instead denies their existence *without* the necessary exertion to confirm their absence. With the advent of real difference, the effort required for that difficult dialogue is evaded.

Toulmin's domestication and cooptation of the women's movement exemplifies all that feminists suspect of pluralism: in just a few lines, he reduces an international human rights movement committed to issues as basic as suffrage and control of one's body to *his* increased freedom to cook. Having given this "silly" example, he proceeds to speak of feminism's worth in freeing him from sexism, racism, and classism, a freedom that few could claim in honesty. When Toulmin declares that "nothing" is interfering with his ability to take people as they are, the statement begs to be read as a denial of difference and of social and language structures. Toulmin seems unaware of the unavoidable difficulties both in understanding other people and in speaking and thinking in a language that is always historically structured and partial in its representations. The concepts of difference, margin, and center elude him. When Olson prods Toulmin to reflect on feminism in a larger frame than his own life, Toulmin acknowledges that "women very often still get a raw deal," but he amends that to say social relations are better, though *maybe* not in exotic countries such as *France*. In his discussion of feminism, Toulmin gives no evidence that he even attempts to conceive of lives outside the Anglo-American male experience.

Finally (for issues of space rather than exhaustion), Toulmin's admitted failure to read his critics calls into question his commitment to the sharing of ideas. At one level, this failure replicates his refusal to invest in reading French postmodernism, but in refusing to read his critics, he also is curtailing dialogue about his own thinking. Given Toulmin's avoidance of critique, Lyotard then seems not so absurd when he asserts that "the institution of knowledge functions . . . like an ordinary power center whose behavior is governed by a principle of homeostasis" (63). That is, the ability of any group to participate in knowledge-production depends on its ability to conform to the existing norms; a player can participate, be read, only if he or she conforms. Thus, consensus, as described by Lyotard, is an inherently conservative activity, especially conservative if the center does not read either its critics or its margins. Toulmin, in this interview, performs exactly the behaviors that precipitate Lyotard's call for a change from a goal of consensus to that of justice (66).

While the practice of pluralism can be far more complex than a cooptive move to consensus (and often is), pluralism and consensus, for Toulmin, seem to require a tame feminism, a tame Wittgenstein, the denial of twenty years of postmodern writing, and the omission of his critics. His practice demonstrates the limits of the "micro-social" (what Toulmin calls "me and my friends") in the process of deliberation and ironically gives ample evidence for the incommensurability of discourses theorized by Lyotard.

The Pluralistic Discipline of Rhetoric and Composition
I once heard the philosopher Stanley Cavell, a good man, say that he wrote as a better man than he was; that was part of the wonder of writing and, in part, why he wrote. Toulmin, too, writes a better man. The dichotomy between his hopeful writings on commensurability and pluralism and his ability to recognize and address difference is significant and probably unconscious, but the split between his theory and his practice presents the dangerous inadequacies of pluralism. In taming Wittgenstein and feminism and ignoring

deconstructionists and his own critics, Toulmin demonstrates why the struggle to think our own future agenda or agendas will require more than placing our scientific inheritance "within the context of our inheritance from the humanities." While his efforts to free disciplinary knowledge from rationalism are valuable, a new humanism will require more than a promise of open-ended reason. Open-ended reason is just a new yardstick when what is needed are ways to comprehend our positions and our diverging discourses in the multidimensional world of human action. After modernism's failure to find foundations, humanism must turn to the further development of self-critique and justice—if only to reveal the Other's outlines and our own.

Rhetoric and composition itself is a pluralistic discipline; our methodologies—close reading, ethnography, discourse analysis—diverge as well as intersect; our formal training in education, English, or communication reflects the multiple intellectual aims that form our questions. As the discipline develops, our research becomes more specialized and harder to evaluate from across the field; we sometimes fail to recognize each other's outlines, situations, and aims and how they are circumscribed by institutional discourses. Thus, the disciplinary tensions underlying our current practice, tensions between current-traditional and sophistic rhetoric, between *paideia* and liberation pedagogy, between theory and practice, are increasing. These tensions can be productive if the discipline uses them to demarcate sites for deliberation and growth, if it uses them to hone tools of self-critique and justice. But the tensions also can divide us.

Differences—whether as disruptions to the community or as sites for critique, demarcation, and growth—call for special recognition, a careful self-reading; but as Toulmin demonstrates, that kind of reading is difficult. For a careful self-reading to happen, rhetoricians and compositionists will need to conceptualize—in pragmatic, situated ways—where differences position us both within the structure of the university and in our disciplinary work.

Faced with the impulse to adjudicate difference and given the theories discussed so far, we have at least three postures toward persuasion to consider: anti-pluralism, convergence pluralism, and tolerant pluralism. Each posture has political strength, but in the complexity of human life, rarely is any one posture enough for extended play, or could it be effective in all situations; the three postures are only possible conversational moments which shift with the rhetorical situation; they are codicils to persuasion by good reasons.

In sparse gesture or outline, let me demonstrate how the postures already play in institutional and disciplinary practice; while this is offered only as an outline, not an argument, I believe it is a useful reminder of the politics implicit in the activity of persuading. Too often a seductive persuasion with undesirable outcomes is blamed on a sophistic rhetor, and the role of the audience in controlling a situation is minimized. But the demagogic rhetor before the ignorant crowd is far from the only rhetorical dynamic.

Anti-pluralism, the refusal of persuasion, has been offered as a necessary though self-conscious position by feminists such as bell hooks and Gayatri Spivak. By insisting on one's difference, one maintains its value and a voice for its value; one successfully keeps a novel value before the speaker. In English departments, rhetoricians and compositionists do this by insisting on the value of student texts and public discourse as opposed to the texts of high culture. In refusing literary models, they create a position separate from the more populous factions of English departments, and since the center most easily contains the margin by its own adaptation, some literary factions recently have responded by defining themselves as cultural studies and granting intellectual status to the study of ordinary language.

Convergence pluralism, Toulmin's theoretical model, seeks a synthesis and ordering of values and practices, but in the process of convergence, it minimizes the values of marginal positions. Its hope for political harmony usually entails accepting the power of the majority as well as cacophony and conflict along the way. An example: in English departments, rhetoricians often are privileged above experimentalists and ethnographers because the methodologies of rhetoric more closely approximate those of the *literati*. For purposes of convergence, rhetoric may become writing's departmental voice; still, it is worth noting that the rhetoric of English departments often identifies with hermeneutic techniques, methods of reading, rather than with the pedagogical or political art of performance. Thus, the convergence requires adaptation even within rhetorical practice; that is, rhetoric becomes more theoretical and interpretive. The pattern of privileging is reversed in education programs where often composition's methodologies and pedagogies dominate. In each case, however, the character of a larger community decides what is valuable for rhetoric and composition and slights the criteria of our own broad practices.

Tolerant pluralism, exemplified by Kolodny's acceptance of different ideologies, is a fragile and transient posture. The suspension of judgment, a therapeutic stance, may facilitate the solving of problems and support movements toward justice. But in addition to the practice of open responsiveness, which requires the temporary abandoning or minimizing of our personal disciplinary aims and priorities, tolerant pluralism requires "talking to, arguing with, and learning from," and that is difficult. Rhetoricians and compositionists come together in organizations such as NCTE or MLA, but they find even their internal diversity uncomfortable. After all, what sessions do you attend? What do you retain or use from a session based on a different methodology? I think it is safe to say, "talking to, arguing with, and learning from" happens. But most often it happens across small difference, not large.

These three postures toward persuasion clearly are in need of more discussion than this essay can provide, but I think it safe to conclude that once speakers acknowledge that they are not operating in a formal system of logic or rationalism, once they have accepted Toulmin's arguments for reason over rationality and the situatedness of knowledge (and who hasn't in 1993?), the next step seems to be the consideration of power and difference. As Toulmin's interview shows, ignoring these postmodern concerns diminishes the justice and wisdom of a good man's arguments.

Without a doubt, Toulmin's work has been significant in reestablishing the value of practical reason in the process of deliberation, but throughout his interview, he enacts the split between the professing of pluralism and the practice of recognizing and respecting difference. At his best, Toulmin recognizes the struggle, saying "all knowledge is related to a human interest of one kind or another." But that insight does not lead him to the observation that reason also is a social construct, no more than the elaborate invention of some "me and my friends," certainly no guarantee of dialogue or justice. A good man can speak well, but that never, by itself, stops business from proceeding as usual.

Temple University
Philadelphia, Pennsylvania

Works Cited

Ede, Lisa. "Clifford Geertz on Writing and Rhetoric." *(Inter)views: Cross-Disciplinary Perspectives on Rhetoric and Literacy.* Ed. Gary A. Olson and Irene Gale. Carbondale: Southern Illinois UP, 1991. 219-23.

Gardiner, Judith Kegan, et al. "An Interchange on Feminist Criticism: On 'Dancing through the Minefield.'" *Feminist Studies* 8 (1982): 629-75.

Hooks, Bell. *Yearning: Race, Gender, and Cultural Politics.* Boston: South End P, 1990.

Lyotard, Jean-François. *The Postmodern Condition: A Report on Knowledge.* Trans. Geoff Bennington and Brian Massumi. Minneapolis: U of Minnesota P, 1984.

Rooney, Ellen. *Seductive Reasoning: Pluralism as the Problematic of Contemporary Literary Theory.* Ithaca: Cornell UP, 1989.

Spivak, Gayatri. *In Other Worlds: Essays in Cultural Politics.* New York: Methuen, 1987.

Toulmin, Stephen. *Cosmopolis: The Hidden Agenda of Modernity.* New York: Macmillan, 1990.

———. *Human Understanding.* Princeton: Princeton UP, 1972.

———. *The Uses of Argument.* Cambridge: Cambridge UP, 1969.

Novissimum Organum:
Phronesis on the Rebound

C. JAN SWEARINGEN

Human understanding, reasonableness, and the interdependence—even identity—of rhetoric and hermeneutics: these seem to me the most resonant chords struck in *JAC*'s interview with Stephen Toulmin. Not long before *Cosmopolis* appeared, *The Return to Cosmology* examined a group of twentieth-century thinkers, among them Teilhard de Chardin and Gregory Bateson. Toulmin emphasizes that they restored systemic and teleological dynamics to desiccated fields that had lost their way in forests of subspecializations and micromethodologies. Through persistence in emphasizing collective uses of concepts and their ongoing evolution in contexts, Toulmin integrates, harmonizes, cross references, recontextualizes, and dreams of being one among the most recent creators of *nova organa*, with a glance back at Aristotle and Bacon, and aside to contemporary figures like Teilhard. Aristotle's and Bacon's are two of the better-known precursors. The designation *novum organon* is apt, for a number of reasons. It emphasizes that in animating and orchestrating the instrument, creativity, the *novum* in the *organon*, comes into being. We can do with a few nova ova just now amid necromantic theories and theorists proclaiming the death of all matter human and humanistic.

Toulmin's objections to proponents of literary analysis and criticism as sciences are reminiscent of I.A. Richards' attempts to defend metaphor and rhetoric alike against the new sciences of logical positivism and linguistic philosophy. Defending rationality against the onslaught of postmodern theories, and noting that their decontextual, ahistorical contours are oddly scientistic, Toulmin provides additional sketches for reunifying and redefining the relationships among philosophy, rhetoric, ethics, and logic. There is an edifying humor in the observation that a certain strand of modern Western thought has veered off the road of human companionship—mutual understanding, contexts, and history—since Descartes, a line of descent (among solipsists) that links otherwise dissimilar figures. The genealogy includes Derrida, who on many counts would seem the arch nemesis of Cartesian mentalism. Similarly, we are reminded, Chomsky severed linguistic science from the larger contexts of human understanding and experience and manifests an aggressively dismissive attitude: "Anybody who asks about the evolutionary precursors of language doesn't understand what language is." *Per contra*, Toulmin affirms the merit of studies of alphabetic versus ideographic cultures. Such studies can suggest subtle nuances in cognition and aesthetics that are shaped by language learning: "Learning to write in Chinese is much more like learning to paint." In a similarly contextual appraisal, Toulmin illuminates the debates within contemporary linguistic science from the historicizing perspective of the evolutionary hinge point at which Descartes and Montaigne part company. Placed in this line of descent, the recent developments of logical positivism and analytic philosophy can be seen as only the most recent, and not the sole, source of the linguistic turn. It is precisely this impasse that has led logicians—and proponents of argumentation within speech communication, rhetoric and composition—to restore to argumentation that limber practical wisdom that Aristotle termed *phronesis*.

Toulmin, Hermeneutics, and Theory

When Stephen Toulmin came to our Ph.D. program not long ago as Distinguished Humanities Lecturer, we had little idea how rich a fulcrum he would provide for our integrated graduate programs in rhetoric, philosophy, and literature—an exemplum of the *novissimum organon* that he gives fuller exposition here. Among our local philosophers are those for whom "rhetoric" has bad overtones. Yet they are nothing if not deeply interested in an argumentation that goes beyond p's and q's, in hermeneutics that goes beyond Heidegger, in forms of reasoning that are shared by rhetoric and philosophy and that link the sciences and the humanities. Many of our literary scholars and students had come to understand "rhetoric" as "theory," and specifically postmodern theory, even though those who teach the first-year English course are familiar with the "other" rhetoric: Aristotle and Isocrates; Cicero and Augustine; Bain, Blair, Campbell, and Whateley; Burke and Young, Becker, and Pike; and of course "the Toulmin method." The model of a *novissimum organon* amplifies the conceptual basis of local curricular ties that bind hermeneutics, logic, and rhetoric as forms of reasoning and methods of self-understanding and discoursing shared by all disciplines.

Toulmin's eager revisionism with regard to the Toulmin method invigorated our thinking concerning the place of argumentation in our first-year composition course. In a three-semester sequence that integrates reading, writing, and critical thinking, we use the Toulmin method in concert with Aristotle's topoi, Burke's Pentad, Ricoeur's interpretation theory, and tagmemics as prolegomena for reading as well as for the thinking and writing tasks that encompass a number of genres. Bacon and Montaigne mingle with Tillie Olsen and James Joyce; autobiography is aligned with history; both genres are tested against multiple concepts of the relationships among understanding, self-understanding, and reasoning. Graduate teaching assistants who had been struggling with the Toulmin method were refreshed to see Toulmin distancing himself from that method: *c'est ne pas moi.* At the same time, he urged them to use the parts that work, to find and design working parts, and not to be afraid of methods just because they are methods. These emphases place self-revision and self-revelation among the models for the kind of thinking and the modes of discourse that a *novum organon* should and can propound. "Once you get into ethics, politics, poetics, rhetoric, and the other things that Aristotle also regards as worth including in his entire series of linked projects, the thing becomes inescapably hermeneutic." Representing argumentation as hermeneutic and hermeneutics as argument encourages palintropic thinking about discoursing, reasoning, and understanding that merit special attention in an era that cries for central clearing houses, safe houses, and common languages (Berthoff, "Rhetoric"; Pratt). Finding patterns that connect is a taxing but also an exciting challenge just now as we devise ways to open up reasoning and discourse to academic disciplines and new student populations undergoing rapid metamorphosis, just as they were in the twenties, when Toulmin begins his account of the Cambridge years of G.E. Moore, I.A. Richards, and Wittgenstein.

Thinking extensively before setting pen to paper, and ample revision and editing thereafter are represented as self-revising abilities developed in order to save the reader work and thereby reduce the possibility of misunderstanding. Toulmin's reader-friendly mode of exposition is instructively inseparable from the issues he addresses in this interview. As in the essays of Montaigne, the thought and exposition lead from a tributary into a stream. Dewey, Wittgenstein, Habermas, Leibniz, and Descartes speak to one another in, through, and about their contexts, temporality, eras, and epochs. "What I found particularly unsatisfactory [about Wittgenstein] was his failure to pay any attention to the long-term intellectual significance of history." These and other reflections upon Wittgenstein at Cambridge illuminate the many points at which the twenties parallels our own era: virtually opaque esoteric mystical theories cohabiting academia with multiculturalisms, linguistic turns, philosophies of science and sciences of philosophy warring over words and worlds. It was in a similar era of ignorant armies clashing by night that I.A. Richards took such pains to address rhetoric as a remedy for misunderstanding and its remedies (Berthoff, *Richards*, esp. 106-17). Like Toulmin's, Richards' self-designated task is expressly political and pedagogical; one parallel between the two eras is marked by their shared concern for reducing misunderstanding through practical uses of reason, for restoring contexts, and for understanding how concepts evolve within contexts.

Perhaps the widest circle of all in the perspectives Toulmin weaves together here concern the various and persistent rifts that eternally divide contextualists and decontextualists, evolutionary temporalists and atemporalists. In an odd brotherhood, Descartes, Wittgenstein, Chomsky, and Lyotard are linked by a rejection of context, causality, and history. They have lost the vehicle for considerations of ethics, politics, poetics, and rhetoric that Toulmin emphasizes are the quintessentials of *phronesis,* or practical wisdom (also see Cooper; Nussbaum). Mystical opaque theory is currently appealing to left-wing intellectuals at a time of widespread political disenchantment (Berthoff, "Rhetoric"; Norris 25). Toulmin's genealogy of postmodern theory joins other recent accounts of Lyotard as among the most recent exponents of a Kantian aesthetics that in radical figures such as Baudrillard leads inescapably to political quietism: "Any politics which goes along with the current postmodernist drift will end up by effectively endorsing and promoting the work of ideological mystification, such as we find in Iran-Contragate or the Falklands war" (Norris 127). Programmatic mystification is, Toulmin observes, a far cry from the classical Pyrrhonists, whose Occamish razors sheared away with continuous questions that led them to examine how the current state of affairs came to be. Like Aristotle's, Toulmin's *organon* provides avenues for cross-referencing and practical application of such examinations, and it helps to guide discourse as well as to locate theory within an evolving conceptual world today. Teleology is an important element in the concept of *phronesis* that was so central to Aristotle's organon. It is not at all surprising that practical wisdom and some of its modern cousins such as dialogical hermeneutics and existentialism have been adopted as touchstones in recontextualizations of philosophy and rhetoric. Theory with a little *t*, after all, is simply the ability to see and think about, reflect upon. Children make great theorists because "they have not yet been educated into accepting our routine social practices as 'natural.' Children who remain discontent grow up to be emancipatory theorists, unable to conquer their amazement at what everyone else seems to take for granted" (Eagleton 34).

Toulmin emphasizes that new demands will be placed upon rationality and reason now that theory with a capital *T* has been dismantled. In the wreckage of postmodernisms, if dear Prudence is to come out and play she must have companions, instruments, a musical tradition, and license to compose and innovate. One knows oneself, Epictetus said, as a singer in a chorus in harmony with others. It is encouraging to see continuity, history, evolutionary progressions, and context receive an *accent grave* in this discussion. Social constructionist paradigms of the composing self and the composing process are superseding the process, cognitive, personal, and expressive models developed in the 1980s. Process and cognitive models, many claim, emphasize too strongly the isolated Romantic individual seeking truth and self within the mind, an emphasis that may be seen as leading to mechanistic or narcissistic isolation of writer and text alike (Crosswhite; Fishman and McCarthy; Tingle). These and other pitfalls of Romanticism are also being reappraised within reviews of the complex compound of social liberalism, democratized hermeneutics, epistemological minimalism and anti-idealism, and aesthetic libertarianism. Like Wittgenstein, who tended to "attack Descartes with Cartesian weapons," Lyotard and his tribe "are really rejecting Descartes for Cartesian reasons." Beneath all this, Toulmin suggests, lies a regressive solipsism. In one of Wittgenstein's early notebooks appears the query, "What is history to me? Mine is the first and only world." Toulmin remarks that Wittgenstein did not really get around this narcissism until after 1930, and even after that, Toulmin finds his treatments of ethics and history unsatisfactory because they cannot provide the kind of under-standing that interests Toulmin most: an account of human reason that will incorporate an explanation of how concepts change. A radically Pyrrhonhist or Cartesian view, Toulmin points out, disallows the formulation of such an explanation. On this point they are much like radical postmodern theories of linguistic determinism that generate interrogative deconstructions of meaning and knowledge alike. "The Saussurian paradigm—a form of struc-tural-linguistic a priori—stands behind Baudrillard's wholesale reduction of economic, political, and social issues to questions of symbolic exchange and the 'dissimulating' agency of the sign" (Norris 188). Cartesian and Wittgensteinian solipsism eschew "the historically changing character of argument forms and basic concepts." It was upon reaching the limits of Wittgenstein's world that Toulmin first conceived the goal of *The Uses of Argument*: to seek accounts of rationality and reasonableness.

Argumentation, Wittgenstein, and Pragmatism

The Uses of Argument was first received in England as "an antilogic book" and almost died at birth; yet, Toulmin recounts, it was soon being used "up and down the Mississippi Valley" and was selling well in unexpected quarters: speech and communication classes in argument, and then in composition courses. Not initially conceived as a work on rhetoric or argumentation, and certainly not as a model of either with classroom applications, it has enjoyed surprisingly long and happy life. In our uses of *Uses* we have found it by and large better adapted to the task of analyzing arguments than of creating them. But as in the quip that is as old at least as Cicero—that argumentation models are tools for dissecting and not for composing arguments—this has been true of most uses of argument from Aristotle to Perelman and Olbrechts-Tyteca. Toulmin's self-revision on this point proved especially fruitful in discussions with our graduate teaching assistants. In our uses of *Uses* we had already cut the warrant loose so that more than one warrant could be found for a given argument, depending on shared values and diversity of audience views that could at times function like a group of floating *koinoi topoi*. Fully drawn contexts, we have discovered, permit several warrants—not any at all, but several—to mingle in many instances of argument and persuasion, just as Shakespeare's plays operate on two levels at least: humor for the groundlings; more sophisticated syntax and lexicon for the educated. The tacit dimension (*pace* Polanyi) implied by warrants is a rich mine of inferences, interpretations, and plural examinations of how any one argument functions. Thus we were well primed when Toulmin arrived on the scene to similarly loosen up backings by specifying the very different kinds there are.

In its original context, *Uses* arose as an investigation into argument in epistemology and in particular into empiricist epistemology from Locke to Kant, up to Mach and Russell and on through to G.E. Moore and his Cambridge generation. Wittgenstein's arrival at Cambridge, and his reception by G.E. Moore, has been recounted by I.A. Richards in an interview conducted with Reuben Brower: "Wittgenstein started asking Moore questions. For the first time in our many years' experience of Moore, Moore was submissive, gentle, doing his best to understand. It was a complete reversal. Mohammed was gone to the mountain. And from that moment came Wittgenstein's dominance over Moore and over Cambridge" (Brower 10-11). How, Brower asks Richards, did meeting with Wittgenstein affect how he thought about language? Richards reports, "I was very negative. Wittgenstein was a personality who required utter devotion. People who saw much of Wittgenstein acquired what I irreverently christened 'Saint Wittgenstein's Dance.' They twitched and they pulled faces and they stopped to stare upwards" (11). Of Moore, Richards recounts, "When Wittgenstein would start a sentence ten times, Moore would write it on his pad ten times up to the point where he broke it off. Absolute devotion. Most peculiar. It gave me the creeps" (11). This might seem irrelevant gossip were it not for the fact that Wittgenstein's appearance on the Cambridge scene is generally regarded as an important shift away from the empiricist epistemology that Moore developed and toward the minimalist and analytic philosophy of language that led to the crippling demand that Toulmin defines: "that substantive arguments meet formal criteria of a sort that seemed to me (and to Aristotle) inappropriate." If that criterion was not met then the Wittgensteinian maxim was invoked: "whereof one cannot speak one must remain silent." Toulmin's *Reason in Ethics* and *Philosophy of Science* were early attempts to redress the carving away at understandings of substantive argument that were reducing it to logical positivism or nothing.

It would seem that William James' and Dewey's pragmatism provides an American antidote and counterpart to the movement away from logical minimalism. Paradoxically, Toulmin notes, one aspect of Dewey's emphasis parallels Wittgenstein's notion of a language game: language functions within collective enterprises, "not just language but *Lebensform* provide situations within which different language games can operate." Widely claimed as forefathers by contemporary neopragmatists such as Richard Rorty, James and Dewey invoked what today are termed social constructionist models of language use. And yet, Toulmin observes, "Rorty still has a highly individualistic attitude toward all philosophical issues and even toward language; anybody's welcome to invent their own language, so to say, and if you want to talk a different language that's your privilege." Once again, it seems, certain traces of Romantic expressivism and Cartesian solipsism have worked their way into ostensibly collectivist and ethically pragmatic theories. To get at this, Toulmin extends his gaze once again further back, to Descartes and the confinement that theoretical philosophy has imposed upon argumentation and the validity of arguments—since the seventeenth century (!)—within the narrow constraints of the *Prior* and *Posterior Analytics* of Aristotle. In other words, the modern confinement of logical argument is untrue to Aristotle and is no doubt one source of the modern association of Aristotle with logical formalism and syllogistic method. Toulmin argues for an alternate Aristotle, the Aristotle of the full *organon*, an Aristotle who has also been invoked in Martha Nussbaum's recent readings of Aristotle's ethics in terms of the concept of *phronesis*. Within rhetoric and composition, a similar emphasis has been defended by James Kinneavy, among others (Swearingen). In such an expanded vision of Aristotle, logic, language, and the human uses of human reason, rhetoric too receives amplification.

In what to me is among the most illuminating passages of the interview, Toulmin proposes, "Whether the argument was valid or not is a question that can be established and to which the answer can be given without peradventure, whereas once you get into ethics, politics, poetics, rhetoric, and the other things that Aristotle also regards as worth including in his entire series of linked projects, the thing becomes inescapably hermeneutic. What we call 'rhetoric' has to be understood as including dialectic, topics, all those bits of the discussion about argumentation that are not analytic. Whether it's prudent to go on calling these things 'rhetoric' when there are still many people for whom the word *rhetoric* has all kinds of bad overtones, is another question" (21-22). Prudence long ago opined that rhetoric in the eyes of the beholder might indeed a harlot be. Yet as the teacher of the uses of the tropes and figures and reasonings, Dame Rhetoric with her sword and mirror simply reminds us, with the help of Prudence, that it is no more or less than ourselves that we see: all those long lost bits of the discussion that are not analytic.

University of Texas
Arlington, Texas

Works Cited

Berthoff, Ann E. "Rhetoric as Hermeneutic." *College Composition and Communication* 42 (1991): 279-87.

——, ed. *Richards on Rhetoric, I.A. Richards: Selected Essays (1929-1974)*. New York: Oxford UP, 1991.

Brower, Reuben. "Beginnings and Transitions: I.A. Richards Interviewed by Reuben Brower." Berthoff 3-22.

Cooper, David E. *Existentialism: A Reconstruction*. Oxford: Blackwell, 1990.

Crosswhite, James. "Authorship and Individuality: Heideggerian Angles." *Journal of Advanced Composition* 12 (1992): 91-109.

Eagleton, Terry. *The Significance of Theory*. Oxford: Blackwell, 1990.

Fishman, Stephen M., and Lucille Parkinson McCarthy. "Is Expressivism Dead? Reconsidering Its Romantic Roots and Its Relation to Social Constructionism." *College English* 54 (1992): 647-61.

Norris, Christopher. *What's Wrong with Postmodernism? Critical Theory and the Ends of Philosophy*. Baltimore: Johns Hopkins UP, 1990.

Nussbaum, Martha C. *Love's Knowledge: Essays on Philosophy and Literature*. New York: Oxford UP, 1990.

Polanyi, Michael. *The Tacit Dimension*. New York: Peter Smith, 1983.

Pratt, Mary Louise. "Arts of the Contact Zone." *MLA Profession 91* (1991): 33-40.

Swearingen, C. Jan. "Pistis, Expression, and Belief: Prolegomenon for a Feminist Rhetoric of Motives." *A Rhetoric of Doing*. Ed. Stephen Witte, Roger Cherry, and Neil Nakadate. Carbondale: Southern Illinois UP, 1992. 123-43.

Tingle, Nick. "Self and Liberatory Pedagogy: Transforming Narcissism." *Journal of Advanced Composition* 12 (1992): 75-89.

Commentary: The Performance Model of Teaching and Scholarship

DAVID BLEICH

This collection of interviews, somewhat shorter and narrower in scope than its predecessor, raises many issues of interest, but the one that stood out most in my reading might be called the "performance model" of teaching and scholarship, a term Jane Tompkins uses explicitly. While all of those interviewed feel to one degree or another that change is in the offing in the academy, most show a continuing devotion—partly conscious, partly unconscious—to the traditional identity of the university faculty member as an individual who must perform intellectually and individually for students, who must perform through individual publication for the university administration to secure salary and promotion, and who must perform individually in the profession to secure a measure of "national and international reputation." In part, the interviews point the interviewees toward themselves; in part, the ideology of individualism has too much historical, cultural, and psychological momentum to respond to demands for immediate change. It repays reading these interviews, therefore, as a measure of how the performance model of teaching and scholarship appears in these different sorts of scholars and teachers. We can see arguments for and against this model, and we can see, finally, that one need not throw it out altogether. Rather, these interviews suggest that an underlying ideological change toward collectivist values in the academy will change what performance means and looks like; conversely, teacher/scholars such as Madeleine Grumet (*Bitter Milk*, 1987) have long advocated a more conscious use in teaching of the resources of theater: dialogue, gesture, role-playing, in addition to soliloquy.

Perhaps a good way into questions of performance and change in the academy might be to compare the interviews of Jane Tompkins and Stanley Fish, a relatively unusual instance of a married couple in the same field, in the same department of the same university, and now appearing in the same format being asked the same questions about more or less the same subjects.

Pedagogy, Writing, and Feeling
Recently, Tompkins has attracted attention with several essays on how she discovered the deficits in her previous approaches to university teaching and

how she now approaches teaching with more eagerness and spirit. Her new feeling has become so strong, in fact, that she is writing a book on pedagogy. Because Tompkins is holding a secure and respectable position at Duke, some have taken skeptical notice of how this Ivy League graduate, this established critic and scholar, this person who first supported, then rejected, then readopted reader-response criticism, has decided to explain to us the private and potentially embarrassing details of her on-the-job education. In her response to the Tompkins interview, Susan Jarratt explores some reasons why the new Tompkins has raised doubts. While I share some of Jarratt's responses, there is no denying that Tompkins took risks describing herself, her history, and her feelings as she did. I welcome Tompkins to the community of teaching-aware critic/scholars, of which there are increasing numbers. However, I doubt that it was naivete and ignorance that held up Tompkins' personal enlightenment until very recently. It is hard to understand, for example, that Tompkins taught writing for fifteen years, as she reports, yet only now has discovered the close connection between teaching writing and the problems of teaching generally in the university. It also cannot have been total ideological domination that kept her in the dark. For a long time she benefitted from and promoted the androcentric values that have suddenly caused her trouble and precipitated a shift in her perspective. However, one can see in her discussions how she is now living, in a sense, in the midst of change, as both the old values and the new exercise a strong pull on her allegiance. Sometimes she is quixotic, as when she offers that writing groups should be a way to "exist in the academy." And yet, it is stimulating and helpful to listen to Tompkins thinking through her changes with us.

One way to describe what happened is that now Tompkins has actually learned the subject of literary response in both its full subjectivity and in its political ramifications. By writing as she now does, she is enacting in her professional life what some literary response advocates have been urging. Tompkins' interview shows skills, talents, discourse styles that are becoming increasingly useful—and, to many, necessary. Her interview shows that when you try to articulate your feelings in everyday language, people notice; that when you try to be faithful to your personal history, you are likely to embarrass yourself at one point or another; that when you speak in your own more informal voice, others answer in similar voices, as do Susan Jarratt and Elizabeth Flynn. We may or may not like either the voices or the things they say, but there is no doubt but that the three voices of Tompkins, Jarratt, and Flynn have the loose ends and ragged edges of interpersonal candor, and in a certain way these voices are familiar; they do in fact give us a new model—no longer that of a pure individual performance—of how to conduct our scholarly and professional work. Tompkins' voice makes it easier for us to detect the historic corruption of the masculine academy, and she makes herself available to join in to the project of changing the specific schools created by the academy as an institution.

One issue she discusses at some length which dramatizes this situation is her attitude toward writing. When asked if she thinks of herself as a writer, Tompkins, like bell hooks, tells us, "Yes I do." In answering the question, Tompkins offers a qualification that, while surprising, rings true: "Yes I do, but only very recently have I thought of myself that way." It is nice to see a professional mainstay ready to share the less sunny details of her professional history. At the same time, her tone of confession, along with the quiet sense of celebration about finally expelling from deep within the guilty secrets, makes us want to know just what is going on, anyhow. Confession is itself part of performance syndrome. It reminds us of the narcissism in many academic discourses.

Tompkins claims to write for herself:

> I've recently come to understand writing as a way that people like us have of taking care of ourselves. When we can't get to our writing, we feel deprived and we feel hungry for it, not just because we're afraid we won't get our articles written so that we won't get our job or our promotion (although certainly those fears apply), but because there's a need that we have to perform this activity *for ourselves*. It's almost like a grooming activity, or something that you do in the mode of self-care, like getting a massage or working out. It's a form of attention that seems to be directed outward toward an object outside of yourself, but somehow the effect strangely is to have attended to yourself in some way. That's the way I'm coming to understand it. . . .
>
> I also see writing as a form of self-development and self-discovery, as a way you can come to know yourself and learn about yourself, or just as a mode of learning pure and simple. In that regard, my sort of proof text is a line from Robert Pirsig's *Zen and the Art of Motorcycle Maintenance*: "The motorcycle you're working on is the motorcycle of yourself." When Pirsig talks in an extended passage in that novel about something he calls "gumptionology," which is the science of what it takes to fix a motorcycle, I read that as being about writing and have always so read it. That approach to writing—that is, you think you're working on the motorcycle and you're really working on yourself—is one that I've recently come to.

Tompkins is generous and thoughtful about explaining how and why she writes for herself. She mentions a source for her thinking in Pirsig's book, and she is imaginative in presenting to us the fact that writing is deep, that it has to do with hunger, need, and self-knowledge. Her personal perspective helps to give her own writing both a heartbeat and a backbone. On the other hand, it is emotionally and ideologically misleading to put so much weight on writing "for" oneself. Writing, like feelings and affect as described by Naomi Scheman in "Individualism and the Objects of Psychology" (1983), is already placed between and among persons. Like language, it has no meaning by itself: the person speaking for more than a short space without others present is generally understood to be mentally incompetent.

The source for Tompkins' highly individualized description, for her perception of writing as playing so large a role in an individual's moral search for an upright and more fully known inner self, is similar to Freud's source in his axiom of self-knowledge as the foundation for knowledge. I share with

Tompkins this impulse or cultural tendency to say that self-knowledge is where the buck stops, to assume an invisible bond between individualism and scholarly work. Lately, this bond has been exposed by the wide combination of constituencies who have been harmed by the invisibility of individualism. Many of us unquestioningly accepted the "myth of the independent scholar," as described by Patricia Sullivan in the forthcoming essay collection, *Writing With: New Directions in Collaborative Teaching, Learning, and Research* (SUNY P, 1994). However, I think that if, today, one is nevertheless ready to compare oneself to a motorcycle, to use this mechanical device as a figure of and for one's self, that one may in fact be committed to the false romanticism of the earnest but isolated man, the individual who feels such an exaggerated responsibility to achieve and succeed *alone* that the tasks he finds for himself are laughable in their impossibility.

Throughout Tompkins' discussion, for every move away from individualism, there is an almost equal move back in its direction. She reports being involved in a writing group at Duke, where the members of this group meet regularly to give each other "feedback." As she gets going on this topic, things soon become exaggerated: "I strongly recommend writing groups as a way not just to write but to exist in the academy.... The earlier you can show something to somebody, the better off you are as far as I'm concerned." What Tompkins describes has always been done by some in the academy—namely, showing friends your work for them to help out. And her reason for doing it in a group is no different from the reasons it usually had—namely, to help oneself. The group described by Tompkins, and those recommended by Elbow and endorsed by Tompkins, are actually only collections of individuals who have unionized to enhance their status as individuals. There is finally no *collective* purpose or novelty in what Tompkins describes. It does not challenge the individualist ideology, and I wonder how many members of such groups are conscious of their relation to ideological change.

Tompkins reaffirms that her approach in teaching is "to have personal experience count for a lot; personal response to literature (or whatever the subject matter) is to be central to any consideration of it. As soon as you have legitimized personal response, private experience, as a source of knowledge about a text, it seems to me you've also legitimized feeling or emotion, since at least for me the two are almost identical." This, of course, is where literary response was first in the late thirties with Louise Rosenblatt and then in the middle sixties and early seventies by us later arrivals to the issue of feelings in teaching and learning. Yet, how can we tell that Tompkins' perspective represents something new or at least more responsive to contemporary issues? It is hard for me to tell. Tompkins describes her view as advocating a situation in which "students are in effect being coerced into taking responsibility for their own learning. I prefer the word *responsibility;* they're forced by me because I step back and won't do it myself." I wish that Tompkins had not so strongly endorsed individualist thinking ("their own learning"), or used terms like "force" and "coerce" so casually. In a classroom, as in other collective situations, most responsibilities are shared. When teaching changes, the *relationships* between teachers and students, as well as among students, change. Tompkins' view still sounds traditional: come on, kids, let's start taking some responsibility. Responsibility is what Hillis Miller finally settles on as the solution to the political challenge: "For me, the political goes by way of the ethical, and it's easier for me to understand the teaching or writing situation along an ethical model, a model that is of a one-to-one reciprocity of responsibility." While Tompkins is different from Miller in attitude, approach, and tone, she is not terribly different in ideology. None of us disputes the necessity of individual responsibility on the part of all classroom members. But both Tompkins and Miller seem conscience-driven, each to exaggerated positions, neither able to find the language and inner energy, the level of *gesellschaftsgefühl* (social feeling) that offers the appropriate responses to the social and political challenges they are discussing.

Fish and Androcentric Individualism
The difference between Tompkins and Fish can be seen most clearly, perhaps, in the matter of the performance model of teaching. Whatever else is to be said about Tompkins, the record clearly shows that she has taken steps to change both her writing and her teaching. As she says in the interview,

> Just as I've tried to step back from what I call the "performance model" of *teaching*, where your ego is very much at stake, to a different mode where presumably your ego is not so much on the line (although, in fact, it still is), I've become more aware of the extent to which *writing* for people in our profession is a kind of ego activity. I'm not in the least degree free from that myself, but the recognition that that's the case makes me question somewhat the role that writing has played for me.

Comparing himself with Tompkins, Fish characterizes her talks about teaching as "performances" and her audiences as approaching a "cult following." He, meanwhile sees no need for change in his teaching, and he does not connect his writing with his teaching:

> I would first have to feel some dissatisfaction with my current mode of teaching or with the experiences of my classroom, and I don't feel that. For me the classroom is still what she has formally renounced: a performance occasion. And I enjoy the performances; I enjoy orchestrating the class in ways that involve students in the performances, but no one is under any illusion that this a participatory (or any other kind) of democracy in a class of mine.... [Although Tompkins' kind of teaching is] a wave of the future ... I'm sure that I would never do it myself—too much egocentrism, too much of a long career as a professional theatrical academic.

The unstated premise of this argument is that egocentrism and professional momentum are sufficient reasons for rejecting challenges from people one respects. In other words, owing to his stake in the total status quo of the university and the society, he will not examine the authoritarian mores commonly practiced in the classroom by accomplished male academics.

One need not discuss at any length what the results, in the interview, of this perspective turn out to be. But just let me list some of the beliefs that follow from how Fish answers the challenge of new forms of teaching: (1) the belief that it is worth arguing about whether theory has consequences; (2) the belief that you can speak about collaborative learning (or interpretive communities) as a known abstraction without specifying just which people and which communities one is discussing; (3) the belief that defining your own intellectual identity—a pragmatist, a sophist, a localist, for example—matters; (4) the belief that sports offers appropriate analogies for issues in intellectual life; (5) the belief that people care about one's disputes with other well-known individualist scholars; (6) the belief that a good way to refer to other people's work is to indicate that they *influenced* you; (7) the belief that you can endorse feminism and then not change anything you do as a result of your endorsement. (I think Fish shares this last trait with every other male scholar interviewed in both volumes of this series.)

The "performance model" of teaching and academic action produces the familiar beliefs listed above, which characterize not just Fish's work, but that of many male, and some female, academics of a variety of stripes. This model also leads him to have a "position" on feminism which, in case it (feminism) should fail, would then be cited as a triumph of his "position." The feminist issue broached in the Fish interview is: are there differences between men's and women's ways of knowing, and how does one understand feminists who use this distinction? Fish disputes that there are differences but says that it is not wrong for feminists to assume differences. In the interview, Fish tries to elaborate this "position." Fish says that the distinction between male and female epistemologies could not really exist if it is possible for people to "step back from" the epistemology they are already in. He thinks that feminists don't recognize that stepping back from one's epistemology while also having one adds up to a contradiction. His position, which wants to avoid contradiction, is that it is impossible to step back from one's socially constructed epistemology, and that, therefore, there "cannot be such a distinction between ways of knowing." This argument suggests that no matter what Fish claims in this essay or that essay, he has no view of why claims have been made by feminists about different ways of knowing. Here is what Tompkins has to say when asked whether she agrees with Fish's "position":

> I don't really think much about epistemology any more. My thinking is not at that level. The question is what's behind a question like that? What are the real-world consequences of it? How does it play out in terms of what you do in the classroom or how you teach people to write or what sorts of models you give them? I think it's true that because women are socialized differently from infancy they find themselves much more comfortable in certain kinds of learning situations than in others. If you want to call that a difference in epistemology, I don't really care, but I think that in a *practical* sense it's true. I've experienced it myself; I've seen it. . . . There are differences in optimal learning environments for some men and some women.

The key here is that Tompkins rejects Fish's terms, not with "nevers" or "impossibilities" or "contradictions" but with "I don't think about it" and "I don't care." She moves the discussion from Fish's abstract ground back to her own experiences and to guesses as to what may be true for some men and women. I can read Tompkins' language into my situations, but not Fish's language. Either I must enter into his discourse and decide not to bring in my actual experience and speak of practical occasions, or I must pay no attention to what is said. To me, finally, his terms are of minor interest with regard to male and female ways of knowing, but Tompkins' terms are worth studying. Her terms keep the issue alive by making it depend on the cases one actually finds and experiences. I feel I am in the same play as Tompkins is, but Fish is speaking a language that no longer works in a feminist-inclusive discourse community. Regardless of his ritualized disclaimers, he wants fixed terms, lasting truths, and the previously unquestioned but now doubtful standard, *noncontradiction.* He is on the edge of the conversation.

While Fish sees the likely reverberations of feminism as a public phenomenon, his career-long removal of himself from the lived consequences of his intellectual life comes into play here so that he does not consider the extent to which feminism is already a critique of the way he has functioned in the academy and the way he performs during this interview. A specific documentation for this claim might be in Tompkins' responses; a more general documentation is the relative narrowness of his discourse style—repetition; feelings shown mainly about intellectual disputes or antagonisms, rarely about situations in which people's lives matter; concern mainly with abstractions and argumentative consistencies.

An especially disappointing phase of his interview is his attack on liberalism, calling it "a brief against belief and conviction." This judgment is a strange one indeed for Fish, who now wants to present himself as the champion of *"conviction, belief, passion."* Fish chooses the need for personal attention, again, for performance, over the need for loyalty to causes that have helped him build his own voice. Having listened for years to the Reagan lies about a political view that has promoted and achieved social, public decency in America for several generations, do we need to hear echoes of these lies even faintly endorsed by Fish who, in other contexts, is a liberal and nothing else? Is this where the "performance model" leads?

A Question of Ethics
A stark contrast to Fish's performance is Patricia Harkin's response to J. Hillis Miller. This short piece is one of the highlights of this volume. In feeling and idea, she brings out the unconscionable inertia of thought, sympathy, and understanding found among those who have yet to face our commonly inherited and troubled academic history, in much the same way that white people face "prejudice" but refuse to face the two-hundred years of slavery which produced the prejudice.

Harkin reads Miller's judgments as those of a scholar incapable of removing himself, even hypothetically, from the privileges of his position. In English departments this means that professors of literature are unable to disabuse themselves of the idea that it is the *responsibility* of the writing teacher to teach all students "to write clearly and effectively for a given purpose." Especially important about Harkin's reading of Miller is that it discloses accurately the fact that seemingly benign and well-meaning faculty members in English and in other subjects simply do not acknowledge, face, or respect what has happened in the study of writing. Harkin says, "My ethical problem is typical of the position of writing program administrators in departments of English. Should composition programs separate from departments of English or try to continue communicating within a situation in which they are treated with condescension? For the moment, I'll choose the latter, adopt Miller's belief that the 'political goes by way of the ethical.'" By proceeding along the "ethical" path, Harkin points out a phenomenon in the Miller interview that is similar to what happens in the Fish interview: to wit, "the more he explains, the more confusing he gets":

> Olson asks how, having deconstructed the writing/reading opposition and thereby permitted us all to see how "reading is itself a kind of writing, or writing is a trope for the act of reading," Miller would prevent composition from being resubsumed under "English as reading." He responds by urging us to "persuade the rest of the English department that it's their responsibility to teach reading." "Composition people," he says, "have got to depend to some degree on the people in the English department and other language departments to do some, if not most, of the teaching of reading," even in the sense that includes writing. But then (is he changing his mind?): "Insofar as that's a *rhetorical* skill, it goes along with Stanley [Fish's] suggestion that they ought to be called departments of rhetoric." Even within what Miller calls "rhetorical reading," he seems still to preserve the hierarchy in which literary studies is privileged over composition.

I suppose Harkin is being euphemistic when she calls this paragraph confusing. Miller, throughout any discussion, sticks to the dogged sense of arrangement in English departments: on top the literati like himself—readers and theorists; on the bottom, writing teachers; theory and literature will always be higher than writing and teaching; say whatever one must to conserve this paradigm. In Fish's case the governing paradigm is the appearance of abstract critical consistency; in Miller's it's literary superiority.

Truth and the Problem of Objectivity
In spite of his own commonsense casual self-presentation, Davidson moves as certainly as Fish and Miller do into ungainly motions in the service of giving a philosophically proper performance. Even though his philosophical perspective on language is almost completely the opposite of Chomsky's, he shares with him that quiet understanding that what actually happens in the world of lived experience need not be a substantive part of a philosophical or other disciplined inquiry into language. To show this, as well as other

features of Davidson's discourse and approach to language, let me cite this one relatively long passage, given in response to Thomas Kent's request that Davidson explain his idea of "triangulation":

> Well, the idea of triangulation is partly metaphorical, but not wholly. The basic idea is that our concept of objectivity—our idea that our thoughts may or may not correspond to the truth—is an idea that we would not have if it weren't for interpersonal relations. In other words, the source of objectivity is intersubjectivity: the triangle consists of two people and the world. Part of the idea is this: if you were alone in the world—that is, not in communication with anybody else—things would be impinging on you, coming in through your senses, and you would react in differential ways. Now, here's where the metaphor comes in. If you were to ask, "Well, when you're reacting in a certain way, let's say to some pleasant taste, what is it that pleases you?" We would say, "It's the peach." However, in the case of the person who has no one with whom to share his thoughts, on what grounds could you say, "It's the peach that pleases" rather than the taste of the peach, or the stimulation of the taste buds, or, for that matter, something that happened a thousand years ago which set all these forces in motion which eventually impinged on the taste buds. How far out are the objects that he is responding to? There would be no answer to that question at all: nothing for him to check up on, no way to raise the question, much less to answer it. So, the idea of triangulation is this: if you have two people both reacting to stimuli in the world and to each other—that is, to each other's reactions to the stimuli—you've completed a triangle which locates the common stimulus. It doesn't locate it in one person's mouth; it doesn't locate it in one person's eyes; it doesn't locate it five thousand years ago. It locates it just at the distance of the shared stimulus which, in turn, causes each of the two creatures to react to each other's reactions. It's a way of saying why it is that communication is essential to the concept of an objective world.

Davidson seems to be demonstrating the necessity of three terms—objectivity, interpersonal relations, and communication (that is, language)—to one another's meaning and function. He is trying for a more inclusive philosophy of language that is neither a pure mathematical abstraction nor an immersion in pure pragmatic experience. Although the explanation is coherent and clear and may well represent a step forward for traditional analytic philosophy, it is hard to see why such an explanation is needed at all.

For one thing, the question of objectivity is not how it exists but *what things can be objectified and by whom.* Davidson's explanation doesn't help with this ethical and political question. The question of whether relationships play a role in language seems also self-evident: neither relationships nor language would make any sense as items to begin with without the other entity. Davidson is laboring to get them back together because people like Chomsky have separated them in the first place. Finally, why did people doubt that objects exist without language and relationships? I think because in philosophy, the tradition of thought teaches us to separate issues from experiences as well as issues and experiences internally from one another so that, in imagination at any rate, they exist as independent items. After a while the academic separation of subjects and issues for study makes it seem to academics and their students that these subjects and issues are in some primordial objective world actually separate from one another.

If, on the other hand, a somewhat different set of assumptions about knowledge prevailed, I am not sure people would worry about how to decide just what it is that pleases us. In cases where such questions may come up, such as sexual activity, it will not help to read the passage by Davidson. In fact, this is not a frivolous point. The public discussion of sexual pleasure does finally contribute to teaching people how to find out how and why they enjoy or fail to enjoy sex. But the terms, style, and language of the sexual discussion are not Davidson's. His case is entirely hypothetical, or put another way, abstract. Even if one accepts the need for his style of discussion, it would be more helpful to find an instance that someone actually reported. In our world—the one and only real world—such questions are *not in philosophy*. Or, put otherwise, philosophy has chosen not to treat such questions but instead to treat the questions described by Davidson in just the way he treats them. As Susan Wells diplomatically observes in her commentary, "Davidson is much less helpful" on "issues raised by the institutional situation of discourse" than he is on "questions of truth."

While it may sound strange to say that questions of truth are in a different category from questions of feminism, this pattern appears in the present volume exactly as it appeared in the previous one. Traditional academic thinkers seem spontaneously activated by issues where one needs to discover just what is "the case," but are shut down, more or less, by the political weight of feminist issues. In deciding what is true, the conscientious scholar takes a long time and many words to judge what or who is "right" about specific issues. In contrast, it took about two tries by the interviewer to exhaust the same people's views on feminism, even though no one rejected it or claimed it was a false perspective. While you may want to blame the interviewer for this shortfall, the interviewees themselves determined the length of their contributions for every question posed, including those on feminism.

Davidson's performance is true to this pattern: feminism is a valid issue, but it is not really close to my field—language "differences don't seem to me to be a major barrier to communication between the sexes. I think that the real barriers are economic and political questions of power." The idea that the interviewer is purposely *placing* feminism in the field under study is ignored either by accident or purposely. The subject of feminism simply exercises as much influence as any subject that the interviewee *already considers outside his field.* Thus, the fact that there are disciplines and departments itself works to reduce the claims of feminism, a self-consciously transdisciplinary movement.

Feminism and Philosophy

One would think the situation would be different for Stephen Toulmin, who has considered in some depth how disciplines behave and who has advocated the loosening of disciplinary boundaries. Olson cites *Human Understanding* in one of his questions: "For the very boundaries between academic disciplines are themselves a consequence of the current divisions of intellectual authority, and the justice of those divisions is itself one of the chief questions to be faced afresh." However, Olson offers four openings on the subject of feminism with Toulmin, and none of them moves him toward relating the women's movement to *work that he is doing or has done.* Rather, Toulmin can only see feminism, as Olson re-articulates, in terms of the "personal impact on [his] life." He speaks about cooking at home, about traveling back and forth between England and America, about his wife's profession, and about male chauvinism in France. To give Toulmin the most possible respect on this matter, one would have to say that his intellectual paradigm does not accept feminism. Feminism is not nothing to Toulmin (and Davidson and Miller), but it is not a part of the real vocabulary of issues.

Because feminism and other provocative political issues do not play a role in Toulmin's thinking, his perspective sometimes seems lacking in energy. A major point comes toward the end of his interview, where he compares the role of rhetoric as a subject to the role of philosophy—more or less a subject that is not independent and meant, perhaps, to combine with other subjects: "I think philosophers often do their best work when they turn their skills to helping to hoe other people's vineyards, which of course is John Locke's old crack about being an underlaborer clearing away the underbrush that stands in the way of understanding." This thought is one of several where connections to feminist concerns ask to be announced. Among "male" (that is, populated mostly by and run by men) disciplines, there are enterprises which have functioned as "helping" sciences; in fact, many sciences consider other sciences in just this role—as, for example, physicists sometimes consider mathematics a helping science, or biologists consider chemistry a helping science. Sometimes such thinking goes on at the level of informal jokes; sometimes it is taken seriously. Behind it is the presumption of hierarchy in knowledge *which is common to both the humanities and the sciences,* as Miller's interview and Harkin's commentary show.

At that moment in the interview, Toulmin might have cited Sandra Harding's critique of the established hierarchy in the sciences and perhaps entertained her disquieting view that the hierarchy of "physics on top social sciences on the bottom" should be *reversed,* not revoked. However, whether Harding was cited is less germane than the need to consider, when the topic of "helping" disciplines is raised, that this is a political fact and not a casual or random arrangement of interests. While the importance of subjects may be changing in the industrialized West today, we all understand that subject matters are linked to economic and social interests and have long been tied to the interests and power of military institutions. In reading Toulmin's and Davidson's interviews, I get the feeling that there is no social or political urgency to the conceptualization of disciplines. Criticisms brought in by the interviewer are more often than not reduced to friendly informal disagreements, giving a purely local character to disputes that, for most of us, will bear on how society takes shape in the future. Toulmin has a "joking relationship" with Habermas; Davidson has been "the target of Chuck's [Charles Taylor's] attacks a number of times"; Fish wonders "whether or not one conveys *anything* to Dinesh [D'Souza]." The turn to the personal in these interviews is not the same as the turn to the personal in the Tompkins and hooks interviews. It is, rather, an escape from the public pressure into the intimacy of disputes that have been converted into good-natured private exchange, thus relieving the exaggerated pressure accruing to public male disputes by virtue of their gender exclusivity. These four figures—Fish, Miller, Davidson, and Toulmin—are not particularly disturbed by this cycle of exaggerations and reduction of issues that results from functioning under performance individualism. I am not sure many of us men know just how our professional lives would change if some of these taken-for-granted mores—enacted, perhaps, in the very interview situation represented in this volume—moved toward more collectivist styles, toward ways where performance can be valued without being demanded, where the discourse between the private and the public is more fluent, less obsessive, more ordinary.

Hooks and Passion

A partial change will likely come from a different sense of what performance can include. Bell hooks' works, aimed at a greater share of the general readership than other academically oriented writings, along with her presentational style in the interview, are performances with new shapes. In her name, Gloria Watkins introduces something that we have not seen in academic life: a *nom de plume* for public intellectuals (if it were a traditional change of name, like that of Ntozake Shange, the copyright on her books would go to bell hooks and not to Gloria Watkins). Can one say which is the "performance" name? Are there any longer "real" names for female spouses? Do Cassius Clay and Lew Alcindor still exist? Among those seeking to restore the dignity assaulted by history and society, changes of name and identity have become new sorts of acts of self-possession. While bell hooks describes how audiences have made her a writer, her own performance name has created the audience. By taking a new name, you can create a new audience and you can better preside over the performance. This is a performance different from what we are familiar with in academic life.

Hooks introduces new terms into her self-description. She is asked to elaborate on her sense that being a writer is tied to her "spiritual evolution":

> A lot of people ask me, "How do you write all these books?" I used to joke, "Oh, it's because I don't have a life." But I think the real answer is that I spent a lot of time alone, and I believe that the act of writing isn't just about spending the time alone writing; it's also the time you spend in contemplation. My development as an intellectual and as a critical thinker is tied to spirituality because growing up as a working-class black woman, the only arena of my life that gave me the sense that I had the right to a space of contemplation was religiosity and spirituality. In fact, it was telling me that everybody needs to go into the desert and to be alone. Given the kind of racist, sexist iconography in our culture that always presumes that black women should serve the interests of

others, whether it's black children or black men or the larger society, it's very hard for black women to claim that space that is the precursor to writing, the space where you can think through ideas. This is a way in which those two experiences of spiritual practice and writing converge for me. Also, I'm really engaged with Buddhism.

This account starts out in what looks like familiar territory to me, and then winds up in space beyond my comprehension. For the last several years, I have heard the use of the term "spirituality" to refer to what in secular circles used to be called religious feeling and/or faith. Academic writing, for me, has never been separate from the active, mutually responsive relationships in my teaching experiences, and while I have definitely needed "time alone," it was simply to sit down and actually do the writing. I did not need the time alone to contemplate, to meditate, or otherwise to make contact with the supernatural. Hooks' joke, "Oh, I don't have a life" does ring true, however. Judging from her written work and performance style, it seems possible that she feels "called" in the old-fashioned sense to speak, to gather her audience, and even, as men have longed to do, to become a prophet. This does take time, calculation, and freedom from family responsibilities. It does focus one's attention on one's individuality. As hooks claims, if white men follow this calling, so can black women. Whether one should take the calling to be a prophet in the same vocational sense we take the term "professor," I don't know. But it is a role played by hooks, and it is done with more theatricality than others with similar styles now being taken seriously in the academy. One might contrast the informal presentation of hooks with the solemn gestures of prophecy found in the work of Bloom and Hartman.

This religiously accented combination of choices has grown from a different history, a different level of anger, and a different sense of what the total culture might become. That I am unresponsive to religious noises does not matter. I may try (but may not succeed) to forget about any prophetic noises this interview seems to make to me and consider its messages on other grounds. It is clear, for example, that when hooks discusses teaching, performance is at the forefront, but the kind in which there are fourteen handpicked students instead of forty on an all-are-welcome basis. In this classroom, there is "the place of desire and love" found when "my students often express great passion for me in their writing, in their journal writing, and I often feel great passion for them." This classroom is host to a "place of passion" and should be used "to diffuse hierarchy and to create a sense of community." Yet, the students in this classroom complain:

Students would actually come up to me and whine, "There's a way that you hug this student or talk to that student, and I want you to look at me the way you look at Johnny." I kept hearing this sort of sense of diminishing returns that if I have a lot of energy for one student I can't have any energy for others. I said, ... Why can't you think that I have this space of care that can enlarge to include everyone?" That was a real challenge for them because, again, we were seeing how either/or thinking, hierarchical thinking, was at work: if I really have passion for one student, I can't have passion for another. How can there be passion when students are different?

I don't think this is going to become my discourse, even if sexual harassment were not on everyone's mind, including hooks'. The vocabulary and attitude may or may not be the same as that of the cult leader or the charismatic preacher, but the situation she describes seems similar: there is enough passion in *me* for everyone. The passion in the classroom cited by hooks seems unexamined, merely mentioned or reported, and not considered in the contemplative way she seems to advocate for her private intellectual life. The exhortations she offers seem dangerous to me, and not new in any case. For a prophetic academic to come on the scene and "share passion" seems too risky to entertain in classrooms in which, as we all know, the kindling temperature for open antagonism among different genders, classes, and ethnic groups is becoming lower and lower. Although I have been soliciting feelings and sharing my own in classrooms for thirty years, I see that my own sense of feelings themselves must change in the face of changing classroom populations and increased political alertness among all students. I feel that hooks' description of the classroom and its "erotic" potential has become only a metaphor, and it is part of the imaginative performance she is presenting. Since I have never met bell hooks and have never heard her speak, I don't know that I am ready to read the interview's coherence in a way that distinguishes the performance from the conversation.

Hooks seems to be sustained in part by what sustained my parents when they came to America and found that many of their ways, defeated in Europe, were tolerated in America. Similarly, hooks has ways that combine her own style with the existing academic style and its taste for figures like her. Yes, hooks' audience is predominantly white, though ultimately unlimited. I read her ways as having understood this very early in her writing career, made the appropriate calculations, adjustments, and write-offs, and found (made?) her audience, which combines the suspicious with the friendly and is predicated on the expectation that the field of writing includes only verbal wrangling. Similar things could be said of Stanley Fish's performance style. As a Jew with a Jewish performance style, he earned his stripes studying an especially Christian author, Milton. His "audience," which he understood as soon in his career as hooks did in hers, was predominantly "other." There is a sense in which, on the one hand, he *has* to be outrageous to get attention, and, in another, it represents a certain aggression against this necessary audience. But whatever else is true of bell hooks, there is no implication of violence in her performance. In this sense, too, hooks' strong voice takes us in a new direction. As we observe our classrooms, as have Tompkins and Fox and Middleton, we notice that conflict and opposition among students is more, and not less, frequent the more we teachers decide to face the fundamental injustices in society. Students feel more "empowered" to be angry with one another, to sulk, to feel resentful, to shout, even to walk out of the classroom if intolerably provoked. In spite of my doubtful response, a distinctive feature of hooks' interview is her willingness to cite, even if it turns out to be teacher centered and metaphorical, the dialogue of student complaint. What students say matters, and hooks' citation of their words puts the issue on the table. This is a valuable step because most academic discussions do not include, much less learn from, what students say.

Opposing racist and androcentric society means, in part, learning to oppose one another without violence lurking in the background, without having to wonder about bodily injury or mutual annihilation. Psychotherapists have long since shown that self-conscious "acting out" can transform violent impulses into verbal and gestural ones. Madeleine Grumet has begun to put her plan into practice at Brooklyn College. We might consider that the performance model in the academy is not itself an object of criticism, but that it has been appropriated by and traditionally served the interests which aggravate the existing injustices of society. Now its shape is changing, as it moves away from the exclusively solo lecturer—the prophet, the preacher—toward the collection of voices characterized recently by Susan Miller as "new discourse city" (*Writing With: New Directions in Collaborative Teaching, Learning, Research,* SUNY P, 1994). In this city, there are performances by many more actors; the murders are only gestures of antagonism. The words, however, are real.

Conclusion: The Interview Project

The reader may note that I have been a kind of "designated respondent" for these two unusual volumes of interviews. The foregoing commentary was originally considered as an introduction, but the editors and I thought that it might do better in its present place. This change bears on the meaning and value of these two volumes of interviews, originally collected as part of the *Journal of Advanced Composition* but then collected as a "set" in themselves. In a sense, the interviews are now part of two genres: the *journal*, with its various contents, and the *volume of collected works*, with its more homogeneous contents. My understanding of what these volumes and the interviews meant changed over time; as a result, the *genre* of my contribution changed from an introduction to a concluding commentary.

In their status as volumes of work, the interviews themselves provide a commentary on the "originally" published work of those who were interviewed. While one thinks at first of the interview as getting us "closer" to a person, we see from these two volumes not that we are necessarily "closer" but that we get a new view altogether. I consider it helpful to find the higher degree of language-use detail that we find in the interviews, including the errors, hesitations, uncertainties, and choices that may have been considered before the interviewees decided on their "final" texts for publication. The interviews, as was once said about psychoanalysis, "predict the past."

One of the main purposes of this project to begin with was to discover how those not in the "writing" business might already be contributing to it. Of course, part of my own response to the collection has been the complaint that their contribution has been rolling along a one-way street: writing teachers read the work of these figures, but these figures are not too interested in what writing teachers do. However, this collection is valuable for this very reason: the "sociology of knowledge" in the writing business is documented by these two volumes. We see the relationship between teachers of writing and teachers in related fields whose work is being read by writing teachers and included in the scholarly perspective of literacy studies. We see the questions being raised by classroom teachers every day: Who is a writer? What does it take to write? How does what we have to say relate to whether we like to write? When we want to know, who do we ask? How far "outside" ourselves do we go to "find out"? What do those outside our group or community think of our work? What do we think of theirs? How do we write about those whose work we reject? What is the role and meaning of leadership in academic life? And, in the immortal words of George Bush, "Who do you trust?"

By presenting these interviews, these volumes suggest a level of discussion that seems more like the provisional character of oral exchange in living human relationships. These volumes perhaps suggest the possibility that others in our profession can be interviewed, not just those whose names we have already heard. New volumes of stories and commentaries by *unpublished teachers, scholars, and students* may be what can now invigorate academic life. We may well need to turn our forums of publication more directly toward those (writing teachers, students) about whose struggles most of the accomplished interviewees have already given their opinions. The *genre* of the "interview volume" could serve new constituencies, who, in turn, will convert into living realities some of the attitudes of intellectual and political generosity often found in schools and universities but which lately have been patronized by those who don't know how to include others in their own performance.

Philosophy, Rhetoric, Literary Criticism: (Inter)views and its predecessor, *(Inter)views: Cross-Disciplinary Perspectives on Rhetoric and Literacy*, could be read so as to help us to promote more actively the interrogative voice, to help us to neutralize the obsessions with the declarative, with who is right, with point scoring, with holding the floor, with competition. These volumes could be seen as providing ways to desacralize "the text," even though the interviews themselves have been textualized. In spite of the fact that our opinions and responses to these interviews raise further problems and frustrations, these volumes may provide a ground to include ourselves in the critique of our works.

University of Rochester
Rochester, New York

Gary A. Olson is professor of English at the University of South Florida, where he teaches in the graduate program in rhetoric and composition and edits the *Journal of Advanced Composition*. Besides publishing articles in such journals as *College English*, *College Composition and Communication*, and *CEA Critic*, Olson has edited and coauthored numerous books and textbooks, including *Writing Centers: Theory and Administration* (NCTE, 1984) and *Advanced Placement English: Theory, Politics, and Pedagogy* (coedited with Elizabeth Metzger and Evelyn Ashton-Jones; Boynton/Cook, 1989). *Philosophy, Rhetoric, Literary Criticism: (Inter)views* is a sequel to *(Inter)views: Cross-Disciplinary Perspectives on Rhetoric and Literacy*, edited by Olson and Irene Gale and published by Southern Illinois University Press in 1991.